American Electoral Behavior : 1952-1988

Michael M. Gant
The University of Tennessee, Knoxville

Norman R. Luttbeg
Texas A&M University

F. E. PEACOCK PUBLISHERS, INC.
ITASCA, ILLINOIS

To Sharon Callison Gant
and Alice Thomas Luttbeg,

with love and respect.

Contents

3

4

5

Preface

Like most books, *American Electoral Behavior: 1952–1988* is linked through many avenues to past conceptual and empirical efforts. Generally, we owe primary intellectual debt to those scholars who have gone before us, and whose work we not only cite, but also has shaped our own thinking. Specifically, this book is an outgrowth of an earlier book written by one of the authors, Norman R. Luttbeg, and David B. Hill entitled *Trends in American Electoral Behavior,* also published by F.E. Peacock. In turn, that book, and therefore *American Electoral Behavior,* finds its earliest roots in a graduate seminar in Electoral Politics led by Professor Luttbeg at Florida State University in 1974.

We have included in this text analyses of all presidential elections from 1952 to 1988, paying particular attention not only to patterns of behavior, but to the current state of that behavior as observed in 1988. We also have attempted to provide as complete a review of the scholarly literature as possible in the context of a text designed primarily for undergraduate students. Two features of this text make it, we think, especially valuable. First, we have included a section on the meaning of party identification—arguably the most important concept in the study of electoral behavior—which focuses on the debate between the "traditional" and "revisionist" interpretations of the concept. Second, we have included a chapter on congressional elections, especially those for the House of Representatives.

The history of the study of American electoral behavior extends back at least to the early twentieth century. But there is no argument among electoral scholars that the publication in 1960 of *The American Voter,* by Angus Campbell, Philip E. Converse, Warren E. Miller, and Donald E. Stokes, was a watershed event. The pre-*American Voter* era was marked by widely disparate methodologies, most of which were rather primitive, and a variety of approaches, which produced a somewhat limited understanding of how and why Americans voted in national elections. While *The American Voter* was not especially sophisticated in its methodology, and did not present a coherent theory of the electoral process, its description of the voter's decision-making process was so persuasive, the framework used still dominates contemporary research.

To be sure, many challenges to *The American Voter* model have arisen, most notably that of the rational choice theorists, but most of these challenges can be viewed as refinements, rather than refutations, of the basic model. In analyses of voter behavior, the one constant theme from the early 1950s to the present is the extent to which *stability* or *change* is the better description of the American electorate. This, too, is our theme. In many ways, change has characterized the electorate: The proportion of citizens not identifying with the Democratic or Republican parties has increased substantially. Citizens of the 1980s are much more distrustful of the government and government officials than in the 1960s. Issues, as opposed to party or image, appear to have much greater impact on how people vote now than in the "issue-less" 1950s. Turnout in all elections has declined substantially over the past thirty years.

And yet, we would argue that these changes have occurred within a broader context of *stability*. The vast majority of Americans still identify with one of the two major political parties, which in turn dominate the electoral arena. The single most important predictor of how people vote is still party identification. While turnout has declined, it is not at all clear that this is a trend which should concern us, either as scholars or citizens; the Republic still stands.

The American electorate has changed, but not that much. This conclusion may be frustrating, especially to the undergraduate student. While most of the analyses in this book are relatively straightforward, their implications are not so clear-cut. What we have tried to do is present enough evidence, from enough perspectives, to allow readers to make up their own minds as to the state of American electoral behavior. We do not promise to provide all the answers, merely to advance the questions, and to provide enough information so that the readers can arrive at their own answers.

The authors must accept the blame for any errors of omission or commission found in the text. But we wish to acknowledge those who have helped us complete this book. All data analyses are based on the National Election Studies conducted by the Survey Research Center/Center for Political Studies of the Interuniversity Consortium for Political and Social Research at the University of Michigan, and funded by the National Science Foundation. Neither the Center, the Consortium, nor the Foundation bear any responsibility for the analyses or interpretations presented herein.

We want to thank the University of Tennessee, Knoxville, and Texas A&M University for their support during the writing of this book. Linda Gaddis, Phyllis Moyers, Debby Pierce, and especially Naina Pinkston provided invaluable assistance in the typing and preparation of the manuscript. Professor Gant's colleague William Lyons of the University of Tennessee, Knoxville, read and commented on portions of the manuscript and was most encouraging when encouragement was needed most. We also want to thank Barbara Norrander of San Jose State University and Thomas Holbrook-Provow of the University of Wisconsin, Milwaukee, whose comments were extraordinarily helpful as we were revising the manuscript.

Finally, we want to thank Ted Peacock for his continued willingness to publish a book which is, in part, less than orthodox; and especially our editor, Leo A.W. Wiegman, whose forebearance, good humor, and professionalism made our task even more enjoyable than it ordinarily would have been.

To all, thanks.

Michael M. Gant
The University of Tennessee, Knoxville

Norman R. Luttbeg
Texas A&M University

Introduction

In contemporary political research, a recurring theme is change in the American electorate: change from a model of electoral behavior formulated by scholars who studied elections of the 1940s and 1950s. The actual extent of change in American electoral behavior, as evidenced in presidential and congressional elections from 1952 to 1988, is reviewed and analyzed in this book. It should prepare you to decide whether stability or change best describes the behavior of the American voter in recent elections.

In the first chapter we introduce certain methodological considerations related to electoral research. We describe the prevailing model of voter behavior drawn from pre-1960s electoral research. Our method of presentation for this model, rather than simply discussing major research findings and theoretical designs, is to review findings and theories within the historical context of their development by electoral scholars. There is a twofold rationale for this. First, the early history of American electoral research shapes our perspective on the meaning of how Americans vote today. Our second reason stems from our belief that researchers often have personal biases about how the electorate should behave which influence their research designs and interpretations. With an historical perspective on the electoral research literature, we can more easily identify various schools of thought and thereby gain a more critical and discriminating appreciation for any given scholar's research and theoretical contributions.

Chapters 2 through 4 are devoted to certain topics which have been identified by scholars as evidence of electoral change. In Chapter 2 we examine the proposition that the role of political parties in American electoral politics has declined dramatically. Making such a determination involves evaluating the role of parties as political organizations and then assessing the impact of political party labels on voting. The latter line of investigation involves comparing partisanship with two other crucial factors in voters' decisions to reject or ignore their parties' leads—perceptions of the candidates (candidate image) and political issues.

Chapter 3 is a study of declining political participation in this country. While there are many ways citizens can take part in the political process—contributing money to candidates, running for local office—the most common is voting. Turnout and the factors which influence whether or not people vote are the focus of Chapter 3. In particular, we are concerned with the long-term trend of declining voter turnout in national elections.

Chapter 4 is an exploration of political trust in America. *Political trust* here means the trust in elected officials or institutions of government expressed by citizens. In addition to examining the changes in trust over time, we also assess the effects of such changes, if any, on other aspects of political life, especially political participation. Group variations in political trust are discussed as well.

At the conclusion of chapters 2 through 4 we have included a trend assessment in an attempt to say something new about the electorate. Each trend assessment section is devoted to a thorough and systematic exploration of whether these trends are empirically interrelated. Several interrelationships, which we will discuss, have been the subjects of considerable speculation; but few attempts have been made to test the validity of these assertions. The rigorous testing of interrelationships between changes in partisanship, participation, and trust and confidence in government are the primary goals of the text.

In Chapter 5, we discuss those factors which exert the greatest impact on congressional elections, especially elections for the House of Representatives. We find that incumbency and partisanship largely shape the outcomes of congressional elections, and have disproportionate influence on how people vote in these contests. In other respects, the basic model we use to understand voting in presidential elections is only of moderate importance in analyzing elections for Congress.

Chapter 6 considers several additional trends at work in American society, such as increased levels of education, which may exert some influence on electoral behavior. This final chapter also enumerates our own conclusions about the extent of change in the electorate and its importance.

While we believe stability is more characteristic of the behavior of the American electorate, every effort is made throughout this book to present the research findings of scholars who suggest that there have been far-reaching, fundamental changes in the behavior of the electorate, beginning in the early 1960s. You will soon recognize, however, that substantial controversy surrounds the study of how people behave politically. In several instances, our own conclusions about change are quite different from those of other scholars whose work we discuss. That supposed experts disagree may cause you dismay. We hope not. We candidly state, though, that the electorate's behavior is elusive, and our research abilities sometimes seem dwarfed by the magnitude of the questions we seek to answer. The noted political scientist V.O. Key best expressed this sentiment when he lamented that speaking "with precision of public opinion is a task not unlike coming to grips with the Holy Ghost."[1]

Note

1. V.O. Key, *Public Opinion and American Democracy* (New York: Alfred A. Knopf, 1961), p. 1.

Studying the

American Electorate

During the past decade political scientists and other election analysts have debated the nature of change in the behavior of American voters. Almost all scholars agree there has been fundamental change in certain areas of voting behavior. For example, many Americans have become less partisan, less participant, and less trusting during the course of the past two decades. What is unclear, however, and what divides scholars is conflict over the significance of and interrelationships between these trends. Furthermore, scholars disagree over the extent of change in the sophistication of the electorate and the relative importance of factors that influence voters' choices of candidates.

This book attempts to introduce students to change in electoral behavior and unresolved issues in electoral research. In order to accomplish this goal each chapter reviews a significant trend in electoral behavior. Each trend is described fully and documented. While describing each trend, we will point out areas of controversy where political science research has provided inconclusive answers to important questions about electoral behavior.

One probable cause of inconclusiveness in electoral research is the relative newness of political science as an empirical academic discipline in the United States. While there have been fifty presidential elections in our nation's history, only the eleven elections beginning with 1948 have been analyzed with the assistance of national opinion surveys conducted by social scientists. Therefore, we have relatively few cases upon which to base firm conclusions about citizen's opinions and voting habits.

Of course, we can study presidential elections prior to 1948 by analyzing aggregate voting statistics or studying journalistic accounts. Also, we have the results of a few small-scale attitude surveys which were conducted in small communities during national presidential campaigns of the 1940s. Some of the private pollsters were even doing pioneering work in the 1930s. But none of these sources provide today's political scientists with data which have the accuracy, depth, or richness required for modern social science research.

Political Research: Academic vs. Private

The idea that adequate analyses of the electorate can be hindered by a scarcity of scientific opinion studies may be puzzling in view of the large number of polls taken during any presidential campaign. Unfortunately, most such polls are of very limited utility to the political scientist. This is because there are some fundamental differences between private polls (like those conducted for newspapers and individual candidates) and academic polls.

Such differences are more subtle than readily apparent. In general, though, private polls are more concerned with determining *what* the public thinks. The emphasis is on substance and content. *Survey research*, the name academics have given to their own polling, has an additional purpose. Political scientists try to understand *why* citizens hold certain attitudes, and what behavior is likely to follow from certain attitudes.

One of the differences between survey research and private polling can be demonstrated by comparing the questions each uses to measure the party iden-tification or partisanship of persons interviewed. Pollsters generally ask inter-viewees only whether they are Republican, Democrat, or independent. While this approach is adequate for many purposes, it does not allow one to distin-guish between degrees of attachment to the parties. For example, labeling two individuals—one who says he is a Democrat but rarely votes or pays attention to politics, and one who says she is a Democrat and always votes for Demo-cratic candidates and occasionally works for the party—both as "Democrat" clearly omits a lot of useful information.

In order to measure party identification more accurately than pollsters, sur-vey researchers use more refined measures of partisanship for their studies. Usually this takes the form of discerning intermediate increments or shades of the pure partisan topology. For example, a survey researcher traditionally classifies those interviewed according to the category below that best describes their partisanship:

Strong Democrat (SD)
Weak Democrat (WD)
Independent-leaning Democrat (I-D)

Independent (I)
Independent-leaning Republican (I-R)
Weak Republican (WR)
Strong Republican (SR)

Such careful differentiation of partisanship obviously produces more useful information about the concept. For example, political scientists have found important differences both between weak and strong identifiers within each party and between independents who lean toward a party and those who do not lean. Figure 1-1 provides illustrations of these sorts of differences. One can see, for example, that strong partisans of both parties stand out as the most interested in political campaigns, the most concerned with election outcomes, and the most likely to vote. On the other hand, weak partisans of both parties are hardly distinct from independents leaning toward one of the parties. And both of these groups stand apart from "pure" independents, especially in whether they care who wins the election and whether they vote. Clearly, much of this subtlety would be lost if we simply grouped all Democrats, all Republicans, and all independents together as pollsters frequently do.

There are other differences between pollsters and survey researchers. Because pollsters usually must employ the least expensive means of getting their information, they may cut costs in ways that subtly affect the accuracy of the opinions they seek to assess. One example involves choice of survey participants. The person initially chosen to be interviewed (a *respondent*) may, for example, not be home when the interviewer visits or telephones the home. Pollsters frequently forego returning to such a home, or calling back, and instead interview a neighbor or another respondent who is at home. The practice of substituting respondents may seriously bias the sample and produce a misleading profile of public opinion. We know, for example, that respondent substitution often results in disproportionate numbers of interviews with homemakers and retirees who happen to be home more than family wage earners.

Telephone interviews are another example of the way pollsters cut costs. A typical telephone interview costs 50 to 60 percent less than a home interview, and therein lies its attractiveness. But telephone interviewing has two drawbacks that make it generally unacceptable to academic survey researchers. First, the telephone format usually requires that interviews be relatively short, usually no more than thirty minutes, and limited primarily to closed-ended questions. Such questions offer the respondent a fixed choice of responses, and spontaneous or original responses are seldom allowed. This format obviously does not permit the interviewer to go into any depth in following up on interviewees' responses. For example, telephone interviews may show that

Figure 1-1

Political Attitudes and Behavior by Partisanship, 1988

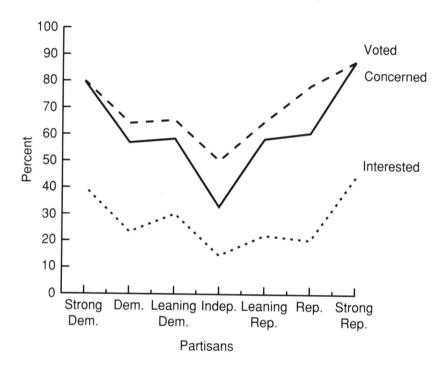

concerned—"cares a great deal which party wins the election."
voted—reported voting in 1988 presidential election.
interested—"very much interested in the political campaigns."

Source: National Election Study, 1988.

the public distrusts a particular candidate. But without probing, open-ended, follow-up questions, the telephone interviewer may not find out *why* the candidate evokes low levels of trust. Survey researchers use fixed-choice questions too, but interviewers may spend over an hour with each respondent in their homes, probing and following up on key questions, often with the benefit of visual aids.

A second problem with telephone interviewing is its built-in biases against the poor[1] and those with lower levels of education. The rural or inner-city poor often cannot afford the cost of home telephone service. No telephone survey can honestly claim to represent the whole of "public opinion" as long as one segment of the citizenry is systematically excluded from the sampling process. It would be difficult to study nonvoting with a telephone poll, for example, because more nonvoters than voters lack telephones, and therefore could not be interviewed.

The size of the sample used by pollsters and survey researchers is also important. In this area private pollsters like George Gallup made pioneering contributions during the early days of opinion research. Through a long trial-and-error process Gallup determined that the optimal sample size for a national opinion survey is about 1,500 interviews.[2] Such a sample size keeps sampling error to no more than plus or minus ($\pm$) 3 percent. This means that if a national sample of 1,500 individuals shows that 25 percent of the respondents oppose additional taxes, then the actual opposition among all Americans will fall between 22 and 28 percent, 95 percent of the time. Thus the researcher can be reasonably confident that a 1,500-person sample closely reflects what would be true of the entire population.

Table 1-1 presents the margin of error associated with various sample sizes. These figures are applicable to national surveys as well as samples from smaller populations. Pollsters and survey researchers seldom use samples as large as 4,000 because of the high costs associated with interviewing such a sample. Survey researchers practically never use national surveys smaller than 1,200, but pollsters are increasingly resorting to smaller samples.

The final distinction we will make between pollsters and political scientists is the research style of the two groups. Pollsters generally pay for their research through subscription sales of poll results. Poll subscribers, like newspapers and their readers, are usually interested in election predictions or opinions on a divisive issue, rather than analysis of trends in response to a particular question or the processes of candidate choice or opinion change. Therefore, polls of private polling organizations tend to be extremely topical. Questions are dropped once the issue has faded from public interest, or rewritten to be germane to the issue as presently discussed, with no concern as to how the rewording complicates the assessment of trends. Political scientists, conversely, emphasize continuity in their research, eschewing the trendy style of pollsters. By using identical survey items over long periods, political scientists can collect survey data that generally allow more sophisticated analyses of change in the electorate.

Our discussion of the differences between pollsters and academic survey researchers is not meant to disparage private pollsters. Our only intent is to show that pollsters are doing a different kind of research. Pollsters like George Gallup, Louis Harris, and Daniel Yankelovich, among others, have, in fact,

Table 1-1

Sampling Error Associated with Various Sample Sizes

Number of Interviews	Margin of Error (in percentage points)
4,000	± 2
1,500	± 3
1,000	± 4
750	± 4
600	± 5
400	± 6
200	± 8
100	±11

Note: Based upon sampling error as calculated from experience with the Gallup sample.
Source: C. W. Roll, Jr., and A. H. Cantril, *Polls: Their Use and Misuse in Politics* (New York: Basic Books, 1972), p. 72.

made important and lasting contributions to public opinion research. Where appropriate, we will make use of such research produced by private polling firms. But for the most part, the wealth of polls offers little aid in efforts to understand the political involvement of citizens.

Landmarks in Electoral Research

One book stands at the fore of past academic research into electoral behavior: *The American Voter*, by Angus Campbell, Philip E. Converse, Warren E. Miller, and Donald E. Stokes, from the University of Michigan. This book was published in 1960 as a definitive study of the presidential elections of 1952 and 1956.[3] To date, over 100,000 copies of this classic volume have been sold.

The American Voter stands as the major landmark in electoral research for two reasons. First, its research techniques and questions have been adopted widely in subsequent research. Second, the substantive findings serve as standards against which new research must be judged. Thus, when we speak about change in the electorate, we are generally talking about movement away from the model of voting behavior postulated in this early volume.

Because of the pivotal importance of *The American Voter*, it will serve as the dividing point of our chronological review of the electoral research literature. First, we will review the findings of studies at Columbia University which predate *The American Voter*. Then we will discuss the American Voter model developed at the University of Michigan and summarize its major contributions. Some of the research that has followed *The American Voter* will be presented as extensions of the model.

The Early Years

It can be argued that the roots of the study of American electoral behavior and public opinion can be found in the efforts of political historians of the late nineteenth and early twentieth centuries. Of these, none was more influential than Frederick Jackson Turner.[4] Turner's work, especially his classic study of antebellum American politics,[5] was motivated by ". . . the strong conviction that maps showing the distribution of demographic, economic, and political variables could be used as powerful tools in explaining the past political behavior of the people of the United States."[6]

Turner's primary research tool was *cartography* (the use of maps). In turn, his work highlighted the impact of characteristics that could be summarized for aggregate political units (such as counties or precincts) and then mapped. He concluded that such socio-economic characteristics as income, occupation, place of residence, and the like played powerful roles in shaping political behavior. His work, among others, helped shape the *social determinism*, or Columbia, model of electoral behavior, developed at Columbia University in the 1930s and 1940s. It was at Columbia that most of the very early voting studies by social scientists were conducted.

Stuart A. Rice's *Quantitative Methods of Politics*, published in 1928, was the first Columbia contribution.[7] One observer noted that Rice's work was "the first noteworthy attempt to connect quantitative research on voting behavior with more general social science problems, such as the study of social change and the determinants of attitudes."[8] However, Rice's study was based almost exclusively on aggregate data or small, nonsystematic samples of student attitudes. No use was made of opinion surveys, as polling was largely unheard of until the mid-1930s, long after Rice's work.[9] Because of this limitation, Rice had to make many highly speculative interpretations of his findings as they related to individual attitude formation and change. It was twelve years before anyone at Columbia initiated a study of individuals' political attitudes using survey research.

The People's Choice. The first major surveys directed by Columbia researchers were sponsored by the university's Office of Radio Research. This department was later renamed the Bureau of Applied Social Research as its scope of interest expanded. A sociologist named Paul Lazarsfeld directed the first Columbia efforts, assisted by a group of sociologists including Bernard Berelson and Hazel Gaudet.

Early in his career Lazarsfeld had developed an interest in theories of individual preference and choice. In particular, he and his colleagues were involved in research on consumer product preferences to determine what impact marketing and media (radio) campaigns had upon consumer's choices among competing products. But Lazarsfeld could not locate a foundation or other philanthropic organization willing to fund a project with such a commercial focus. This prompted him to redirect his research interests. The result was his decision to study the impact of political campaigns on voters' choices among competing candidates. The Rockefeller Foundation and Time, Inc. agreed to fund such a study of the 1940 presidential contest between Franklin D. Roosevelt and Wendell Willkie.[10]

Lazarsfeld chose to carry out his research in Erie County, Ohio, and 600 citizens of that county were selected to participate in the main part of the study. The research team employed a *panel design*, one in which respondents are interviewed several times, so that changes in attitudes and candidate preferences could be followed throughout the campaign. The respondents to Lazarsfeld's survey were interviewed seven times, before and immediately following the campaign. The results of this study were published in 1944 under the title *The People's Choice.*[11]

Lazarsfeld's interest in consumer choice shows through in his research design. He hypothesized that campaigns were successful in "selling" products—the products being candidates for the presidency. He believed that if a candidate was properly marketed by the media and other campaign events, much as a new shampoo or toothpaste is advertised, then the public (voters) might purchase (vote for) the candidate.

This consumer preference model of electoral behavior proved to be a disappointment. It was discovered that most voters had long-lasting "product" or "brand name" loyalties, in the form of pre-existing commitments to one of the political parties. These loyalties served to stymie the effectiveness of the campaign in its efforts to "sell" the candidates. Traditional loyalties to their political party's nominee were so great that almost eighty percent of the residents of Erie County knew whether they would vote for the Democratic incumbent (Roosevelt) or his Republican challenger (Willkie) long before the campaign had run its course. Because of this early commitment to one candidate or the other, the citizens of Erie County exhibited little interest in, or knowledge of, the campaign.

One aspect of the Erie County research proved to be more productive. As sociologists, Lazarsfeld and his associates had asked the 600 persons studied about their social group affiliations and personal background. Such questions were routinely asked in the early days of survey research, in order to check how representative a sample was of a population. The answers to the personal background questions, such as income, occupation, and the like, were compared with figures from the U.S. Census. If the figures from the survey were close to, or matched, the figures from the Census, the sample was considered to be representative of the population.

Three of these variables—the individual's religion, social status, and place of residence (urban or rural)—were important in predicting vote choices. It was found that Catholics tended to be Democrats while Protestants tended to be Republicans. Low social status and high social status were associated with the Democrats and Republicans, respectively. Rural citizens were more likely to be Republican and urban dwellers were more often Democratic. These three factors were combined into an index of Political Predisposition that proved to be a good predictor of an individual's vote. For example, about three quarters of those individuals who were wealthy (high status), Protestant, and rural residents were very likely to vote Republican in 1940.

In analyzing citizens' predispositions, Lazarsfeld found that some individuals had been "cross-pressured."[12] This meant that one factor indicated they might vote Republican while another predicted a Democratic vote. For instance, a Protestant, urban resident was cross-pressured between the "Republicanism" of the Protestant religion and a "Democratic" urban living environment. Cross-pressured individuals were among the very last to make up their minds about whether and how they would vote. As they approached election day they took one of two alternative courses of action. Some simply withdrew psychologically from the contest and disavowed all interest in the campaign or voting. Others sought more information with which to make a voting decision. The researchers thought that the media might reach these persons, but it was found that they sought advice from personal friends, work associates, and family more often than from the media. Thus, cross-pressured voters resolved their dilemmas by going along with the decision of the majority of others in their immediate environment.

The one provocative question dealt with by the authors of *The People's Choice* was what role, if any, the media played in the 1940 campaign in Erie county. They concluded that the media had little, if any, direct effect on the mass public.[13] However, Lazarsfeld's research group hypothesized that the media did affect voters through a *two-step flow of communication*. This process was based on the finding that the media campaigns of each party did reach the most highly partisan activists supporting the respective nominees (Step 1). These strong partisans responded to the media's messages by increasing their partisan commitment. At that point they became *opinion leaders* who tried to mold and shape the opinions of the less partisan citizens around them (Step 2).

We have gone into fairly substantial detail about this landmark in electoral research. This attention to one early study cannot be said to stem from any particular virtue of the researcher, however. It may have been fairly exotic for the 1940s, but today it ranks as a rather ordinary project. The importance of *The People's Choice* likewise does not lie in its methodological sophistication. A study of attitudes in one county in Ohio could be suspect in its application to voters elsewhere. Nevertheless, *The People's Choice* remains an intriguing and important study due to the timelessness of many of its conclusions. In the nearly three decades since this study, political scientists have consistently replicated many of its major findings, such as the link between partisanship and secondary group affiliations like religion. They still find that citizens make a voting decision very early in a campaign and that many are not interested in the campaign or any other aspect of politics. Thus, this first important study has continuing relevance in the electoral research literature.

Voting. It is clear that *The People's Choice* turned out to be a far different book than Lazarsfeld and his colleagues originally envisioned. Instead of affirming the "consumer preference" model of voter behavior, the final product was an analysis of the role of group influences in individuals' decisions. In turn, the characteristics found to have the greatest impact on the vote—religion, social status, and place of residence—were originally included primarily as a check on the representativeness of the sample, and not for compelling theoretical reasons.

To determine whether their findings could be extended beyond Erie County, Ohio, in 1940 and to build a more elaborate theory of the influence of groups on individual behavior, the Columbia research team undertook a second major study in 1948. This research, under the direction of senior researcher Bernard R. Berelson, assisted by Lazarsfeld and William N. McPhee, was a sophisticated replication of the earlier Erie County, Ohio, project. More persons were surveyed during the campaign (1,000), and the study was located in Elmira, New York. The research was reported in *Voting*, which was published in 1954.[14]

Berelson and his colleagues found little in Elmira that contradicted the earlier Ohio study. Perhaps the most important similarities of the two studies lie in their analyses of the phenomenon of cross-pressured voters. Berelson again found voters who were cross-pressured to vote Republican and Democratic, with religion and social status as the sources of these pressures. The cross-pressured voters were found to be late deciders, and were more likely to have changed their party identification between 1944 and 1948. Elmira was strongly Republican, and this was found to exert enormous influence on cross-pressured voters; most of them eventually went along with the majority in Elmira and voted for Thomas E. Dewey, the Republican nominee for the presidency.

The authors of *Voting* also made an important observation in Elmira regarding a concept termed *perceptual screening*.[15] Perceptual screening occurs when a voter holds a distorted perception of a candidate's or party's position on some issue. This misperception is not intentional; instead, the voter subconsciously brings about agreement between his own opinion and his perception of a candidate's opinion. For example, as shown in Figure 1-2, Republicans who favored the Taft-Hartley Act were more likely to believe that Governor Dewey was in favor of the act than were Republicans who opposed the act. (Dewey, in fact, opposed the act.) Republican supporters of Taft-Hartley obviously misperceived Dewey's position. Many Democrats supporting Taft-Hartley misperceived their nominee's position on the issue, too. Harry Truman had vetoed Taft-Hartley in 1947, and campaigned against it in 1948. Still, of those Democrats favoring the legislation, 40 percent were of the opinion that Truman favored Taft-Hartley. This type of perceptual screening occurred on other issues, such as price controls and public housing, as well.

Voting also articulated an important theory of political participation. In Elmira, as in Erie County, many citizens were not particularly interested in politics. Neither did they participate in the political life of Elmira. Berelson's commentary on this political apathy was unique and almost without precedent.[16] Rather than condemn political inactivity, as had most democratic theorists prior to the 1940s, Berelson extolled its virtue. He argued that political apathy and inactivity make a democratic political system more stable and flexible than would be the case with high levels of citizen involvement. He reasoned if everyone in a community like Elmira were to become very active in politics, making demands on the government, then the system would collapse under the pressure of internal political conflict. This rather unconventional endorsement of apathy was controversial, and the debate that ensued continues today.

Despite the importance of *The People's Choice* and *Voting*, Columbia waned as a center of electoral research. Many scholars were dissatisfied with the social determinism model employed by Berelson, Lazarsfeld, and their colleagues. Specifically, while voting is an *individual* political activity, the Columbia researchers described voting as an act stemming from *group* influences. In turn, little attention was paid to political factors, such as issues or the appeal of candidates.

To rectify these, and other, shortcomings, students of voting behavior introduced new models and new research techniques—especially national sur-

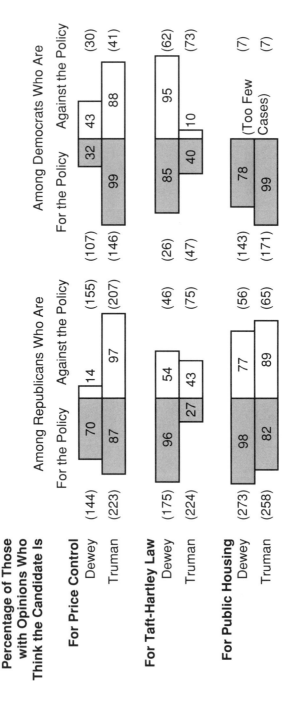

Figure 1-2

How Voters' Own Stands on the Issues Affect Their Perception of Candidates' Stands

Percentage of Those
with Opinions Who
Think the Candidate Is

Note: For simplification and clarity, the "No stand" and the "Don't know" responses have been omitted from this chart. The omission does not affect the point of the data.
Source: Bernard R. Berelson, Paul F. Lazarsfeld, and William N. McPhee, *Voting* (Chicago: University of Chicago Press, 1954), p. 221.

veys. Further, sociologists at Columbia moved to redirect their research on consumer preference back to projects more clearly related to product marketing and the media. The center of political research moved westward to the campus of the University of Michigan.

The Michigan Model of Voter Behavior

During World War II the U.S. government realized it would be useful to know more about Americans' attitudes toward various aspects of the war effort. For example, the administrators of the War Bond program needed to know more about why citizens bought and sold bonds. To assist in such opinion research, the Department of Agriculture offered the services of its Division of Program Services to other governmental units.[17]

After the war, many of these opinion researchers left government service because of severe budget cuts. Rensis Likert, Angus Campbell, George Katoris, and Leslie Kish left the Division of Program Surveys to establish the Survey Research Center (SRC) at the University of Michigan.[18] The Survey Research Center is now known as the Center for Political Studies (CPS) and has come to be the preeminent electoral research organization in the world.

Since 1948, the CPS has conducted national opinion surveys in conjunction with every presidential election. It also has sponsored (since 1954) a national opinion survey in off-year congressional elections between presidential elections. The sampling error associated with these studies is quite small, with better than 1,200 persons interviewed in each survey. Together, these surveys constitute the single most valuable research data available to scholars of electoral behavior. Since many of the same questions have been used in the surveys throughout the years, these data provide us with an unparalleled view of the changes in Americans' opinions and attitudes over more than two decades.

Three early books and several articles out of Michigan define what is called the social-psychological, or "Michigan," model of voting behavior. The core volume, entitled *The American Voter*, was published in 1960. It was preceded by *The People Elect a President* (1952), and *The Voter Decides* (1954), and followed in 1966 by *Elections and the Political Order*, an anthology of essays and scholarly articles.[19]

These books differed from the Columbia research in their approach to understanding political attitudes. This difference was explained through a concept called the *funnel of causality*. Richard G. Niemi and Herbert F. Weisberg have summarized this concept, illustrated in Figure 1-3, as follows:

> The phenomenon to be explained—voting—is at the tip of the funnel. But it depends on many factors that occur earlier. The funnel's axis is time.

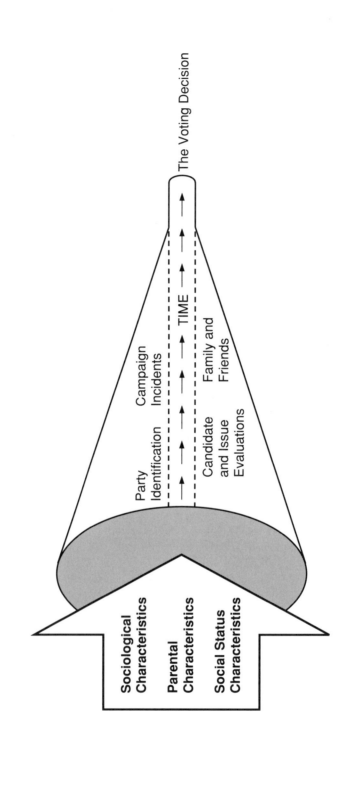

Events follow one another, converging in a series of causal chains and moving from the mouth to the stem of the funnel. Thus a multitude of causes narrow into the voting act. At the mouth of the funnel are sociological background characteristics (ethnicity, race, region, religion, and the like), social status characteristics (education, occupation, class), and parental characteristics (class, partisanship). All affect the person's choice of party identification, the next item in the funnel. Party identification in turn influences the person's evaluation of the candidates and the issues, which takes us further into the funnel. Then . . . (come) incidents of the campaign itself. . . . Even closer to the tip are the conversations which the voter has with family and friends about the election. Then comes the vote itself.[20]

Michigan researchers concentrated, then and now, on those variables that are closest to the voting decision. This approach can be attributed to the influence of social psychology on modern political science. Today's typical political scientist believes that "the immediate determinants of an individual's behavior lie more clearly in his attitudes and his perceptual organization of his environment than in either his/her social position or other 'objective' situational factors."[21] This perspective is distinctly different from that of Columbia sociologists Lazarsfeld and Berelson who—like others of their discipline—dealt primarily with sociological or group variables, variables which are further back in the funnel and away from the immediate voting decision. While group based behavior is certainly important to contemporary political scientists, they are not motivated primarily by such an orientation.

Findings and Interpretations.   Several interesting findings and interpretations were advanced by the Michigan researchers. We will concentrate on findings of *The American Voter*, the study of the 1952 and 1956 elections. But where appropriate we will discuss later findings that elaborate on *The American Voter* and complete certain elements of the American Voter model.

The fundamental and most enduring findings of the model relate to the importance of *party identification* in shaping not only electoral behavior, but political attitudes and opinions as well. Party identification has been defined as "a psychological commitment or attachment to a political party that normally predisposes us to evaluate that party and its candidates in a favorable light."[22]

The most noteworthy effect of party identification is that it predisposes individuals to vote for their own party's candidate. In 1952, for example, 99 percent of those who were Strong Republicans voted for Dwight Eisenhower, the GOP nominee, and 84 percent of the Strong Democrats voted for Adlai Stevenson, the losing Democratic nominee. Overall, 78 percent of all voters in 1952 supported the presidential candidate of the party with which they identified. The figure in 1956 was 83 percent.

Thus, only 22 percent of those identifying with a political party in 1952, and 17 percent of those doing so in 1956, "defected" or voted for the opposition political party's candidate for president. Similar patterns have been found in succeeding election studies, with the greatest discrepancy between party identification and vote choice being found in Democrats' support for their nominee. Democrats, through the years, have not supported their presidential nominee with the consistency that characterizes Republican support for their nominee. Nevertheless, partisan loyalty has been the norm in both parties.

The partisan voting finding led to Philip Converse's articulation of the concept of the *normal vote*.[23] Converse argues that partisan attachment is the prevailing *long-term force* in voting. In elections which are characterized primarily by party voting, the result is a normal vote. However, as Converse and others have noted, not all elections are marked by strong party loyalty. In such elections *short-term forces* prevail over partisanship and cause a deviation from the normal vote. The short-term forces most discussed in the literature are *candidate images* and the *issue orientations* of voters. (These will be discussed in this and later chapters.)

The normal vote concept has become the basis for classifying presidential elections as maintaining elections, deviating elections, and realigning elections.[24] A *maintaining* election is defined as one in which the normal vote is maintained and therefore the majority party captures the presidency. An example of a maintaining election is 1976, the year the Democratic (and majority) party nominated and elected Jimmy Carter to the presidency.

A *deviating* election occurs when short-term forces cause many majority party voters to support the minority party's nominee. This defection to the minority party by voters does not mean they will identify permanently with the minority party, however. The years 1980, 1984, and 1988 are prime examples of deviating elections. On these occasions, enough Democrats voted for Republicans Ronald Reagan and George Bush to thwart the normal vote and to elect the minority party's candidate to the presidency. Furthermore, it should be noted that the victories for the GOP did *not* swing the majority of Americans toward a permanent identification with the Republican party.

We would argue that the concepts of maintaining and realigning elections are of minimal importance to the study of contemporary presidential elections. In the ten presidential elections held since 1952, the Democratic (majority) party candidate was victorious in only three – 1960, 1964, and 1976. Further, since 1968, the Democrats have held the presidency only for Carter's single term in office. At the same time, however, Democrats have held substantial majorities in both houses of Congress (with the exception of a brief period of time in the early 1980s, when Reagan fashioned a small Republican majority in the Senate), as well as in state legislatures and governorships.

Many commentators have suggested we are in an era of a "permanent Republican presidency," and the evidence for this proposition is compelling. If such is the case, then presidential elections can no longer serve as accurate barometers of partisan sentiment. While the concepts of maintaining and deviating elections may be useless, the concept of *realigning* elections may still have analytic utility. Such elections are characterized by a "more or less durable" shift in the underlying pattern of partisanship in the electorate. This massive shift would result in the majority party dropping to minority status while the minority party vaults into power. For example, if the campaigns of Reagan and Bush had succeeded in converting many Democrats into Republicans, or persuading new voters to enter the electorate as Republicans, the elections of 1980, 1984, or 1988 would have been realigning elections.

There have been no realigning elections since the 1930s. The Democrats have maintained their majority status throughout the period following Franklin D. Roosevelt's formation of the "New Deal" coalition of blacks, Southerners, the urban working class, and intellectuals. But, some political scientists have speculated in recent years that a realigning election is imminent, for at least two reasons. First, many political scientists have concluded that party fortunes are cyclical in nature; that is, a new party gains majority status on a semi-regular basis, perhaps every thirty or forty years. Thus, some feel the Republican party's time for majority status is overdue.

A second reason for expecting a realignment is the argument that conservative Southern whites will eventually leave the Democratic party for the more conservative GOP. In fact, the Republican presidential candidate has carried the old "solid South" in every presidential election year since 1964, with the exception of native Southerner Jimmy Carter's victory there in 1976. But the Republicans are still the minority party nationwide. These facts suggest either that Southern white Democrats have *not* changed their partisan allegiance, but are merely voting Republican for the presidency and, perhaps, Democratic in other elections; or, Southern white Democrats *have* realigned, but this movement is insufficient to produce a new party balance nationwide. At any rate, it is apparent that realignment has not occurred. We will consider realignment and realigning elections in greater detail in Chapter 2.

The authors of *The American Voter* found that partisanship had a significant impact on voting behavior other than choice of candidate. It was discovered that partisanship (Republican or Democratic) stimulates political participation. Independents were generally less likely to participate in electoral politics than either partisan group. In 1952, for example, only 8 percent of Strong Republicans and 24 percent of Strong Democrats failed to vote in the presidential contest. However, 28 percent of those identified as independents failed to cast a presidential ballot. Strong partisans were also found to be more psychologically involved in electoral politics, expressing more interest in the campaign in 1956 and greater concern over the election's outcome. These findings led some early researchers to conclude that independents were not "good" citizens when contrasted with their partisan fellows. This unflattering characterization of independents has not died easily. We will consider such changes among independents in Chapter 2.

While strong partisans were found to be more involved than independents, neither group was overly active in the campaign itself. Ten percent of citizens or fewer were actively involved in any phase of the 1952 and 1956 campaigns. For example, only 3 percent of the public reported doing any work for either a party or a candidate in those years.[25] The few who were participating were Republicans, by and large.

The American Voter concluded that most citizens restricted their political involvement to the one act of voting, and this act was influenced largely by almost blind allegiance to party affiliation. Thus the voter was understood as an uninvolved, dependent creature; this was not the rational citizen that theorists had envisioned populating a democracy.

Probably the most nagging fact regarding this aspect of how Americans vote for president is that the Republican candidate won both in 1952 and in 1956. In October of 1952, 57 percent of the sample considered themselves Democrats or at least independents who leaned toward the Democratic party, while 34 percent were similarly committed to the Republican party. If party identification is the key determinant of how people vote, Stevenson, the Democrat, should have won overwhelmingly, but Eisenhower was the victor. In 1956, 51 percent versus 37 percent were Democrats, yet Eisenhower won again. Indeed, in presidential elections between 1952 and 1988 the Democrats in the electorate have always outnumbered Republicans, yet Democratic presidential candidates have lost seven of ten elections!

Extension of the Model.   Donald Stokes, a co-author of *The American Voter*, attempted to explain such apparent deviations from the partisan loyalty model. In "Some Dynamic Elements of Contests for the Presidency," Stokes examined data collected between 1952 and 1964 that facilitated comparisons of voters' attitudes toward: (1) the parties and candidates as they related to domestic and foreign policy, (2) the parties as managers of national affairs and in benefiting groups, such as working men and farmers, and (3) the candidates' personal attributes and style.[26]

Stokes found that the latter attitudes, issue-free opinions about the candidates, fluctuate most from election to election. And he concluded these fluctuations allow the party whose candidate has the better image to win the election.

This conclusion does not challenge the notion that most people vote according to their partisan identification, but it suggests that enough majority party voters desert their party to allow the minority party nominee to be elected on occasion. For example, in 1952 and 1956 Eisenhower got the support of most Republicans and Stevenson got the support of most of the more numerous Democrats, but Ike's personality won him the election by attracting enough Democrats and independents to claim the victory. Issues, Stokes found, varied little in their impact on these elections and did not determine who won the elections.

Philip E. Converse extended his work from *The American Voter* in an article on the nature of mass belief systems.[27] He found that most Americans do not hold truly meaningful political attitudes, and concluded that most individuals' opinions or *belief systems* consist primarily of "nonattitudes." Nonattitudes are defined as attitudes or groups of attitudes that lack consistency, are internally contradictory, and are unstable over time. The implicit conclusion drawn from Converse's work is that most Americans are not equipped to participate in issue-oriented politics. This depiction of an electorate moved by considerations of partisanship and candidate image, without concern for issues, is perhaps the central concept of the social-psychological model of voter behavior.

The crucial nature of partisanship in citizen politics led researchers to study the origins of partisan loyalty. They wanted to know where and from whom people learn their partisan attitudes. The learning of political attitudes such as partisanship is called *political socialization*.

In the 1952 and 1956 surveys, respondents were asked if they could recall the partisan affiliation of their parents. An individual who remembered that both parents were affiliated with the same party was in most instances also affiliated with that party. In 1952, for example, of those persons remembering that both parents were Democrats, 72 percent were Democratic themselves. Only 12 percent had chosen to be Republicans rather than adopting their parents' choice. A similar pattern of transmission of partisan values was found for offspring of Republican parentage.[28]

These early findings of adoption of parents' party identity by children were criticized by some because of the reliance on individuals' recall of their parents' political leanings. Some researchers felt that recall could be unreliable because those interviewed may not have recalled their parents' identification accurately but merely claimed consistency.

Concern about the reliability of recall data led to a second demonstration of parental transmission of partisanship. This more objective socialization study was conducted by M. Kent Jennings and Richard G. Niemi.[29] In a 1965 study they interviewed both children (high school seniors) and their parents. Again,

Table 1-2

Parent and Child Agreement in Party Identification

Parents	Child		
	Democrat	Independent	Republican
Democrat	33%	13%	4%
Independent	7	13	4
Republican	3	10	14

N = 1,852

Source: M. Kent Jennings and Richard G. Niemi, "The Transmission of Political Values from Parent to Child," *American Political Science Review,* Vol. 62 (March, 1968), p. 173.

it was found that children adopt the party orientation of their parents. These data, presented in Table 1-2, show that only 7 percent of the high school seniors held a party identification opposite that of their parents.

The American Voter Model: A Summary

The major points of the American Voter model can be summarized as follows:

1. Identification with a political party is the single most important influence in determining political behavior, especially voting.
2. Partisan identification is adopted primarily from one's parents at such an early age that personal issue positions cannot be involved in the choice of parties.
3. Politics is not an abiding concern of Americans, resulting in very few people participating in most political acts, with the exception of voting.
4. Given this low concern or salience of politics, few vote on the basis of issues. Partisans largely rely on partisan cues. Less partisan citizens, lacking a disposition to loyally support a political party and its candidates, vote on the basis of personalities or do not bother to vote at all.[30]

This model is controversial, to say the least. As Gerald Pomper observes, "Although the findings are sometimes distorted when retold, the central thrust of these studies is denigrating to the electorate."[31] The ordinary citizen, as described by early Michigan studies, was uninformed, often irrational, and hardly the model of those who assert the value of the common man's role in democratic government.

The Changing American Voter

Some political scientists were dismayed by *The American Voter*—especially its conclusions regarding the apathy and irrationality of the electorate. V.O. Key, one such political scientist, responded to *The American Voter* with a book entitled *The Responsible Electorate*.[32] About his book, Key stated that its "perverse and unorthodox argument . . . is that voters are not fools."[33] Contrary to Michigan researchers, he concluded that American voters were neither "straitjacketed by social determinants" nor "moved by subconscious urges triggered by devilishly skillful propagandists." He characterized the electorate as being "moved by concern about central and relevant questions of public policy, of governmental performance, and of executive personality."[34]

Key's challenge to *The American Voter* was focused largely on the 1930s and 1940s. Other critiques, based on analysis of change in the electorate since 1960, argue that the findings of *The American Voter* are time bound. These critics point out that the American electorate has changed substantially through the years since the presidential contests of 1952 and 1956. Events like the Cold War, the civil rights and student movements, Vietnam, recession, and Watergate have had a profound effect on the electorate, these critics contend.[35] Some argue that the Eisenhower years of the 1950s was a peculiarly benign time, one in which few political events stirred the electorate. Because of the quiescence of the 1950s, some have concluded that it is no wonder that *The American Voter* found such a docile citizenry.

What changes have occurred since the 1960s in the electorate? Political scientists have claimed three: 1. a decline in partisanship and the role of parties in the electorate, 2. a decline in political participation, especially voting, and 3. a decline in political trust. We will briefly examine some of the studies which have suggested the existence of these trends in this section, and chapters 2, 3, and 4 will each examine one trend in considerable detail. We will also consider the proposition that the three trends are somehow related.

Decline of Partisanship and Party

The decline in partisanship is probably the most often cited change in American electoral behavior since 1960. This trend is documented from several perspectives. First, researchers have found evidence of increases in the number of persons classifying themselves as independents, rather than as Democrats or Republicans. For example, according to the election studies conducted by the CPS, 23 percent of all respondents considered themselves independents in 1960, compared with 34 percent in 1984, an increase of about 48 percent.

Second, researchers have found widespread occurrence of something called *split outcomes*. Split outcomes occur when a state or congressional district votes for the nominee of one party for one high office, and the nominee of the other party for another high office. For instance, in 1980 about one third of all congressional districts split between the parties of the winning House of Representatives candidate and the presidential candidate who received a majority of the vote in that district.[36] Such disparities in electoral outcomes would not be expected if the cues the political parties were providing voters were as strong or compelling as they have been in the past.

A final perspective on the decline in partisanship involves a purported increase in the role of issues and candidate images in voting behavior. Because voters increasingly vote on the basis of these last two factors, they have less need to depend on their partisanship, some researchers have argued. Key, Pomper, and others have made important contributions to the documentation of increases in issue awareness and issue voting. More recent Survey Research Center election studies by Converse, Warren Miller, and others also acknowledge the increasing role of issues and images in voting behavior. Debate continues, however, over the actual extent of the decline of partisanship as a determinant of voter behavior, and whether issues or candidate images have replaced party as a determinant.

Decline in Political Participation

The existence of trends in participation depends largely on one's perspective. Since 1960, as Figure 1-4 shows, there has been about a 13 percent drop in voter turnout. But 1948's turnout of 51 percent may suggest that the early 1960s saw abnormally high turnout, and that we may now be returning to normalcy. It is also interesting that some observers erroneously predicted that both 1976 and 1980 would see presidential election turnouts of less than half of the eligible American electorate. Against this prediction and the seemingly unstoppable decline in turnout, the actual turnouts of 53 percent in 1980 and 1984 appear

Figure 1-4

Voter Turnout for Presidential Elections Expressed as Percentage of Voting Age Population, 1948–1988

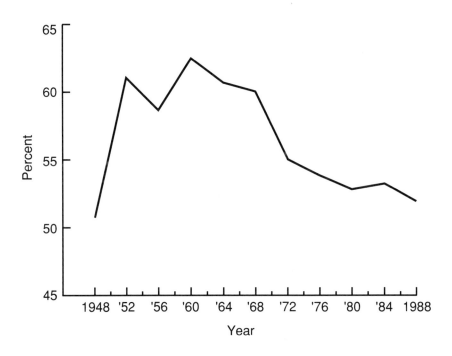

Sources: U.S. Bureau of the Census, *Statistical Abstract of the United States: 1978.* Table No. 835, p. 520; The Federal Election Commission, *The FEC Journal of Election Administration,* Volume 16, Summer 1989, pp. 4, 6.

more respectable. And yet, turnout in 1988 fell to approximately 50 percent of the eligible electorate, suggesting the decline in turnout continues unabated.

In order to place this trend in perspective, it is also useful to note that participation in most other election activities has changed very little. As we will show in Chapter 3, the number of persons working in political campaigns or attending political rallies has declined very little between 1960 and 1988. Thus, the turnout decline may not necessarily represent a broader tendency on the part of voters to withdraw from all forms of political participation.

Many political observers are nevertheless greatly concerned about the decline of presidential voter turnout since 1960. If it were to persist, nonvoters would outnumber voters (if they do not already), and the meaning of winning elections might well become obscure to a candidate. As it is, however, only presidential elections, of all elections in the United States, whether at the national, state, or local level, currently enjoy turnouts of greater than or equal to 50 percent. So in some respects, presidential elections are given preferential attention by voters even today.

Decline in Political Trust

Between 1960 and 1984 there was a steady, although not constant, decline in Americans' trust of government and its leaders. There were two dimensions of this change. The first involved an increasing public sentiment that government leaders were corrupt and served primarily special interest groups. In turn, this suggested that Watergate was the source of such beliefs. Arthur Miller, however, has demonstrated that this trend began before Watergate became a household word.[37] Thus the cause of the decline in trust went deeper than a Watergate explanation allows.

A second dimension of declining trust involved *political efficacy,* the belief that the individual has some influence over government. Fewer and fewer Americans expressed this feeling of control over their government, as studies at the Center for Political Studies have revealed. Such changes in political trust are particularly engaging when one considers that distrust of government was an unheard-of phenomenon in the 1950s. *The American Voter* scarcely mentions the concept of Americans being dissatisfied with their government. In fact, most trust questions were not included in CPS surveys until the 1960s. This rapidity of change makes the topic of trust perhaps the most engaging of the three trends in electoral change, especially in light of the fact that in 1984 the downward drift in political trust appeared to reverse itself.

The Importance of Electoral Change

In the preceding section, we identified three commonly noted trends in electoral behavior which have occurred since *The American Voter* appeared: declining partisanship, participation, and trust. The importance of these trends lies in their relationship to the stability of our nation.

Theorists and social scientists around the world have long marveled at the stability of American democracy. Except for one major upheaval—the Civil War—American history is unique in its domestic tranquility. No other democracy on earth can match this record.

Most observers of this phenomenon agree that America's stability is not due to fate or simple luck; certain factors have engendered it. The first of these factors is our political party system. It is argued that our two-party system provides a more stable government than a multiparty arrangement that requires coalitions to achieve a majority. Certainly, two-party countries throughout the world have enjoyed stability, and the United States is a prime example. Multiple-party systems, as in Italy and France, and single-party systems, as in many of the emerging countries, have not been stable.

Furthermore, some of those who question whether government is responsive to the public in this country contend that the two parties usually agree on most of the major issues facing the nation. Disagreements between the parties are more in terms of means than ends. These ends are policies which serve the interests of economic and political elites. Because elites and the parties narrow the range of questions open to political debate, they stimulate stability in political affairs.

We must note that not all multiparty systems are unstable, nor are all two-party systems stable. Some countries in Scandinavia, for example Sweden, have multiparty systems and are stable. For a time Austria had a two-party system but was unstable. What is important are the divisions in society reflected by the political parties. In the United States, these divisions are over means, not ends; this is the primary reason we believe the two-party system in the United States contributes to the stability of the political systems.

Political participation also creates stability in America, according to some researchers. Participation, such as voting, is thought to make citizens feel more efficacious, meaning that they can be more confident that their votes count. Furthermore, by participating citizens are said to gain a sense of being integrated into the political system. Cynics retort that voters are merely co-opted by the system; however, as long as participating citizens believe that they are participating meaningfully, the result is a more stable system. A content citizen is not likely to follow the lead of demagogues and revolutionaries.

Finally, political trust can be considered one of the foundations of a democratic system. It is reasonable to suggest that unless citizens trust the political system, they will not actively support it, psychologically or otherwise. At least in theory, a democratic political system is supposed to fulfill the needs and desires of the citizenry. If citizens perceive—correctly or incorrectly—that the system is not working to their benefit, and as a consequence lose trust in the system, this suggests the political system may not long persist.[38]

In summary, the declines in partisanship, participation, and trust have all been linked to the concept of political stability in America. These trends are all in directions that suggest diminished stability, and therein lies their importance. Will these trends actually bring about increased instability in the electorate? As we examine each pattern in the succeeding chapters, we will consider this question.

Notes

1. Charles W. Roll, Jr., and Albert H. Cantril, *Polls: Their Use and Misuse in Politics* (New York: Basic Books, 1972), pp. 96–102; Donald S. Tull and Gerald S. Albaum, "Bias in Random Digit Dialed Surveys," *Public Opinion Quarterly* 41 (1971): 389–95.
2. Roll and Cantril, *Polls*, pp. 65–75; Herbert F. Weisberg and Bruce D. Bowen, *An Introduction to Survey Research and Data Analysis* (San Francisco: W. H. Freeman, 1977), pp. 40–41.
3. Angus Campbell, Philip E. Converse, Warren E. Miller, and Donald E. Stokes, *The American Voter* (New York: John Wiley and Sons, 1960).
4. For an excellent description of the early history of the study of American voting behavior, see Joel H. Silbey, Allan G. Bogue, and William H. Flanigan, eds., *The History of American Electoral Behavior* (Princeton, NJ: Princeton University Press, 1978), pp. 3–19.
5. Frederick Jackson Turner, *The United States. 1830–1850: The Nation and Its Sections* (Gloucester, MA: Peter Smith, 1958).
6. Silbey, *et al., The History of American Electoral Behavior*, p. 8.
7. S. A. Rice, *Quantitative Methods in Politics* (New York: Alfred A. Knopf, 1928).
8. Peter H. Rossi, "Four Landmarks in Voting Research," in *American Voting Behavior*, eds. Eugene Burdick and Arthur J. Brodbeck (New York: Free Press, 1959), p. 7.
9. *Ibid.*
10. *Ibid.*, pp. 15–16.
11. Paul F. Lazarsfeld, Bernard R. Berelson, and Hazel Gaudet, *The People's Choice* (New York: Duell, Sloan & Pearce, 1944).
12. Lazarsfeld *et al., People's Choice*, p. 53.
13. Rossi, "Four Landmarks in Voting Research," p. 19, reports that Lazarsfeld told him in a private interview that this finding was unanticipated by the researchers.

14. Bernard R. Berelson, Paul F. Lazarsfeld, and William N. McPhee, *Voting* (Chicago: University of Chicago Press, 1954).

15. *Ibid.*, Chap. 10.

16. *Ibid.*, Chap. 14.

17. Richard W. Boyd and Herbert H. Hyman, "Survey Research," in *Handbook of Political Science*, vol. 7, *Strategies of Inquiry*, eds. Fred I. Greenstein and Nelson W. Polsby (Reading, MA: Addison-Wesley Publishing Co., 1975), p. 311.

18. *Ibid.*, p. 312 ff.

19. Campbell *et al.*, *The American Voter*; Angus Campbell and Robert Kahn, *The People Elect a President* (Ann Arbor, MI: Survey Research Center, Institute for Social Research, University of Michigan, 1952); Angus Campbell, Gerald Gurin, and Warren Miller, *The Voter Decides* (Evanston: Row, Peterson & Co., 1954); Angus Campbell et al., *Elections and the Political Order* (New York: John Wiley & Sons, 1966).

20. Richard G. Niemi and Herbert F. Weisberg, *Controversies in American Voting Behavior* (San Francisco: W. H. Freeman & Co., 1976), p. 12.

21. Rossi, "Four Landmarks in Voting Research," p. 37.

22. Herbert B. Asher, *Presidential Elections and American Politics*, fourth ed. (Chicago: The Dorsey Press, 1988), p. 41.

23. Philip E. Converse, "The Concept of a Normal Vote," in *Elections and the Political Order*, eds. Campbell et al., pp. 9–39.

24. *Ibid.*; also see Gerald Pomper, *Elections in America* (New York: Dodd, Mead & Co., 1974), pp. 104–11.

25. Campbell *et al.*, *The American Voter*, p. 91.

26. Donald E. Stokes, "Some Dynamic Elements of Contests for the Presidency," *American Political Science Review*, 60 (March 1966): 19–28.

27. Philip E. Converse, "The Nature of Belief Systems in Mass Public," in *Ideology and Discontent*, ed. David E. Apter (Glencoe: Free Press, 1964).

28. Campbell *et al.*, *The American Voter*, p. 147.

29. M. Kent Jennings and Richard G. Niemi, "The Transmission of Political Values from Parent to Child," *American Political Science Review*, 62 (March 1968): 169–84.

30. This listing of findings from *The American Voter* is by no means exhaustive. For an excellent, although outdated, review of the literature on voting behavior spawned by *The American Voter*, see Gerald M. Pomper, "The Impact of The American Voter on Political Science,"

Political Science Quarterly, (Winter, 1978): 617–28, especially his listing of "twenty-five disputed propositions."

31. Gerald Pomper, *Voters' Choice* (New York: Dodd, Mead & Co., 1975), p. 5.
32. V. O. Key, *The Responsible Electorate* (Cambridge, MA: Belknap Press, 1966).
33. *Ibid.*, p. vii.
34. *Ibid.*, pp. 7–8.
35. See especially Pomper, *Voters' Choice*; and Warren E. Miller and Teresa E. Levitin, *Leadership and Change: The New Politics and the American Electorate* (Cambridge, MA: Winthrop Publishers, 1976).
36. Michael M. Gant and Dennis Black, "The Determinants of Split Results at the Congressional District Level." Presented at the Annual Meetings of the Midwest Political Science Association, Chicago, April, 1987.
37. Arthur H. Miller, "Political Issues and Trust in Government," *American Political Science Review*, 68 (September 1974): 951–72.
38. For an excellent treatment of democratic political systems, and the role of citizen trust and support in the viability of these systems, see David Easton, *A Systems Analysis of Political Life* (New York: John Wiley & Sons, 1965).

2

Voter's Choice: The Decline of

Party and Partisanship

The decisions of citizens to vote for or against a particular candidate are generally recognized to be affected by three factors: party identification, issue positions, and candidate image (how the candidates are perceived). Through the 1960s, party identification was considered the strongest of these factors, followed by (depending on the election) candidate image and issues. But since the early 1970s, many political scientists have noted that issues and image have played an increasingly important role in voters' decisions, at the expense of the influence of partisanship.

In this chapter we explore two distinct themes. Our first theme is the relative impact of partisanship, issues, and candidate image on vote choice in presidential elections during the period 1952–1988. Especially, we want to explore how the mix of these factors has changed. Our second theme, and the one which we will introduce first, is the declining role of political parties in electoral decision making by voters. Unlike many scholars, we believe far too much has been made of this decline.

Our focus, then, is on party identification, and the reasons for this are three-fold. First, as we noted above, party identification has long been the most important influence on the vote.[1] Indeed, even today most Democrats vote for Democrats, and most Republicans vote for Republicans.[2] Second, as described by *The American Voter*, party identification did not seem to have much to do with politics. For example, many people "became" Democrats or Republicans because of their parents identification as such and not for any overt policy based reasons. Third, in the American political system, citizens can influence policy—what government does—primarily through elections. Thus, if people vote on the basis of party identification, elections will not serve their most important purpose of establishing a political link between citizens and leaders. Consequently, the democratic ideal of "government of the people, by the people, and for the people" will exist largely as a myth. We wish to explore whether this is still true in the 1980s.

The Nature of Partisanship

There are two understandings of, or perspectives on, party identification in the United States. The "traditionalist" perspective is most strongly associated with the "Michigan model" of voter behavior. The "revisionist" perspective challenges many of the traditional understandings of the concept.

The Traditionalist Perspective

According to the traditional perspective on partisanship, party identification is "a psychological identification, which can persist without legal recognition or evidence of formal membership and even without a consistent record of party support . . . [it is] the individuals' affective orientation to an important group-object in his environment."[3] This means that party identification is primarily an *emotional* attachment to one party or another, and *not* the result of the individual's consideration of which party might be more likely to better serve his or her interests. This is so because party identification is formed very early in life, is usually consistent with one's parents' partisanship, and is therefore not based on policy concerns. In short, "a person can be said to choose his party attachment only insofar as he chooses his religion."[4] Politically, being a Democrat or Republican is not very different from being an avid reader of mystery novels, a devoted follower of the Cleveland Browns, or a committed member of the local garden club.

Nevertheless, it is common to think of Democrats as more "liberal" than Republicans. Does this not suggest that issues strongly influence one's decision to become, or at least remain, a Democrat or Republican? Not according to the authors of *The American Voter*: "the role of party identification seems primarily to be that of an antecedent factor that colors . . . attitudes as they are formed."[5] Party identification comes first and shapes attitudes on specific policies. People are *not* Democrats because they are liberal; they are liberal *because* they are Democrats.

Because issues do not have much impact on the *development* of party identification, new issues will not bring about *changes* in party identification. Only cataclysmic events, such as the Civil War or the Great Depression of the 1930s, can bring about substantial changes in party identification. Partisanship is, therefore, quite stable; it is "an attachment which is not easily changed."[6]

Finally, issues play no important role in determining how people vote, since issues have so little to do with partisanship. To be sure, people with different issue positions vote differently. For example, George Bush and Michael Dukakis took dramatically different positions on the issue of abortion during the 1988 presidential campaign. It would not be surprising to find that "pro-lifers" voted for Bush, while "pro-choice" advocates voted for Dukakis. But according to the traditionalist perspective, this link between vote choice and issue position is false, or *spurious*. Republicans are more favorably disposed toward Bush *and* more likely to be anti-abortion. Any relationship between issues and voting is almost entirely due to party affiliation.

In sum, this interpretation of party identification might dishearten those who view elections as a means for people to control government. People do not pay a great deal of attention to politics and tend to vote on the basis of party. Thus, the results of voting—the election of one candidate or the other—have very limited impact on government, according to this interpretation.

The Revisionist Perspective

In recent years, a different interpretation of partisanship has been advanced. This alternative or "revisionist" perspective is based on the concern that "we have been misled by conceiving of party ID as a childhood-instilled, affectively-based allegiance to the elephant or the donkey."[7] In this view, party identification is "a citizen's running balance sheet on the two parties."[8] Partisanship is not merely a psychological attachment without political meaning; rather, it reflects the citizen's judgment of the parties' performance on issues important to the citizen.

The thrust of the revisionist is captured in the following four statements. First, the adoption of, or change in, party affiliation is a conscious, considered decision, based in whole or part on the policy positions of parties and candidates. For example, John Jackson's analysis of the 1964 election led him to conclude the following:

> . . . party affiliation decisions are issue-based political decisions, motivated by people's desires to have public policy reflect their own judgments about these policies. . . . People's party affiliations are subject to change if their positions on various issues change, if the parties modify their positions, or if new issues arise. . . . [9]

Similarly, Charles Franklin concludes: "party identification is the result of citizens' judgments of which party is most agreeable with their own preferences."[10] Thus, party identification seems to be affected by the individual's issue positions and is therefore not devoid of political importance.

Second, Republicans and Democrats differ from one another in terms of policy positions. Moreover, citizens can correctly distinguish between the two major parties with respect to the parties' policy positions. Parties, and partisans, espouse different issue positions.

Gerald Pomper demonstrated that during the period 1956–1968, self-identified Republicans and Democrats held dissimilar views on public policy.[11] Citizens were better able to distinguish between the parties on matters of public policy in 1968, compared to 1956. A later analysis of the 1980 election[12] confirmed Pomper's findings and demonstrated that the policy distinctiveness of Democrats and Republicans continues.

According to Michael Gant and Norman Luttbeg's analysis of the 1984 election, however, over one half of the respondents to the Center for Political Studies election survey could not name a correct attribute of either party when asked to describe differences between the Republican and Democratic parties.[13] This does not necessarily imply that the parties are no longer distinct on the issues, but that many people still have trouble seeing these differences. Moreover, this suggests that if people vote strictly on the basis of party, many will do so without knowing what policies they are voting for.

Third, apparent relationships between issue positions and vote choice are real and not due to the effects of party identification on issue positions and vote choice. Later in this chapter we will discuss the topic of issue voting. At this point it is sufficient to note that several studies have demonstrated the effects of issue positions on vote choice, independent of party identification. These studies are based on complex statistical techniques and beyond the scope of this book. At any rate, strong evidence exists that policy concerns have contributed to the voters' decisions, independent of the effects of partisanship, in presidential elections since 1964.[14]

There are two ways in which issue positions can affect how people vote. One way is that people can try to vote on the basis of their own issue positions and what the parties or candidates say they are going to do in the future. This is called *prospective issue voting*; this was the form of issue voting the authors of *The American Voter* had in mind when they concluded that few Americans cast issue-based votes in presidential (or any other) elections.

Another way is that people can vote on the basis of their own issue positions and what the parties or candidates have done in the past. This is known as *retrospective issue voting*, a recurring theme in the revisionist literature.[15] It is easier, and perhaps more efficient, to compare what one wants done with what has already been done, rather than comparing one's desires with future promises, as in prospective issue voting. While the increase in issue voting is due in part to the greater sophistication of the electorate, some of it is also due merely to the fact that some scholars have changed the way they think about issue voting.

In this chapter, in order to more faithfully trace the trends in issue based evaluations of candidates from the 1950s to the present, we will focus on prospective issue voting. At the same time, we caution the reader that other forms of evaluation are possible.

Fourth, party identification is not completely stable, but can be changed by new issues, new party positions on old issues, or new positions by individuals on old issues.[16] Recall that political scientists conventionally measure party identification through the use of a seven-point scale, on which people place themselves.[17] If we define *instability* in party identification as an individual "moving" from one point to another (for example, from "Strong Democrat" to "Weak Democrat," "independent," etc.), then party identification is much more unstable than the authors of *The American Voter* thought.[18] Kenneth Meier's analysis of the 1956–1960 panel study conducted by the Center for Political Studies shows that *over 60 percent* of respondents changed their position on the seven-point party identification scale.[19] An analysis of the 1972–1976 panel study found almost *one half* of the respondents changing their self-placement on the scale.[20] Even within an election year, the instability of party identification is remarkable. Upwards of 40 percent of all respondents change on the seven-point scale between September and November of an election year.[21] In short, the evidence suggests that "party identification is not the fixed . . . force organizing other political behavior that we thought at one time . . . [it] is subject to change as individuals' preferences change, or as a consequence of shifts in the party's [sic] positions."[22]

Whether party identification is a "psychological attachment" that has little to do with politics or a "running tally" of the policies and performance of the two major political parties is still an open question. And while party identification continues to be the single most important concept in the study of electoral politics, the answer to the question may not be as critical as it once was. We suggest this because the influence of party identification on political behavior appears to have weakened over the past thirty years, if for no other reason than fewer people strongly identify with either party than was once the case.

Partisan Decline

The contribution of political parties and partisanship to American politics is believed to be declining.[23] Political scientists and others have concluded that Americans are increasingly reluctant to identify with either major political party. Furthermore, analyses of some presidential elections have shown partisanship to have less effect on Americans' voting decisions. In this section we examine evidence with respect to each of these trends.

Increasing Independency

The distribution of party identification in the United States from 1952 to 1988 is presented in Table 2-1. The most remarkable figures in this table relate to changes in the numbers of independents and strong partisans. In 1952, only 22 percent of the American electorate claimed to be independent, including those leaning toward one of the two parties. But by late 1988, 36 percent of the American electorate claimed to be independent, virtually identical to the high of 37 percent observed in 1978.

While one third of the electorate proclaims independence from parties, it is also true that most self-declared independents willingly admit to leaning toward one of the major political parties. But when we look at those disclaiming any attraction to either party, independents who are not leaning, we still see a substantial change. In 1952 only 5 percent were non-leaning independents, while in 1988 this category had 11 percent, over twice as many. And yet, this figure is substantially lower than the peak in self-identified independence, 15 percent, observed in 1974.

There is no denying that overall the electorate has experienced a moderate cooling of partisan passions. Scanning across the rows in Table 2-1 indicates the decline of strong partisanship in both parties taken together, from 35 percent in 1952 to only 31 percent in 1988, and the growth of leaners from 17 percent in 1952 to 25 percent in 1988. Because the same people were not reinterviewed across the years, these data do not allow us to say for certain that strong partisans have tended to become weak while weak partisans have moved toward independent leaner status. However, *panel-designs,* studies using reinterviews with the same people, measure such partisan movement. The results from such studies show substantial change of this sort, a change balanced by movement in the *opposite* direction.

For example, Edward Dreyer's analysis of the 1952–1956 panel study shows that 17 percent of the respondents interviewed in both 1952 and 1956 became less committed to one of the major parties (for example, shifting from strong to weak identification). This was offset by the 21 percent of respondents who *strengthened* with respect to partisan allegiance.[24] The same sort of movement occurred in the latter half of the 1972–1974–1976 panel study. Eighteen percent of respondents weakened with respect to their partisanship, but 22 percent strengthened during the 1974–1976 time period.[25] These data suggest that individuals already in the electorate are only partially responsible for the decline in partisanship, a possibility we will explore later when we consider the reasons for the decline in partisanship.

Table 2-1

Distribution of Party Identification in Presidential Elections, 1952–1988

Party Id.	1952	1956	1960	1964	1968	1972	1976	1980	1984	1988
Strong Democrat	22%	21%	21%	26%	20%	15%	15%	16%	18%	17%
Democrat	25	23	25	25	25	25	25	23	22	18
Leaning Democrat	10	7	8	9	10	11	12	11	10	12
Independent	5	8	8	8	11	13	14	12	6	11
Leaning Rep.	7	8	7	6	9	11	10	12	13	13
Republican	14	14	13	13	14	13	14	14	15	14
Strong Republican	13	15	14	11	10	10	9	10	14	14
Other	4	3	4	2	1	2	1	2	2	2
Number of cases	1614	1772	3021	1571	1553	2705	2869	1408	2257	2040

Source: National Election Studies, 1952–1988

The Impact on Election Outcomes

Thus far we have discussed partisanship in only one sense—a psychological attachment to one of the parties. But there are other ways of conceptualizing the notions of partisanship and independency that involve the *behavior* of voters. Specifically, there have been marked increases in split-ticket voting and partisan defection in voting. Both of these are accepted generally as symptomatic of increasing independency. We will define these two concepts and examine some evidence which relates to their existence.

Ticket splitting occurs when a voter casts his or her vote for candidates of two or more parties for different offices in the same election. If enough voters split their ballots, there can be a *split outcome* for a given congressional district or state. For example, a split outcome occurs when a majority of a state's citizens vote for the Republican presidential candidate while also electing a Democratic senator or governor. Jack Dennis reported a split-ticket voting rate of only about 5 percent of voters in 1900 but 32 percent in 1960.[26] The Gallup Poll estimates of split-ticket voting (Gallup asks poll respondents whether they voted for "candidates of different parties") have been erratic in recent elections but consistently about 50 percent of the electorate: in 1968, 60 percent; 1972, 54 percent; 1976, 56 percent; 1980, 60 percent.

Stephen Shaffer finds increases in three kinds of ticket splitting between 1952 and 1980: presidential-House, Senate-House, and state-local. (See Figure 2-1.) His analysis indicates that ticket splitting is highest in state-local elections, but the slope of the increase has been roughly the same for all types of electoral races.[27]

A similar trend of increase is evident in *split outcomes*. State elections involving simultaneous Senate and gubernatorial contests had split outcomes only 18 percent of the time from 1932 to 1940, with the average increasing to 21 percent between 1952 and 1960. After 1960, some electoral years saw the percentage of split outcomes top 50 percent.[28] More recent data on split outcomes suggests that the incidences of split outcomes may have peaked for some time, however.[29] As shown in Table 2-2, split outcomes have exceeded 50 percent only once since 1972, averaging about 41 percent since then. This suggests that, at least in some states, the frequency of split-ticket voting has waned since the 1960s.

Perhaps a more interesting type of split outcome involves presidential and congressional contests. For example, a congressional district which gave a majority of the vote to George Bush in 1988, but elected a Democrat to the House of Representatives, produced a split outcome. In 1980 and 1988, about one third of all congressional districts produced split outcomes, with most of the House seats in these districts won by Democrats.[30]

Figure 2-1

Ticket Splitting, 1952–1980

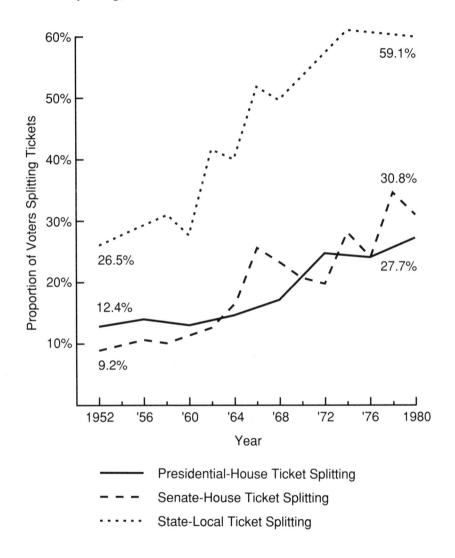

————— Presidential-House Ticket Splitting

– – – Senate-House Ticket Splitting

· · · · · · State-Local Ticket Splitting

Source: SRC/CPS Election Study data reported by Stephen D. Shaffer in "A Multivariate Explanation of Rising Ticketsplitting," a paper presented at the annual meeting of the Southern Political Science Association, 1982.

Table 2-2

Split Outcomes in Gubernatorial and U.S. Senatorial Elections: 1952–1982

Year	States with Simultaneous Elections	Percent: Split Outcomes
1952	22	27
1954	25	24
1956	20	15
1958	22	18
1960	19	36
1962	27	44
1964	18	56
1966·	22	59
1968	15	60
1970	24	46
1972	12	50
1974	25	44
1976	9	33
1978	24	42
1980	9	67
1982	21	29

Source: Ruth K. Scott and Ronald J. Hrebenar, *Parties in Crisis* (New York: John Wiley & Sons, 1979); data for 1978 through 1982 was compiled by the authors.

Another way to approach the question of increasing independency is through the concept of *partisan defection*. In an analysis of the 1960 presidential campaign, V. O. Key implied that psychological identification is not the only, or even the best, way to identify partisans and independents. Instead, Key suggested that independency can be assessed best by examining the voting behavior of citizens.[31] He therefore developed a typology or classification of voting behaviors. The voting electorate was divided into three categories: *standpatters, switchers,* and *new voters.* Standpatters were individuals who voted in the 1960 presidential election for the same party that they had voted for in 1956. Switchers were individuals who voted for a different party in 1960 than the party they had supported in 1956. New voters were individuals who voted for the first time in 1960.

Key was extremely interested in "switchers." He believed that switchers, because they demonstrated willingness to cross party lines, represented an important strain of independency. In 1960 there were approximately 13 million switchers.[32] While not as great in number as the 45 million standpatters, the switchers played an important role in the 1960 election. John Kennedy was the recipient of 10.3 million switched votes, while his opponent, Richard Nixon, only garnered 2.7 million switched votes, and this was the decisive factor in the Democrats' victory.[33]

Key's interest in the importance of switchers led him to explore their motivations and issue orientations. It must be remembered that *The American Voter* had typecast independents as ill equipped to wrestle with the complexities of politics and voting. However, Key found that switchers (one type of independent) were rather politically sophisticated. Some of his conclusions were as follows:

> . . . analyses of the available information indicate quite marked correlations between policy attitudes and vote switching.[34]
>
> To an astonishing degree . . . voters in their movements to and from across party lines and from an inactive to an active voting status behaved as persons who made choices congruent with their policy preferences.[35]
>
> Party switchers move toward the party whose standpatters they resemble in their policy views. . . . [36]

Subsequent studies by other political scientists note increasing political sophistication among independents. Pomper, for example, finds that independent identifiers are as knowledgeable about government as weak party identifiers, though not as knowledgeable as strong party identifiers.[37] An analysis of the 1984 election provides additional evidence that independents are more sophisticated than previously thought. Gant and Luttbeg constructed a measure of issue voting that they defined as voting for the candidate whose policy positions are closer to one's own. They found that independents were as likely to be issue voters as were strong party identifiers. Interestingly, when the authors looked just at those respondents with large amounts of political information, independents were substantially more likely to vote on the basis of issues than were strong identifiers.[38]

Evidence from 1988, however, does not support the contention that independents have grown increasingly sophisticated over the years. In Table 2-3, we present distributions on various measures of political activity and awareness for those of different strengths of partisanship. When compared to strong and weak partisans, as well as independents who "lean" to one party or the other, "pure" independents fall far short on all the dimensions presented in Table 2-3. Independents are much less likely to have reported voting in 1988 or to

Table 2-3

Strength of Partisanship and Political Activity and Awareness, 1988

	Strong Partisans	Weak Partisans	Leaners	Independents
Reported voting	84%	68%	64%	50%
Very much interested in campaign	41	22	26	14
Follows politics most or all of the time	68	56	60	44
Talked about campaign with other people	38	25	28	16
Knew majority party in House of Representatives	67	58	60	46
Knew majority party in Senate	64	51	55	36

Source: National Election Study, 1988.

have expressed much interest in the campaign. Moreover, independents are the least likely to say they follow politics regularly or to talk to other people about the campaign.

Finally, with respect to political information, independents are the least likely to have known that the Democratic party controlled both houses of Congress prior to the 1988 elections. On all dimensions strong partisans exhibited the highest level of political activity and awareness, as would be expected. It would appear that, at least in 1988, the traditional conception of independents as uniformed about, and uninvolved in, politics was largely correct.

Party Identification and Voting, 1988

On the face of it, party loyalty seemed alive in 1988. Most partisans voted for the candidate of their own party, party "switching" was low and, compared to the figures presented above, split-ticket voting was at a fairly low level in 1988.

Table 2-4 shows the proportions voting for George Bush, Michael Dukakis, and other candidates for each of the seven categories of partisanship. It is apparent that when considered by itself, party identification is still a strong predic-

Table 2-4

Party Identification and Presidential Vote, 1988

	Bush	Dukakis	Other	N
Strong Democrat	6%	93%	1%	240
Weak Democrat	27	70	3	198
Leaning Democrat	12	88	*	133
Independent	61	33	6	84
Leaning Republican	84	15	1	147
Weak Republican	83	17	*	181
Strong Republican	98	2	*	223

Total N = 1206

*Less than 1%.
Source: CPS Election Survey, 1988.

tor of the vote. Over 90 percent of strong partisans voted for their party's candidate, and over three fourths of those categorized as weak partisan and "leaning" independents remained loyal to their standard bearer. Of course, when other factors such as candidate image and issues are considered, the relationship between party and vote choice would weaken considerably. But taken by itself, party tells us a great deal about how people vote.

Table 2-4 presents some rather interesting information about the American voter in 1988. For example, we see that "leaning independents" (those who claim to be independent but admit to leaning to one party or the other) are more partisan in their voting than are weak identifiers (and, in the case of Democrats, *much* more partisan). These data also suggest why Bush was victorious in 1988. He enjoyed a sizable advantage among pure independents, gaining almost a two-to-one split over Dukakis. Also, Republicans were more loyal than were Democrats. The defection rate was 13 percent among Republicans and 16 percent among Democrats. For all partisans, the defection rate stood at 15 percent.

Put another way, 86 percent of all partisans were loyal in 1988, a figure that does not conjure up a picture of moribund parties. Moreover, the incidence of partisan switching between 1984 and 1988 was quite low. Specifically, 82 percent of 1984 Reagan voters voted for Bush in 1988, while 91 percent of 1984 Mondale voters voted for Dukakis in 1988, according to the 1988 CPS election study. The lower rate of switching among Democrats is to be expected, given the breadth of Reagan's victory in 1984, a victory which cut across party lines.

Finally, ticket-splitting in 1988 appears to have dropped. In 1988, 35 percent of Bush supporters split their ticket, voting for a Democratic House candidate, while only 15 percent of Dukakis supporters cast a split ballot. Overall, the rate of ticket-splitting in 1988 was about 26 percent, slightly lower than that observed in previous years.

The election of 1988 may have been an anomaly, a blip in the downward curve of the fortunes of the two major parties. Or it may have signaled the reemergence of the Democrats and Republicans in electoral politics. In terms of behavior, partisan attachments were impressive in their strength. But the impact on behavior is at least partially offset by the continually low levels (historically speaking) of partisanship. And, we cannot ignore one very important fact: the Democratic party, despite outnumbering the Republicans nationwide, once again lost the presidency by a substantial margin.

The Decline in Partisanship: Some Explanations

How do we account for the decline of party identification in the United States? Many explanations have been offered for the apparent "dealignment" of the American electorate, several of which are reviewed here. The attempts to account for this phenomenon can be divided into three types of arguments. The first general type is that there has always existed anti-party sentiment in the United States, and in recent years this antipathy has taken the form of *structural changes* in the parties. These changes, in turn, have reduced the vitality and, ultimately, the relevance of the major political parties to American politics and to the public.

The second general type of argument focuses on the *attitudes* of citizens. In particular, it is argued that people have grown increasingly negative toward the parties or, at the very least, view the parties with increasing apathy. Finally, a third general argument has to do with changes in levels of partisanship brought about by such processes as socialization and maturation, and that changes in these *transmission processes* have resulted in the decline in party identification.

Parties as Organizations: Decline or Vitality?

Anti-party sentiment has always been a dynamic element of American politics.[39] Whether such anti-party sentiment exists in the country today is an empirical question. It is clear, however, that anti-party feelings have a long history in this country, and were in fact first expressed by the Founding Fathers. James Madison, for example, wrote in *The Federalist Papers* that the greatest threat to a republican form of government was the existence of *factions*, what we call today political parties.

Ironically, the government Madison helped to create makes the formation of a *two-party system* almost inevitable. Specifically, the use of *single member plurality electoral districts* perpetuates a two-party, as opposed to a multiparty, system. A single member plurality electoral district is simply one in which only one person wins a seat, and that person is the one with the most votes. All seats in the House of Representatives, for example, are single member plurality seats.

The other major way of allocating seats to representatives is through *proportional representation* in which seats are allocated to parties based on the proportion of the vote the party receives in the election. A party, or candidate, does not have to get the most votes to win a seat. In single member plurality systems, parties or candidates do need to win the most votes to win a seat. Unsuccessful parties are weeded out, or forced to join forces with other minor parties, and balance is usually achieved when a two-party system emerges.

Some argue that the result of a two-party system is relatively little difference in party ideologies. And, as we observed earlier in this chapter, even today the American people often have difficulty distinguishing between the two parties. Critics of American democracy and its parties argue that the lack of ideological distinctiveness in our party system serves the interests of the status quo in public policy.

On the other hand, it is just as reasonable to argue that the two major political parties in this country are moderate because most citizens are themselves moderate in their political beliefs. In order to win elections, therefore, parties must make appeals that are also moderate. If Americans were at the extremes, left and right, it is just as likely that the parties would be extreme to appeal to these voters.

In summary, the United States operates with a party system that narrows the range of political choices offered to the citizenry and this contributes, some have argued, to the public's disenchantment with the parties. Other forces are also at work, and the result has been numerous restrictions on the parties as organizations. Some believe that these restrictions have diminished the importance of the parties in the political process and diminished the relevance of parties to individuals. Following are some of the more important structural changes arising in this century.

Loss of Patronage Powers

Because of their dissatisfaction with the parties, the public and some political leaders have initiated several reforms or changes through the years. One of the first reforms directed toward parties involved patronage powers. Until the late 1800s, the winning party was allowed to fill governmental positions from top to bottom with party supporters and activists. The promise of public employment through party patronage strongly encouraged party fidelity and support. But the civil service reform movement swept through America, and government employment was reorganized under state and federal merit systems. Thus, the parties were deprived of one of their strongest incentives for party support.

Unionization of government workers has also circumscribed the number of government jobs that can be manipulated by party officials who seek to reward the party faithful with public employment.

Nonpartisan Elections

Another defeat was dealt to parties by the reforms of the Progressive Movement in the late nineteenth and early twentieth centuries that sought to eliminate partisanship in local elections. Proponents of nonpartisan elections equated party politics with corruption and political bossism. The effect of this movement was the virtual elimination of partisan elections at the local level of government. It has been argued that this weakened the two parties because it cut them off from their roots.

Primary Elections

The single most important function played by political parties, at any level, is to recruit candidates for public office. By doing so, parties furnish the voters with individuals behind whom they can rally and for whom they can vote. If parties did not recruit candidates for public office, it is likely they would cease to exist. Any reform that diminishes this function, therefore, endangers the viability, if not the existence, of the parties. One such reform is the use of *primary elections* to select nominees.

In primary elections, party members participate in the selection of candidates for office by selecting delegates to nominating conventions in public or quasi-public elections. Identification of party members is open to interpretation, but in most states a desire to vote in a party's primary is sufficient evidence of party membership. Some states register voters by party, and a very few state organizations actually maintain membership roles. Today, most candidates for public office are chosen either directly via a primary election or indirectly through the selection of delegates in primary elections. Nominees of the two major parties for the presidency are chosen through the latter method.

Prior to the advent of primary elections which, like nonpartisan elections, were an offshoot of the Progressive movement, parties used caucuses to select nominees. A *caucus* is a private meeting of party members and much more subject to manipulation by party leaders than are primary elections because they are smaller and secret. Through caucuses, the party organization has substantial control over who runs under the party label. With primary elections, such control is virtually absent. Witness, for example, the nomination of Jimmy Carter by the Democratic party, even though he was an outsider and clearly not the favorite of party leaders (that honor belonged to Senator Edmund Muskie of Maine). This shows that under the primary system, parties lose control over their most important function.

The growth of primary elections to nominate presidential candidates began in earnest in the late 1960s. The increase in the number of primaries was in response to a call to open up – "democratize" – the presidential nomination process. The movement succeeded remarkably. In 1988, two thirds of the delegates to the Democratic nominating convention were chosen in primaries, with about 18 percent being chosen through caucuses. For the Republicans, over three fourths of the delegates to the presidential nominating convention were chosen through primary elections, with the remainder being chosen in caucuses.[40]

Some party leaders, especially among the Democrats, concluded in the early 1980s that democratization had worked a little too well. Party leaders, such as elected officials, were often excluded from the national nominating conventions. As a consequence, the national Democratic party designated about 15 percent of the delegates as "super delegates" who were appointed, not elected, in the primaries or caucuses. Most super delegates were state and national party executives, elected officials (such as Democratic members of Congress), and Democratic governors.

The growth of primaries has reduced the importance of the parties in the electoral process. Moreover, during the presidential nomination campaign, voters may develop loyalties to candidates, not the parties, and this loyalty may translate into decreased partisanship in the electorate. More importantly, the parties are less important to the process of selecting and electing. Perhaps that is why the parties are less relevant to citizens.

Candidate-centered Campaigns

Party organizations have also lost some of their attraction for political candidates, especially presidential candidates. Candidates quite naturally still pay some allegiance to party organization until they capture the party's nomination. But with a nomination in their grasp, candidates can, if they choose, ignore the party organization for campaign purposes and replace it with a personal campaign organization.

There are at least two reasons for such a strategy. First, it may be that an increasingly large bloc of independent voters prompts candidates to eschew party labels and personalize their campaigns. Second, personal campaign organizations are loyal only to the candidates. Once the nomination is secured, candidates are reluctant to shed the organizations that proved so successful during the nomination campaign. Candidates, not parties, run the general election campaigns, further eroding the importance of party organizations.

Presidential Campaign Finances

After the abuses of public office known collectively as the "Watergate" scandal, Congress enacted legislation designed to diminish the influence of those contributing large sums of money to the parties and to the candidates. Prior to these reforms, it was not uncommon for individuals to contribute upwards of $500,000 to presidential campaigns. The appearance, if not the reality, of corruption was pervasive.

Today, general election campaigns for the presidency are funded with federal dollars administered by the Federal Election Commission. In 1988, the Democratic and Republican nominees for the presidency each received about $46 million in public funds, with which they ran their general election campaigns. The national parties each received about $8.3 million to run their conventions, campaign for a wide variety of candidates, and conduct other party related campaign activities.[41]

The importance of these reforms are three fold. First, candidates, not parties, receive the bulk of public funds, eroding still further the role of the parties on the general election. Second, candidates need not depend on the party structure (nor anyone else, for that matter) to raise funds for their general election campaigns. Third, the amount of money available to candidates is much lower than was available prior to the reforms. For example, in 1972 Richard Nixon spent over $60 million in his successful reelection campaign against George McGovern. Today, dollars must be spent ever more efficiently, to reach the greatest number of voters possible. This has led to decreased reliance on normal party structures for contacting voters and increased use of more sophisticated campaign technologies. The latter are not only expensive, but they allow the candidates to circumvent the parties and take their message directly "to the people."

New Campaign Technology

The changing nature of campaigning and campaign technology has several facets. Robert Agranoff, a noted expert in the field of campaigning, points out that these changes have particularly altered the nature of what is communicated to citizens during a campaign. He states that today the candidate, not the party, is the chief focus of campaign communications.[42] Many candidates completely eliminate any mention of their party affiliation in media messages. Agranoff notes further that party professionals no longer perform services for candidates in the area of communications. Instead, the candidate relies on the services of communications professionals who acquire their skills in nonpolitical fields.

Professional polling is another facet of the new campaign technology that has weakened the campaign role of parties. Polling results can determine the viability of a candidate's quest for a party's nomination. In the past, party professionals handpicked the "most promising" candidates and helped them secure the financial backing needed to seek a nomination. But today political financiers, the media, and even the public depend on poll results to narrow the field of potential party nominees.

The number of changes in campaign technology are endless and only a few have been mentioned here. But the important lesson to be learned from these changes involves their impact on party organizations. Frank Sorauf has summarized this impact succinctly as follows:

> All the campaign assets they (candidates) once received from the party organization and their workers—skills, information, pulse reading, manpower, exposure—they now can get from pollsters, the media, public relations people, volunteer workers, or even by "renting a party" in the form of a campaign management firm.[43]

Are the Parties Dead?

Undoubtedly, many forces have conspired to weaken the organizations of the two major parties. But to paraphrase Mark Twain, reports of the parties' demise are greatly exaggerated. Virtually all of the changes we have described in this section involve the *national* party structures and activities. Yet most of the work done by parties in this country is performed by state and local party organizations. And there is substantial evidence that these structures are alive and well.

A major study of party organizational strength, conducted by James Gibson, Cornelius Cotter, John Bibby, and Robert Huckshorn, generated some interesting and surprising findings with respect to the vitality of party organizations at the state level.[44] Their study indicates that state and local party organizations have not become weaker and less active since the decline in party identification began. In fact, the authors find that parties at the subnational level are stronger and more active than they were even in the 1950s, when partisanship was at its peak. Further, in the face of decreasing party loyalties, these organizations apparently redouble their efforts, such that as citizen party loyalty erodes, party organizational strength increases. In short, if the vitality of state and local parties are any indication, the party system is not crumbling. The parties are *not* dead.

The second set of arguments we will examine in order to account for the decline of partisanship involves public *attitudes* toward the parties. We first examine evidence relating to the question of whether citizens are negative, neutral, or positive toward the parties. If people are negative or neutral, they would be more likely to identify themselves as independents. Second, we look briefly at the possibility that citizens have *two* party identifications—one for national politics and one for state and local affairs. If this is occurring to any great degree, then when given the opportunity to align themselves with one party or the other, some might unconsciously balance their competing views and identify themselves as independents.

Citizen Attitudes: Positive, Negative, or Neutral?

In the 1970s many Americans were alienated from the parties and the party system, while earlier they had trusted political parties.[45] Perhaps one of the most important expressions of alienation involves a decline in citizens' willingness to place the party above the candidate. Gallup Poll data showed that in 1956, 22 percent of Americans believed "It is better to vote for the party than the man," as compared to only 12 percent in 1968.

In turn, political parties were held in much lower regard than other political institutions in the 1970s. For example, Dennis asked nearly one thousand Wisconsin citizens: "How much faith and confidence would you say you had in each of these to do what is right?" The respondents were asked to rank each of seven institutions[46] between 1 (no confidence at all) and 7 (complete confidence). The mean scores ranged from 4.8 for the Supreme Court to 3.7 for interest groups. The mean confidence score for political parties, 3.8, was lower than for any other institution except interest groups.

Recent studies suggest that Dennis may have overdrawn his portrait of an electorate growing increasingly hostile to the Republican and Democratic parties. Especially, research by Martin Wattenberg presents convincing evidence that citizens are not as negative towards the parties as they are neutral.[47] According to Wattenberg, citizens do not distrust the parties, but they may find the parties irrelevant.

Using the "likes/dislikes" questions relative to political parties, Wattenberg notes that from 1952 to 1980, the proportion of the electorate who are neutral, or apathetic, toward either or both parties has increased substantially. Citizens are not expressing negative comments about the parties; instead, the attitude that parties really do not matter appears to have increased over the time period. Additionally, he classified responses as substantive (those that involved foreign and domestic policy) and non-substantive (those that did not reflect policy content) for both parties and candidates. The proportion of party responses that were substantive declined precipitously, while the same proportion increased dramatically for candidates. While public evaluations of the parties turned negative in the late 1960s, in 1972 evaluations of the parties rebounded, so that by 1984, the level of positive attitudes toward the parties was higher even than in 1952. Americans' dislike for the parties appears to vary greatly.[48]

In Table 2-5 we present the evaluations of the Democratic and Republican parties in 1988 for Democrats, Republicans, independents, and all respondents. Positive evaluators are those who named more things they liked about the parties than they disliked, in response to the "likes/dislikes" questions on the CPS survey. Negative evaluators reflect the opposite pattern. Those labeled as neutral expressed an equal number of positive and negative attributes of the parties.

Only about one quarter of the respondents express negative evaluations of one party or the other. But they are not especially positive toward the parties either. In general, respondents were more positive about the Democratic party than the Republican party, although this undoubtedly was due to the fact that Democrats outnumber Republicans in the sample and that partisans tend to evaluate their own party more positively than the opposition. Since the greatest number of respondents are neutral — those whose positive and negative comments balance out — it appears that citizens are neutral toward the parties, consistent with Wattenberg's thesis.

Inconsistent Party Identifications

There is some evidence that citizens of the United States hold more than one party identification. For example, some might consider themselves a Democrat for state politics and a Republican for national politics. The evidence for the existence of this phenomenon in the United States is sparse. But to the extent it does occur, it can help account for increased independency, split-ticket voting, and partisan defection.

The concept of "partisan inconsistency" is fairly common in the study of Canadian politics. In Canada, the provinces are a much more important part of the political process than are the states in this country. One consequence of this is that "dual partisanship" is a widely observed phenomenon in Cana-

Table 2-5

Attitudes Toward the Parties, 1988

	Attitudes Toward the Democratic Party			
	Democrats	Republicans	Independents	All
Positive	60%	15%	19%	37%
Neutral	32	42	72	41
Negative	8	43	9	22
N = 2000				

	Attitudes Toward the Republican Party			
	Democrats	Republicans	Independents	All
Positive	12%	55%	12%	30%
Neutral	42	37	73	43
Negative	46	8	15	27
N = 2000				

Note: Entries are proportions expressing type of attitude.
Source: CPS Election Survey, 1988.

dian politics. In turn, those holding inconsistent partisanships are much more unstable in their partisan allegiance than are those consistent in this regard.[49]

There have been very few studies of dual partisanship in the United States. In fact, questions to determine whether people hold inconsistent party identifications do not appear on the CPS national election surveys. However, a study based on several local samples, as well as party elite national samples, suggests dual partisanship is an important phenomenon in American politics.[50] According to this study, dual partisanship increased substantially during the 1960s, the same period in which the decline of partisanship can be observed. Further, the authors of this study estimate that about 20 percent of citizens hold inconsistent party identifications between state politics and national politics. There is also some evidence to suggest that the tendency to "split" one's party identification is more prevalent in the South, compared to other parts of the country.[51]

If citizens hold two party identifications, but are given the opportunity to name only one, it is not unreasonable to suggest that some will balance the inconsistency by identifying themselves as independents. Alternatively, they may identify themselves as aligned with the party most salient to them; for these individuals, a fairly high level of split-ticket voting should be observed. Finally, the inconsistency in partisanship would lead to a weakening of the impact of either identification on behavior, resulting in partisan defection and, perhaps, dealignment.

Given the scarcity of evidence regarding the existence of dual partisanship in the United States, these proportions remain speculative. But to the extent the phenomenon exists, it can help account for the weakening impact of party identification in electoral politics.

Socialization and Maturation

According to the Michigan model, many, if not most, individuals adopt the same party identification as their parents. It was assumed that parents transmitted their partisanship to their offspring through a process called *political socialization*. As we noted in Chapter 1, the evidence for the existence of this process was in the form of moderate-to-strong correlations between parental and one's own party identification.

The conventional wisdom also suggests that young people have weaker partisan attachments when they first enter the electorate, but they tend not to be more independent than older generations. Finally, scholars have observed in the past that as people age, their partisan ties strengthen, due to the reinforcing effect of voting, exposure to agreeable information, and the like. As a result, these citizens become more resistant to changes in partisanship, including a move to independence.

What happens if these processes are disrupted? Two studies that discuss the decline in party identification deal with this question. The first, by Edward Carmines, John McIver, and James Stimson, suggests that much of the decline in partisanship is due to the "incomplete transmission of partisanship from parents to children."[52] They suggest that most of the decline in partisanship since 1952 is due to the fact that individuals who entered the electorate after 1964 were less likely to enter as partisans than those who entered during the "steady state" period of party identification of the 1950s and early 1960s.

The reason for this is that parental partisanship was less salient for these individuals, so they did not adopt it and, having "nowhere else to go," they became independents. In turn, this "rejection" of parental partisanship was due, they suggest, to the fact that the issue positions of the newly enfranchised independents were at odds with those espoused by the party of their parents. To resolve the dilemma, they chose independence.

To test this hypothesis, the authors look at the issue positions of people who "should have" become Democrats or Republicans when they entered the electorate (that is, those whose parents were Democrats or Republicans, respectively) but instead became self-identified independents. The authors find that "unrealized Democrats" were more conservative than self-identified Democrats, and "unrealized Republicans" were more liberal than self-identified Republicans. In the face of contrary policy views, therefore, the transmission of parental partisanship is weakened.

A second study, by Helmut Norpoth and Jerrold Rusk, attempts to account for the decline in party identification through the use of three factors: lower levels of partisanship for new entrants into the electorate, desertion of party labels (dealignment), and a weakening of life-cycle effects.[53] Their study covers the period 1952–1976, during which most of the decline in partisanship was observed.

Norpoth and Rusk note first that individuals entering the electorate after 1964 reflected markedly lower levels of partisanship than did those who entered 1952–1964, consistent with the findings of the previous study. They suggest that the lower levels of partisanship exhibited by new entrants can account for approximately one third of the decline in partisanship. Second, they suggest that another 30 to 40 percent of the decline in partisanship is due strictly to the desertion of party labels by those who were already in the electorate by 1964. Finally, when comparing the adoption or strengthening of partisan ties usually associated with the process of aging (the "life-cycle" effect), Norpoth and Rusk find that life-cycle gains were much weaker in the 1968–1976 period than they were in the 1952–1964 era. They estimate that about 20 percent of the decline is due to the suppression of life-cycle gains.

The processes which produced fairly high and remarkably stable levels of partisanship in the 1950s began breaking down in the late 1960s. Not surprisingly, this erosion occurred simultaneously with tremendous political upheaval in this country, including the assassinations of John Kennedy, Martin Luther King, Jr., and Robert Kennedy; the civil rights movement; the war in Vietnam; and the Watergate scandal of the 1970s. Unless new upheavals of similar magnitude occur which would drive citizens *toward* the parties, there is no reason to think the erosion of partisanship will reverse itself. Regardless of how the evidence is read, many people have become dissatisfied with the two major parties in the country or never were sufficiently comfortable with them ever to align with them. Does this suggest that new political parties are in the offing, for example, is realignment a likelihood? To explore this, we turn to our final topic of discussion on party identification.

Realignment: The Necessary Corrective?

Political scientists have long been interested in a phenomenon called *realignment*. Realignment occurs when there is a massive shift in the underlying pattern of partisan identification in the electorate. This change can be so sweeping that the majority party is transformed into a minority party and the minority party becomes the new majority party. The most recent example of a realignment took place during the 1930s, when the Democrats put together a large enough coalition (called the New Deal coalition) to overtake the Republicans in numerical strength and become the majority party.

Researchers have suggested two stimuli for realignment. Sellars and others contend that realignments are cyclical phenomena.[54] Realignments lose their relevance after a more or less predictable period of time, coalitions disintegrate, and cyclical forces take charge to produce a new realignment. This ebb and flow was characterized by Charles Sellars as an *equilibrium cycle* in two-party politics. The second stimulus for realignment is the appearance of some new issue for the advent of a national crisis, like war or depression, that causes a sudden transformation of partisan loyalties. Key characterized elections involving such occurrences as *critical elections*.[55]

In recent years researchers have been looking for the signs of impending realignment. Numerous scholars have indicated that the following occurrences are indicative of the collapse of the New Deal coalition and a coming realignment: (1) the increase in independents, (2) the success of third parties, (3) the increase in issue voting, and (4) declining confidence in the parties as they are presently constituted.[56]

The conclusion drawn from these trends is summarized well by Jerome Clubb, William Flanigan, and Nancy Zingale: "Taken together, this evidence suggests a considerable growth in the size of the pool of voters without well-developed partisan loyalties. Most analysts . . . see this as indicative of an increasing availability of potential new partisans in a realignment."[57] These authors express doubt, however, that a realignment will actually occur because a necessary component of the realigning process is missing. They contend that realignment can occur only after a party perceived as unsuccessful in governing is replaced by a party that is ultimately perceived as successful in governing where the former party failed. Because "successful" governance today would require control of all branches of the government simultaneously (something only the Democrats might accomplish in the near term), and because government's problems might be unsolvable, at least to the public's satisfaction, the requirement for realignment is not likely to be met.

The greatest amount of research directed toward predicting and explaining realignment has dealt with the South. The South has been interesting in this regard because the supposed "solid Democratic South" generally supported the Republican presidential nominees in 1964, 1968, and 1972. This prompted some Republicans to anticipate achieving a "New Majority" status for their party as the South gradually turned away from the Democrats and joined their more conservative allies in the GOP.

There have been several explanations of partisan change in the South. James Sundquist has suggested that a *new* realignment is not occurring in the South. Instead, he sees the South belatedly conforming to class based patterns of partisanship adopted by the rest of the nation in the New Deal realignment of the 1930s. This explanation envisions middle- and upper-class white Southerners becoming Republicans in partisan orientation.[58] Research conducted by Carol Cassel tends to refute Sundquist's thesis. In her study of native white Southerners over the period 1952–1972, she found that group moving away from its traditional Democratic partisanship toward the independent, not Republican, label.[59] A final perspective on change in the South has been advanced by Phillip Converse. He attributes most change in Southern partisanship not to political conversions, but instead to the relocation of northern Republicans as industry and commerce move south of the Mason-Dixon Line.[60]

Political Issues and Partisan Realignment

A stream of research that has recently appeared makes a persuasive case that the old social compositions of the parties *have* changed; that these changes offer the potential for a shift in the balance of power between the two major parties; and that these changes are directly related to the emergence of new issues on the national agenda. The first point to be made is that the current dealignment may lead, in the future, to a realignment of the parties. As we noted previously, Carmines, McIver, and Stimson claim that much of the decrease in partisanship is due to "unrealized partisanship," and this increase in independency is issue based.[61] Given that an increasing number of citizens identify themselves as independents because of conflicts between their issue positions and those of their parents' party, Carmines and his colleagues suggest these citizens would be susceptible to issue-based appeals from the appropriate party. The current dealignment might produce a new "ideologically based realignment of the American party system."[62]

Carmines and Stimson, in a provocative paper on the role of issues in changing the party balance,[63] suggest we must rethink our understanding of the concept of realignment and they offer the following interpretation:

> Mass party realignments . . . may be interpreted as the redistribution of party support associated with the displacement of one political conflict with

> another. . . . Realignments are precipitated by the emergence of new is-
> sues about which the electorate has intense feelings that cut across . . . the
> existing . . . cleavage between the parties. . . . The process may result in
> a new majority party. The new line of conflict may, alternatively, simply
> alter the coalitional structure of the parties.[64]

According to this interpretation, there are two key features of a realignment:
a change in the groups that support the parties must occur and a new issue
must emerge that coincides with the changes in the "coalitional structure" of
the parties. If these two conditions are met, regardless of whether the balance
of power reverses (that is, the majority and minority parties switch positions),
a realignment can be said to have occurred.

The literature suggests both conditions have been fulfilled. First, it is in-
disputable that the group bases of support for the major parties have changed
dramatically since the 1950s, with the most noticeable changes having occurred
within the Democratic party. Robert Axelrod has charted the makeup of
presidential election coalitions (that is, the groups that contribute to the share
of the vote received by the Democratic presidential candidate) for the years
1952–1984.[65] He found that the contributions of non-Protestants, union households, the poor, and residents of the central cities to Democratic election coalitions have declined since 1952. In the case of the poor and residents of central
cities, the decline has been dramatic due to the decreased size of these groups.
Only the South and blacks have maintained or increased their support for the
Democratic party. The Democratic *electoral* coalition has changed markedly
since 1952.

The group bases for *party identification* have also undergone a substantial
transformation since the 1950s. A paper by Harold Stanley, William Bianco,
and Richard Niemi presents estimates of the probability of members of different groups identifying with the Democratic party.[66] In 1984, only blacks and
Jews had a greater than 50 percent probability of being Democrats. The probability for traditional Democratic groups—such as native Southern whites,
Catholics, members of union households, and working class individuals—
ranged from 40 to 46 percent.

More importantly, only blacks reflect an increased likelihood of identifying
with the Democrats, increasing from 53 percent in 1952 to 65 percent in 1984.[67]
The biggest decline was observed among native Southern whites, from 75 percent to 42 percent. With the exception of Jews, the probability of all other
groups being Democratic dropped below 50 percent. Clearly, the coalitional
structure of the parties has changed.

John Petrocik presents additional evidence for this proposition.[68] He notes
that by 1984 the core of the Republican party included middle- and upper-
class Protestant whites and Southern whites. The core of the Democratic party

consisted primarily of blacks and Jews; union members and Catholics are now target groups for both parties. More to the point, Petrocik suggests that this new social composition of the parties encourages a shift in the balance of power between Democrats and Republicans. And, this realignment will probably be issue-based, since the parties will have to offer issue positions appealing to their (new) supporters. In short, Petrocik argues that a "noncritical realignment" has already occurred in the United States.

What prompted this "non-critical realignment"? Carmines and Stimson argue that a new issue that reflects the following characteristics can produce a realignment in the social bases of the parties:

1. The issue must generate intense feelings across the electorate.
2. The behavior of political elites, for example, elected political leaders, must change with respect to the issue and grow more distinct.
3. Citizens must perceive with greater clarity the parties' positions on the issue.
4. Citizens' evaluations of the parties must change in response to the new positions espoused by the parties.
5. Citizens must change party identifications and the positions of Democratic and Republican identifiers must change and grow more distinct.[69]

According to Carmines and Stimson, all of these conditions were met in the 1960s with respect to one volatile and divisive issue—racial desegregation. Since 1960 members of Congress have switched on the issue of racial desegregation, such that Democrats are much more liberal on the issue than Republican members of Congress. In turn, since 1964 citizens have perceived the parties' stands on this issue correctly, with much greater clarity than before 1964. And, in the mass public, Democrats are much more liberal on the issue of racial desegregation than Republicans.

The implication of the transformed group bases of partisanship, coupled with Carmines and Stimson's argument, is that the issue of racial desegregation was the stimulus for a realignment, especially in the South. That *something* has happened to the parties is undeniable, and it would strain credulity to argue that what has happened has no connection to the volatile issue of civil rights. But more traditional scholars might argue that since the Democrats still outnumber the Republicans, a realignment has *not* occurred.

Our view is that, on the surface, the traditionalists are correct. But we would also argue that what it means to be a Democrat or Republican in 1988 is much different than what it meant in 1952. While Democrats may still outnumber

Republicans (and this is no trivial fact), the party system, and the bases for that system, have changed dramatically since the 1950s.

The Evidence of Issue Voting

As noted in the first chapter, *The American Voter* has been criticized as time bound. This is particularly true of its conclusions regarding issue voting. Many researchers have found the 1950s to be a peculiarly issueless period in our nation's history. Consequently, they believe that the findings of the 1950s regarding issue voting hold little relevance for the student of contemporary American electoral behavior.

Several sets of events made the 1960s and 1970s different than the 1950s. Fresh in many Americans' minds was the long and divisive war in Vietnam. This tragic conflict unquestionably served to sharpen many Americans' interest in and knowledge of national issues. But the Vietnam War was only one of many changes in our social and political environment since the 1950s. Social scientists generally agree that these changes, including the civil rights movement, the increasing youthfulness of the electorate, and rising levels of education, must have changed America.

Party Loyalty and Policy Views

Since their 1956 national opinion-election survey, the University of Michigan's Survey Research Center and Center for Political Studies have asked respondents a number of questions about policy matters. The policy areas involved are (1) federal aid to education; (2) government-sponsored medical care; (3) government guarantee of employment; (4) federal fair employment and housing practices; (5) school integration; and (6) foreign aid. For each of these areas, respondents have been asked whether they favor or do not favor action by the federal government. A respondent favoring federal action is characterized as more "liberal" on that issue than a respondent not favoring government action. By comparing responses to these items over time, Gerald Pomper has been able to make some important observations.

The first relationship which is evident from these data is that citizens' policy views and their partisan preferences have become increasingly interrelated through the years. Table 2-6 shows that since 1964 there has been a distinct partisan flavor to policy views. Specifically, self-identified Democrats are much more liberal in most of these policy areas than are self-identified Republicans.

Table 2-6

Party Identification and Policy Position, 1956–1972

Party Identification	Education, Taxation					Medical Care					Job Guarantee				
	1956	1960	1964	1968	1972	1956	1960	1964	1968	1972	1956	1960	1964	1968	1972
Strong Democrat	80.0	66.8	51.0	53.6	52.6	74.2	74.5	78.2	81.3	67.4	75.6	71.2	52.6	53.1	62.6
Weak Democrat	78.1	59.0	44.1	38.3	66.5	67.3	60.2	65.2	72.1	53.1	64.0	62.4	38.4	39.7	44.4
Independent	71.0	53.2	39.3	32.9	55.2	55.8	56.7	57.2	55.3	56.7	55.0	56.6	31.0	27.0	39.5
Weak Republican	68.7	39.1	21.5	22.5	59.3	51.4	47.5	43.5	39.3	36.2	59.5	43.9	25.9	24.9	24.0
Strong Republican	67.7	44.5	15.5	12.0	39.8	45.9	54.2	23.6	42.7	40.9	51.5	52.7	16.1	25.4	20.5

Party Identification	Fair Employment					School Integration					Foreign Aid				
	1956	1960	1964	1968	1972	1956	1960	1964	1968	1972	1956	1960	1964	1968	1972
Strong Democrat	73.3	63.0	56.3	61.9	64.9	38.7	39.8	53.7	58.9	55.3	49.5	51.4	64.7	51.3	38.9
Weak Democrat	71.3	63.1	42.9	43.5	53.0	44.4	37.5	43.2	44.6	43.1	55.4	48.8	59.2	45.8	44.7
Independent	66.6	65.4	50.3	37.7	55.2	48.8	47.1	49.0	37.3	45.6	49.9	53.2	57.5	42.7	47.4
Weak Republican	70.8	62.7	36.3	37.8	51.0	49.3	43.0	50.5	37.4	45.4	48.2	54.0	56.6	47.0	44.0
Strong Republican	66.8	65.9	20.6	31.3	39.4	38.8	41.5	34.8	31.5	34.8	51.4	61.5	49.7	41.8	47.8

Note: The percentage in each cell is that supporting the "liberal" position.
Source: Gerald M. Pomper, *Voters' Choice* (New York: Dodd, Mead & Co., 1975), p. 168. Data from SRC/CPS Election Studies.

The only area in which this generalization does not hold is foreign aid. There seems to be no particular partisan bias in favor of the liberal position on this matter. Further examination of Table 2-6 reveals that the relationship between liberalism and Democratic party identification began in earnest in 1964 and persisted into 1968. However, the relationship appears to diminish in the data for 1972.[70]

Are we to conclude, then, that the trend toward Democrats being more liberal than Republicans is playing itself out? The answer is almost certainly not. One reason for this is that the way in which the policy questions were asked in 1972 differed from the way they were asked in prior years. This may explain to some extent the 1972 finding. Furthermore, other studies of partisanship and ideology which make use of post-1972 data confirm the continued existence of a linkage between the two. One study has combined the 1973–1977 National Opinion Research Center's (NORC) General Social Surveys and demonstrated that Democrats are more likely to identify themselves as liberals while Republicans classify themselves as conservatives. During the years examined, 60 percent of strong Republicans and 41 percent of weak Republicans labeled themselves "conservative." On the Democratic side, only 23 percent of strong Democrats and 25 percent of weak Democrats labeled themselves conservative. While many Democrats, especially weak identifiers, saw themselves as moderates, a plurality of strong Democrats (about 40 percent) classified themselves as liberal.[71] Therefore, it appears that the link between partisanship and political views persisted into the 1970s, although perhaps not as strongly as it was in the 1960s.

Party Differences Perceived

Pomper also found in his longitudinal analyses of the SRC/CPS policy questions that the public has become increasingly aware of policy differences between the Democratic and Republican parties. Furthermore, among those persons perceiving differences between the two parties, there has been an increase over time in the percentage of citizens who correctly perceive the parties' differences.

Data taken from the Gallup Poll are not as supportive of the notion that Americans have more clearly perceived differences, correctly or incorrectly, between the Republicans and the Democrats. In 1960 and again in 1980, Gallup asked a sampling of Americans which political party could best handle the nation's most important problem (which each respondent was asked to identify) and which party would be best for people like themselves. On both questions there was little change in the percentage of those polled that perceived little or no difference between the two parties.[72] There was, in fact, a very tiny increase in the proportion of persons that saw no difference between the parties in terms of their capacity to handle the most important problems.

On the other hand, an analysis of questions from the 1984 CPS election survey that allowed respondents to describe differences between the two major parties tells a different picture. While Gant and Luttbeg find that over one half of the respondents could not name a correct attribute of either party, they found, conversely, that just under one half *could* name a correct attribute of one party or the other.[73] The divergence of these findings from those reported by Gallup suggest that caution is advised when arriving at strong conclusions about changes in popular conceptions of party differences.

Better Belief Systems

Converse, who has been concerned with the quality of Americans' belief systems, found that most Americans did not have a constrained set of beliefs between 1956 and 1960. Converse determined the level of constraint by examining the size of the correlations between individuals' issue positions. Most Americans' beliefs were inconsistent, often internally contradictory, and unstable over time. In fact, Converse found attitude changes among many Americans that appeared almost random in nature.[74]

Converse conceived of constraint as one characteristic of individuals who had an ideology—an abstract representation of the political world. It was felt by the authors of *The American Voter*, which included Converse, that an abstract world view—an ideology—was necessary to process all the information about the political process needed to make voting decisions based on issues. The lack of constraint, as well as the lack of *consistency* (the relationship between positions on an issue across time), has long been held to indicate a lack of ideology. In turn, the potential for issue voting could only be reduced.

More recently, Norman Nie and Kristi Anderson claim to have found some improvement in Americans' belief system. In their analysis of the 1960s and 1970s, they used Converse's general techniques and methods and detected a striking improvement in ideological constraint between 1960 and 1964. This constraint has diminished to a small degree since 1964, but it persists at levels that surpass those noted earlier by Converse. Nie and Anderson also find that levels of ideological consistency have risen more for domestic policy issues than for foreign policy issues.[75]

At least three studies, however, have been critical of Nie and Anderson's conclusions about increased ideological consistency.[76] Two studies suggest that the Nie and Anderson finding was simply an artifact of changes in the format of SRC/CPS survey questions. Another study, by Philip Converse and Gregory Markus, examined consistency of issue attitudes across the 1956-1960 and 1972-1976 panel studies. (In each panel study respondents were interviewed during each of the three election years that fell during the panel.) If Nie and Anderson are correct that ideological consistency is improving, Converse and Marcus reasoned that consistency across the 1972-1976 panel study should be greater than that observed across the 1952-1956 panel study. But this increase in consistency did not occur on issues that were included in both panel periods. Taken as a whole, these three studies cast serious doubt on Nie's conclusions.

Another body of research suggests that people are much better able to think in abstract terms than the authors of *The American Voter* claimed. This line of research does not suggest that individuals have grown more sophisticated in this regard (although Kathleen Knight reported that in 1980 fully 26 percent of all respondents to the CPS election survey could be classified as ideologues[77]). Rather, several scholars have suggested that the conventional way of looking at ideological capabilities—ordering the political world on a liberal-conservative or "left-right" continuum—is fundamentally misguided. In the words of John Kessel: " . . . the ability to discern which party 'is closer to what you want' . . . is more vital for voter rationality than a capacity to understand the denotation of abstract concepts."[78] One study of the 1980 election found that people who could think about *liberal* and *conservative* in abstract terms were no more likely to vote on the basis of issues than those who could not articulate what these terms meant to them,[79] a finding which corroborates Kessel's warning.

As conceived by Converse, an ideology is a cognitive structure which organizes and allows the use of political information in decision making. Given that the dominant way of thinking about politics has been through the use of a liberal-conservative continuum, these scholars conceived of ideology in such terms. But a study by Ruth Hamill, Milton Lodge, and Frederick Blake suggests that other cognitive structures, organized along lines other than a left-right decision, can be equally useful in organizing political information.[80]

The authors find that a *class-based* ideology, with distinctions between rich and poor, is far more widely used to organize political information than other ways of doing so. In fact, the ideological left-right continuum was least often used by subjects in their study. The implications of these findings is that if we confine ourselves to looking for liberal-conservative distinctions, we will often miss equally useful ways people have of making sense of the political world.

Mark Peffley and Jon Hurwitz suggest scholars ought to look for relationships between general orientations (such as a liberal-conservative ideology), general policy attitudes (such as on racial issues), and specific issue positions (such as on busing).[81] The authors proceed in this fashion, and find that attitudes *are* constrained in an "up-down" fashion. Their findings suggest that belief systems are in place, if we only know how to look for them.

The research cited in the next section indicates that the impact of issues on vote choice has strengthened considerably since the 1950s. What counts for issue voting is that people are organizing information in *some* way, even if it is not immediately "comprehendible" to the critical observer.[82]

Voting: The Link with Issues and Images

Another more important facet of the rise of the influence of issues concerns the increasing connection between issue positions and vote choices. The available evidence suggests that issue voting is rising. David RePass argues that if we confine our attention to those issues that are salient to individuals, issues are just as important as party identification in determining the vote.[83] And, as noted earlier, Miller and his colleagues found substantial issue voting in the 1972 presidential election.[84]

Miller and Wattenberg found that, although party identification is still the strongest predictor of the vote, policy concerns have become increasingly important, especially when citizens evaluate nonincumbents.[85] William Lyons and Michael Gant estimate that for the elections of 1972–1984, the rate of issue voting, independent of party identification, ranged from 55 percent to 61 percent.[86] John Jackson's conclusion concerning the role of issues in the 1964 election sums up the position of many scholars on this point:

> Voting decisions are largely motivated by evaluations of where the parties are located on different issues relative to the person's stated positions and to a much lesser extent by party identifications unless people are indifferent between the parties on the issues.[87]

However, increasing levels of issue voting have been accompanied by another phenomenon—an increase in voting on the basis of candidate image. According to Eugene DeClercq, Thomas Hurley, and Norman Luttbeg, this increase in candidate-image voting has matched, if not outstripped, the growth in the role of issues in the voter's decision.[88]

Candidate image is a term describing the personal characteristics of a candidate that a voter finds appealing or unappealing. However, these characteristics are unrelated to the candidate's policy or partisan views. The candidate may be viewed as appealing solely because of personal factors such as physical appearance, intelligence, schooling, family background, or speech.

A second image variable employed by DeClercq and his associates is *party image*. This is another evaluation the authors feel is devoid of specific policy concerns. For example, a Kansas wheat farmer may say that he votes Republican because "Republicans are the party of the farmer." In the view of Declercq et al. such a response lacks any specific policy content. It is possible, however, that the farmer has observed that the Republican party supports farm policies that he personally favors. For example, research by Michael Gant and Dwight Davis indicates that statements such as "The Democrats are for farmers" reflect specific information processed and discarded and shows that these sorts of statements are linked to issue voting.[89] While the evidence is mixed, given that our discussion is based on the research on DeClercq, Hurley, and Luttbeg, we will adopt their interpretation of these responses as they relate to parties, and assume that these statements seldom have policy content when applied to parties.

The question these authors sought to answer was "What has been the relative impact of these four variables on Americans' voting decisions in presidential elections between 1956 and 1972?" The four variables considered were (1) candidate image, (2) issue orientation, (3) party identification, and (4) party image. Their findings, updated through 1984, are displayed in Figure 2-2. While the measure used here is somewhat complex, you need only note that a variable with a beta of 0.4 has twice the impact on how people vote as a beta of 0.2.

The trend lines depicted in Figure 2-2 indicate that, with the exception of the 1972 presidential election, party identification has prevailed over the other determinants of voter choice, but only narrowly so in 1980. After the 1972 election and the precipitous drop in the importance of partisanship, there was much discussion to the effect that party identification would no longer dominate voters' decision making. Nevertheless, partisanship reemerged as the most important factor in 1976, only to fall again in 1980. With this perspective of recent elections, it is difficult to predict the future importance of party identification or any other of the four factors analyzed except that issues are slowly and consistently rising in importance over time. It seems likely that the erratic performance of these factors over the last four elections will continue as we enter an era of dynamic electoral behavior in which the absolute and relative effects of partisanship, issues, and images will fluctuate.

A Trend Assessment: Partisanship

At the conclusion of this and the next two chapters we will offer assessments of selected aspects of each trend under consideration. These assessments focus on some of the more controversial aspects of contemporary political science.

Figure 2-2

Factors Influencing Presidential Voting, 1956–1984

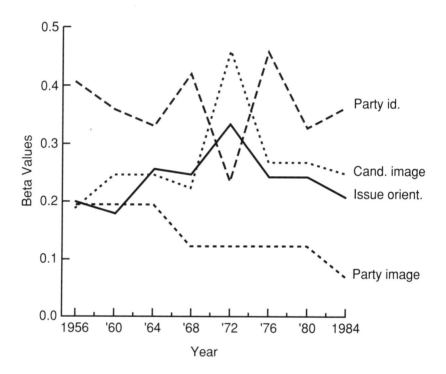

Note: Betas using average standard deviations across elections.
Source: Eugene DeClercq, Thomas L. Hurley, and Norman R. Luttbeg, "Voting in American Presidential Elections," *American Politics Quarterly* 3 (July, 1975). Analysis updated for 1976 by Thomas L. Hurley; Analysis updated through 1984 by Norman R. Luttbeg. Data from NES 1956 through 1984.

The original research discussed here should help students and other researchers better understand the various phenomena of change in the American electorate.

We will seek to assess change in the American electorate over time on five variables: (1) voting defection from party identification, (2) the nature of independency, (3) quality of candidate evaluation, (4) participation, and (5) alienation or loss of trust. The first three are introduced in this chapter.

We use party identification to measure the first two of our five trend variables: defection from party identification and nature of independency. In voting for president, defection or loyalty depends on the correspondence between one's party identification and the party of the candidate for which one votes. For example, a Democrat who voted for George Bush in 1988 would be defecting from the party, as Bush was the Republican candidate. A vote for Michael Dukakis would have been a loyal vote.

The question arises as to how to treat independents who admit to leaning toward the Democrats or the Republicans. Since SRC/CPS research has shown that such "partisan" independents vote overwhelmingly for the candidates of the party toward which they lean, we included them as possible defectors.

In Table 2-7 we present the proportions of individuals in each of the categories of the seven-point party identification scale who voted for the Republican, Democratic, and other candidates in the 1980, 1984, and 1988 presidential elections. The results from 1988, previously presented in Table 2-4, are repeated here to allow comparisons with the previous elections. Three features of this table are worth noting. First, the reemergence of party identification as a voting cue is dramatically illustrated. Partisans at all levels were overwhelmingly loyal to their party's candidate, especially in 1988. The force of Ronald Reagan's personality was such that defection was much higher in 1980, and to some degree in 1984, than it was in 1988. Lacking such a strong personal figure, the election of 1988 saw a strengthening of the impact of partisanship.

Second, in both 1984 and 1988, leaning partisans were more loyal to their party's candidate than weak partisans. This suggests anew that those who claim to be independent, but admit to leaning to one party or the other, may in fact be partisans "in disguise."

Finally, despite the fact that we indicated earlier that one reason Bush won in 1988 was his popularity among independents, Bush actually did worse among pure nonpartisans than did Reagan in both 1980 and 1984. As a consequence, independents moved closer to an even (though not much more even) split between the Democratic and Republican candidates.

As we saw in Table 2-1, both major political parties have lost weak and strong supporters to the ranks of independents. But more than one half of the increasingly numerous independents admit to leaning toward one of the two parties. And most of these leaners continue to vote for the nominee of the party toward which they lean. Therefore, we have elected to refer only to *pure* independents in our evaluation of the increase in independency. Only these pure independents reflect a significant change from the politics of the 1950s. Considering only pure independents makes the magnitude of the trend toward in-

Table 2-7

Presidential Vote by Party Identification, 1980–1988

Party Id.	1980 Election				1984 Election			1988 Election		
	Reagan	Carter	Anderson	Other	Reagan	Mondale	Other	Bush	Dukakis	Other
Strong Democrat	11	86	3	—	11	87	1	6	93	1
Democrat	33	60	8	—	32	67	1	27	70	3
Leaning Democrat	29	45	20	6	21	79	—	12	88	—
Independent	64	22	12	2	71	27	2	61	33	6
Leaning Republican	76	12	10	3	92	6	1	84	15	1
Republican	86	5	9	1	92	6	1	83	17	—
Strong Republican	92	5	4	—	96	3	—	98	2	—

Source: National Election Studies, 1980 and 1988.

creasing independence less dramatic, but pure independents alone seem to merit consideration as voters free from party ties.

Quality of Candidate Evaluation

The third variable to be introduced in this chapter is quality of candidate evaluation. Many central questions concerning the American electorate involve the quality of the decision underlying the voter's choice of presidential candidates. Much of the controversy concerning the implications of studies of the electorate centers on whether issues or candidates' images are now the most important determinant of how people vote. Have positions on issues as taken by candidates and as preferred by voters replaced party loyalty in voting? Or is the image of the candidates, especially trivial aspects such as sense of humor or physical attractiveness, as manipulated in media presentations, now central to the voter's decision among candidates?

Our measure of the quality of a voter's evaluation of a presidential candidate uses questions asked in the SRC/CPS studies since 1952. In each instance, respondents were queried as to whether there was anything that would cause them to vote for or against the Democratic or Republican candidates for president. We scanned three possible responses for pro-Democratic, anti-Democratic, pro-Republican, and anti-Republican reactions to the candidates to ascertain a hierarchy or rank ordering of quality in these responses.

If any one of the possible twelve responses revealed a mention of an ideological standard for candidate evaluation, such as "He is too liberal," that respondent is credited with giving the most sophisticated response and labeled *ideologue*. The next lower level of candidate evaluation involves mention of an issue such as "He favors Medicare." Respondents who evaluate candidates in these terms are assigned the label *issue-oriented*. If a respondent sees a candidate in terms of the groups the candidate will place at an advantage or disadvantage, such as "He will hurt the farmers," the respondent is labeled *group benefits*. Respondents who evaluate candidates with references to party connections, such as "He's a good Democrat," are placed in the *partisan* category.

The last two classes of candidate evaluation lack any evidence that the voter prefers a candidate because of a policy preference espoused by the candidate. The voter who mentions some assessment of a candidate's personality, such as "He looks honest" or "I like him," is labeled an *image* evaluator. The class labeled *no-content* is the lowest rung on our hierarchy of quality of evaluation. Such respondents give *no* response to any question concerning the candidates for president. Obviously, evaluations by ideologues and issue oriented voters reflect a quality that suggests their choice among the candidates could lead to the enactment of policies they prefer. They are judged *high quality* on this basis. The image and no-content evaluators are judged low quality, as no issue positions are furthered by a candidate receiving their vote.

Our use of these categories of candidate evaluation suggests that were the electorate as a whole to exhibit substantially more concern about issues, survey responses as to why voters have decided to vote for or against candidates should reveal this improvement. But this measure is an indirect indicator of the factors impacting on voters' decisions. Certainly, one could argue for new questions which might better measure the issue sophistication of the average voter, and certainly other existing questions can be used to make an assessment. But because these questions are open ended, taking the respondent's own words as an answer, they neither suggest answers nor force the respondent to choose between a limited number of possible answers. Furthermore, by structuring a hierarchy of responses in which the respondent is credited for his or her *most sophisticated response*, we allow every opportunity for a more ideologically sophisticated, issue voting electorate to reveal itself.[90]

Table 2-8 shows that in 1988, some 55 percent of the electorate revealed the highest quality candidate evaluations (7 percent ideologue and 48 percent issue-oriented), while 29 percent gave the lowest quality evaluations (13 percent image and 16 percent no content). Scanning the trend in high quality evaluation since 1952 indicates fluctuations from the low of 17 percent in 1952 to a high of 73 percent in 1984, truly a remarkable figure. Substantial declines in 1968, 1976, and 1984, however, suggest the absence of a continuous trend. Were 1964, 1972, 1980, and 1984 merely peaks, to be followed by a return to the levels of the 1950s? All that can be said with complete confidence is that the pattern of issue-oriented responses is very erratic.

But low-quality evaluations show a consistent decline, from a high in 1952 of 77 percent (62 percent image and 15 percent no-content) to 18 percent in 1984; the uptick to 29 percent in 1988 may again be a random fluctuation. The overall consistency of this decline is entirely a function of the consistent decline of image only responses by respondents. No-content responses show no pattern of change in that they are equal to or greater than the levels observed in the 1950s.

Are Independents High Quality Evaluators?   Figure 2-3 clearly reveals that the pattern noted in Table 2-8 holds regardless of whether the respondent is a Democrat, a Republican, or an independent. If any such pattern of difference between independents and partisans is notable, it is that since 1960 independents have exhibited lower quality evaluations than have partisans. In the 1950s, the quality of evaluations expressed by independents was equal to or higher than those of partisans. While evaluations by independents have im-

Table 2-8

Trend in Quality of Candidate Evaluations, 1952–1988

Percent of Respondents Using Various Types of Candidate Evaluations

Year	Ideologue	Issue Oriented	Group Benefit	Partisan	Image	No Content	N
1952	1	16	5	1	62	15	1899
1956	1	19	6	—	64	10	1762
1960	1	20	4	—	62	12	1181
1964	6	35	5	—	44	9	1571
1968	3	23	5	19	36	15	1557
1972	7	44	9	6	28	10	1372
1976	7	35	3	13	27	9	2870
1980	10	48	5	5	22	12	1614
1984	6	67	5	5	8	10	2257
1988	7	48	5	12	13	16	2040

Source: National Election Studies, 1952–1988.

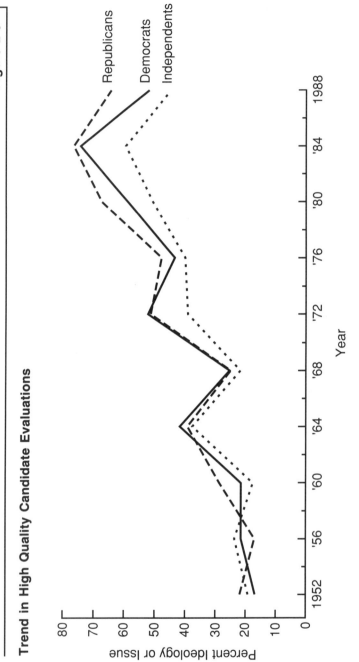

Figure 2-3

Trend in High Quality Candidate Evaluations

Source: National Election Studies, 1952–1988.

proved since the 1950s, they have improved at a slower rate such that in 1988 independents were the poorest performers in terms of the quality of candidate evaluations.

Are Defectors Higher Quality Evaluators?   Defection among partisans in voting for president has varied substantially across elections. In 1952, 22 percent of all partisans (those identifying with a political party or leaning toward it) defected to the opposition party in voting for president. Defection then declined to a low of 14 percent in 1960, followed by a rise to yet another peak in 1972 at 27 percent. Clubb, Flanigan, and Zingale have shown that this rise is almost exclusively due to Southern Democrats who cast their votes for Goldwater, Wallace, and Nixon between 1964 and 1972. In 1976, defection sharply declined to 17 percent only to peak once again in 1980 when about one third of all partisans defected.[91] But in 1984 and 1988 partisan loyalty increased sharply such that defection in the late 1980s was even lower than that observed in *The American Voter*. The percentages of defection are as follows:

1952	22%
1956	17%
1960	14%
1964	16%
1968	25%
1972	27%
1976	17%
1980	33%
1984	14%
1988	15%

No trend line is apparent in these data, suggesting that factors peculiar to a campaign have tremendous impact on the rate of partisan defection. Whatever other factors influence the American electorate, at least eight out of ten partisans continue to vote loyally for their party's nominee for president. The high rates of defection observed in 1968 and 1980 suggest that defection is most true when a viable third party candidate (such as George Wallace in 1968 and John Anderson in 1980) seeks the presidency.

Defectors show no unique increase in the quality of their candidate evaluations. Figure 2-4 distinguishes between those who defect in their presidential vote and those who defect from their party with respect to their votes for the U.S. Senate or the House of Representatives. Four types of voters are thus shown: (1) those defecting in the presidential election and for at least one of the congressional offices (DD on the figure), (2) presidential defectors and congressional loyalists (DL), (3) presidential loyalists and congressional defectors (LD), and (4) *total* loyalists (LL). Congressional defectors during the period 1952–1964 proved somewhat higher in the quality of their candidate evaluations. But all voters seem affected identically by the somewhat jagged trend toward higher quality in candidate evaluations.

In examining Figure 2-4, the reader should consider that the evaluations referred to are evaluations of the presidential candidates, and that high quality evaluations refer to those with ideological or issue content. Interestingly, voters who do not defect at either level are most likely to reflect high quality evaluations, when compared to the other three groups. Clearly, straight-ticket voting is not the blindly partisan activity it was once thought to be. In turn, the next group most likely to exhibit high quality evaluations of presidential candidates are those who voted *against* their party's presidential *and* congressional candidates. But again, these people are not splitting their ticket but engaging in "reverse" straight-ticket voting. It has been suggested that ticket-splitting is an activity which demonstrates the "independence" of voters from party labels. If this is true, this independence does not flow from high quality evaluations, nor presumably, result in high quality votes.

Conclusion

In this chapter we have considered two different aspects of the American electorate's involvement with political parties: willingness to identify with one of the two major parties; and, given this willingness, loyalty to the party in voting for its nominees. If unwillingness to identify with a political party were more common, with an increasing number of citizens declaring themselves independent of parties, and if defection in voting were growing among the remaining partisans, we might well explain such trends by questioning the usefulness of parties in influencing how people vote. The possibility that voters have perceived the parties as failing to reflect issue divisions felt by an increasingly issue-oriented public would seem to be a viable explanation. But our assessment of trends over this twenty-eight year period refutes this explanation in two ways.

First, while independents are more numerous (11 percent in 1988 versus 5 percent in 1952; see Table 2-1), defections show no consistent pattern of increase. In fact, defection has *decreased* since the 1950s, the supposed high-water mark of partisan activity. Perhaps even more conclusively, these data show that neither refusing to identify with a political party nor defection in voting from one's political party relates to the sophistication one shows in evalu-

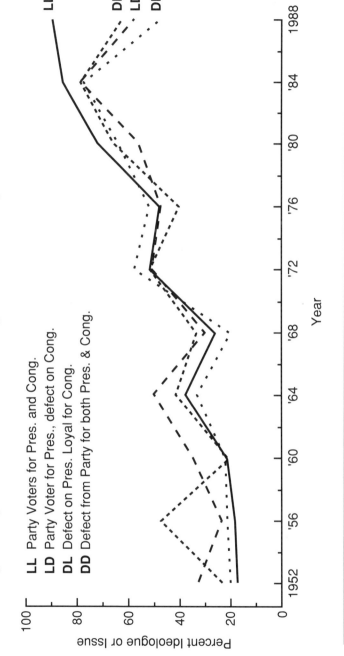

Figure 2-4

Trend in High Quality Candidate Evaluation Among Defectors and Loyalists

LL Party Voters for Pres. and Cong.
LD Party Voter for Pres., defect on Cong.
DL Defect on Pres. Loyal for Cong.
DD Defect from Party for both Pres. & Cong.

Percent Ideologue or Issue

Year

Source: National Election Studies, 1952–1988.

ation of presidential candidates. Voter sophistication, as judged by the use of issues or ideology in evaluating the candidates, has improved, but it is neither the cause nor the result of disenchantment of the public with the major political parties.

The majority political party in terms of identifications, the Democrats, may have lost seven of the ten presidential elections during this period, but no substantial growth in the number of Republicans is evident in the electorate, except for independents admitting to leaning toward the Republican party. Democratic identification has declined, however, from a high of 60 percent in 1964 to the low of 47 percent observed in 1988. Over 85 percent of the electorate remain partisans, including leaning independents, and about eight out of ten partisans vote for their party's presidential candidate. Neither party can expect to win a presidential election purely on the basis of partisan loyalty. Obviously, both need to pursue possible defectors, as well as independents, to win, but the Republican must try harder. Deviations from this overall pattern are not likely to occur in the near future, if the past is any guide. Only substantial changes in the nature of partisanship and independency, or the nature of candidate evaluations, is likely to alter election outcomes.

Notes

1. Angus Campbell, Philip E. Converse, Warren E. Miller, and Donald E. Stokes, *The American Voter* (New York: John Wiley and Sons, 1960).
2. Arthur H. Miller, and Martin P. Wattenberg, "Throwing the Rascals Out: Policy and Performance Evaluations of Presidential Candidates, 1952-1980," *American Political Science Review*, 79 (March 1985): 359–72.
3. Campbell, *et al., The American Voter*, p. 121.
4. Peter B. Natchez, "Images of Voting: The Social Psychologists," *Public Policy*, 18 (Summer 1970): 553–88.
5. Campbell, *et al., The American Voter*, p. 137.
6. *Ibid.*, p. 149.
7. Morris P. Fiorina, "An Outline for a Model of Party Choice," *American Journal of Political Science*, 21 (August 1977): 618. This article, along with John E. Jackson's "Issues, Party Choices, and Presidential Votes," *American Journal of Political Science*, 19 (May 1975): 161–86, are the classic contemporary statements of the revisionist interpretation of party identification. The references in the quote to the "elephant"

and the "donkey" are to the traditional editorial cartoon representations of the Democratic and Republican parties.

8. Fiorina, "An Outline for a Model of Party Choice," p. 618.

9. Jackson, "Issues, Party Choices, and Presidential Votes," p. 181.

10. Charles H. Franklin, "Issue Preferences, Socialization, and the Evolution of Party Identification," *American Journal of Political Science*, 28 (August 1984): 459-78. See also, Charles H. Franklin and John E. Jackson, "The Dynamics of Party Identification," *American Political Science Review*, 77 (December 1983): 957-73, in which the authors arrive at the same conclusion they each developed individually.

11. Gerald M. Pomper, "From Confusion to Clarity: Issues and American Voters, 1956–1968," *American Political Science Review*, 66 (June 1972): 415-28. We will discuss Pomper's findings in greater detail in connection with our consideration of issue voting. We introduce these findings here, however, because of their immediate relevance to the point at hand.

12. Michael M. Gant, "The Political Content of Party Identification: Traditional *vs.* Revisionist Perspectives." Presented at the Annual Meetings of the Southern Political Science Association, Savannah, Georgia, November, 1984.

13. Michael M. Gant and Norman R. Luttbeg, "The Cognitive Utility of Partisanship," *Western Political Quarterly*, 40 (September 1987): 499-517.

14. Studies which are representative of research done on this point include Jackson, "Issues, Party Choices, and Presidential Votes"; Arthur H. Miller, Warren E. Miller, Alden S. Raine and Thad A. Brown, "A Majority Party in Disarray: Policy Polarization in the 1972 Election," *American Political Science Review*, 70 (September 1976): 753-78; Benjamin I. Page and Calvin C. Jones, "Reciprocal Effects of Policy Preferences, Party Loyalties and the Vote," *American Political Science Review*, 73 (December 1979): 1071-89; and, Miller and Wattenberg, "Throwing the Rascals Out."

15. Morris P. Fiorina, *Retrospective Evaluations in American National Elections* (New Haven: Yale University Press, 1981).

16. Franklin and Jackson, "The Dynamics of Party Identification."

17. The categories of this measure are Strong Democrat; Weak Democrat; Independent-Leaning Democrat; "Pure" Independent; Independent-Leaning Republican; Weak Republican; and, Strong Republican. Additional categories, such as "other or minor party" and "don't know," are also used, but the number of people who are placed in these groupings are very small.

18. In all fairness to the Michigan scholars, they did not have access to *panel data*—studies of the same people interviewed at two or more points in time. They based their conclusions regarding the stability of party identification largely on recall data, which are notoriously unreliable, and on the distribution of party identification for the entire electorate, which did not change much during the 1950s. But the distribution of an entire sample will *not* necessarily show whether *individuals* were changing partisanships which the evidence in the text makes clear individuals were doing, and still are today.

19. Kenneth J. Meier, "Party Identification and Vote Choice: The Causal Connection," *Western Political Quarterly* (September 1975): 496-505.

20. Michael D. Martinez and Michael M. Gant, "Partisan Issue Preferences and Partisan Change," *Political Behavior* (forthcoming, 1990).

21. Edward C. Dreyer, "Change and Stability in Party Identification," *Journal of Politics*, 35 (November 1972): 712-22; and Meier, "Party Identification and Vote Choice."

22. Franklin and Jackson, "The Dynamics of Party Identification," p. 968.

23. Perhaps the best summary of the literature on party decline is William J. Crotty and Gary C. Jacobson, *American Parties in Decline*, second ed. (Boston: Little, Brown, 1984); also see Gerald M. Pomper, *Voters' Choice* (New York: Dodd, Mead & Co., 1975); Walter Dean Burnham, *Critical Elections and the Mainsprings of American Politics* (New York: W. W. Norton, 1970); Walter DeVries and V. Lance Tarrance, *The Ticket Splitter: A New Force in American Politics* (Grand Rapids, MI: William B. Eerdmans Publishing Co., 1972); Jack Dennis, "Trends in Support for the American Political Party System" (Paper presented at Annual Meeting of the American Political Science Association, Chicago, August-September 1974). As we shall see, the conclusion that the parties have diminished in importance has by no means universal support, and in fact has come under increasing attack.

24. Dreyer, "Change and Stability in Party Identification."

25. Martinez and Gant, "Partisan Issue Preferences and Partisan Changes."

26. Dennis, "Trends in Support for Party Systems."

27. *Gallup Opinion Index and Gallup Opinion Report*, various issues; Stephen D. Shaffer, "A Multivariate Explanation of Rising Ticketsplitting" (Paper presented at the annual meeting of the Southern Political Science Association, Atlanta, 1982).

28. DeVries and Tarrance, *Ticket Splitter*, pp. 145-46.

29. Ruth K. Scott and Ronald J. Hrebenar, *Parties in Crisis* (New York: John Wiley and Sons, 1979), pp. 145–46.

30. Michael M. Gant and Dennis Black, "The Determinants of Split Results at the Congressional District Level." Presented at the Annual Meet-

ings of the Midwest Political Science Association, Chicago, April 1987; *Congressional Quarterly Weekly Report*, 47 (July 8, 1989): 1711.

31. V. O. Key, Jr. *The Responsible Electorate* (Cambridge, MA: Belknap Press, 1966).

32. *Ibid*, Chap. 2.

33. Philip E. Converse *et al.*, "Stability and Change in 1960: A Reinstating Election," in *Elections and the Political Order*, eds. Angus Campbell, Philip E. Converse, Warren E. Miller, and Donald E. Stokes (New York: John Wiley & Sons, 1966), p. 83.

34. Key, *Responsible Electorate*, p. 64.

35. *Ibid.*, p. 65.

36. *Ibid.*, p. 71.

37. Pomper, *Voters' Choice*, p. 33.

38. Gant and Luttbeg, "The Cognitive Utility of Partisanship."

39. Joyce Gelb and Marian Lief Palley, *Tradition and Change in American Party Politics* (New York: Thomas Y. Crowell Co., 1975), p. 3.

40. Rhodes Cook, "The Nominating Process," in *The Election of 1988*, ed. Michael Nelson (Washington, D.C.: CQ Press: 1989), 25–61.

41. *Congressional Quarterly Almanac*, 44 (Washington, D. C.: Congressional Quarterly, Inc., 1989): 42–43.

42. Robert Agranoff, *The Management of Election Campaigns* (Boston: Holbrook Press, 1976), p. 17.

43. Frank J. Sorauf, *Party Politics in America*, third ed. (Boston: Little, Brown & Co., 1976), pp. 416–17.

44. Cornelius P. Cotter, James L. Gibson, John F. Bibby and Robert J. Huckshorn, *Party Organization in American Politics* (New York: Praeger, 1984); James L. Gibson, Cornelius P. Cotter, John F. Bibby and Robert J. Huckshorn, "Wither the Local Parties: A Cross-Sectional and Longitudinal Analysis of the Strength of Party Organizations," *American Journal of Political Science*, 29 (February 1985): 139–60; and, by the same authors, "Assessing Party Organizational Strength," *American Journal of Political Science*, 27 (February 1983): 193–222.

45. Dennis, "Trends in Support for Party System."

46. *Ibid.*, pp. 23–24. The institutions were: Congress, Supreme Court, Presidency, Political Parties, Elections, Interest Groups, and Federal Administrative Agencies.

47. Martin P. Wattenberg, "The Decline of Political Partisanship in the United States: Negativity or Neutrality," *American Political Science Review*, 75 (September 1981): 941-50. See also his *The Decline of American Political Parties*, 1952–1980 (Cambridge, MA: Harvard University Press, 1984).

48. Thomas M. Konda and Lee Sigelman, "Public Evaluations of the Amer-

ican Parties, 1952-1984," *Journal of Politics*, 49 (November 1987): 814-29.

49. Harold D. Clarke and Marianne C. Stewart, "Partisan Inconsistencies and Partisan Change in Federal States: The Case of Canada," *American Journal of Political Science*, 31 (May 1987): 383-407.

50. Richard G. Niemi, Stephen Wright and Linda W. Powell, "Multiple Party Identifiers and the Measurement of Party Identification," *Journal of Politics*, 49 (November 1987): 1093-1103.

51. Charles D. Hadley, "Dual Partisan Identification in the South," *Journal of Politics,* 47 (February 1985): 254-68.

52. Edward G. Carmines, John P. McIver and James A. Stimson, "Unrealized Partisanship: A Theory of Dealignment," *Journal of Politics*, 49 (May 1987): 376-400.

53. Helmut Norpoth and Jerrold G. Rusk, "Partisan Dealignment in the American Electorate: Itemizing the Deductions Since 1964," *American Political Science Review*, 76 (June 1982): 522-37.

54. Charles Sellars, "The Equilibrium Cycle in Two Party Politics," *Public Opinion Quarterly*, 29 (Spring 1965): 16-38.

55. V. O. Key, Jr., "A Theory of Critical Elections," *Journal of Politics*, 17 (February 1955): 3-18. Also see Gerald Pomper, "A Classification of Presidential Elections," *Journal of Politics*, 29 (August 1967): 535-66.

56. Paul Beck, "A Socialization Theory of Partisan Realignment," in *The Politics of Future Citizens*, eds. Richard G. Niemi and Associates (San Francisco: Jossey-Bass publishers, 1974), pp. 199-219; Paul Beck, "Youth and the Politics of Realignment," in *Political Opinion and Behavior*, eds. E. C. Dreyer and W. A. Rosenbaum (Belmont, CA: Wadsworth Publishing Co., 1976), pp. 366-73; Richard J. Trilling, "Party Image and Partisan Change," in *The Future of Political Parties*, eds. Louis Maisel and Paul M. Sacks (Beverly Hills, CA: Sage Publications, 1975), pp. 63-100; Norman H. Nie, Sidney Verba, and John R. Petrocik, *The Changing American Voter* (Cambridge, MA: Harvard University Press); *Transformations of the American Party System* (New York: W. W. Norton & Co., 1975); E. C. Ladd, Jr., *Where Have All the Voters Gone?* (New York: W. W. Norton & Co., 1978).

57. Jerome M. Clubb, William H. Flanigan, and Nancy H. Zingale, "Partisan Realignment Since 1960." (Paper presented at the 1976 meeting of the American Political Science Association, Chicago, p. 7.)

58. James Sundquist, *Dynamics of the Party System* (Washington, D.C.: Brookings Institution, 1973).

59. Carol Cassel, "Cohort Analysis of Party Identification among Southern Whites, 1952-1972," *Public Opinion Quarterly* 41 (1977): 28-33.

60. Philip E. Converse, "On the Possibility of a Major Realignment in the South," in *Elections and the Political Order*, eds. Angus Campbell, et al. (New York: John Wiley & Sons, 1966).

61. Carmines, *et al.*, "Unrealized Partisanship."

62. *Ibid.*, p. 397.

63. Edward G. Carmines and James A. Stimson, "On the Structure and Sequence of Issue Evolution," *American Political Science Review*, 80 (September 1986): 901–20.

64. *Ibid.*, pp. 901–02.

65. Robert Axelrod, "Presidential Election Coalitions in 1984," *American Political Science Review*, 80 (March 1986): 281–84.

66. Harold W. Stanley, William T. Bianco and Richard G. Niemi, "Partisanship and Group Support Over Time: A Multivariate Analysis," *American Political Science Review*, 80 (September 1986): 969–76.

67. The probabilities presented in the text are not the proportions of the groups who identify with the Democratic Party; these are generally higher than the probabilities calculated by Stanley, et al. The authors calculate these probabilities by removing the influence of other factors. For example, the probability of a black being a Democrat in 1984 was 65 percent, after the effects of such factors as living in the South, being working class, etc., are removed.

68. John R. Petrocik, "Realignment: New Party Coalitions and the Nationalization of the South," *Journal of Politics,* 49 (May 1987): 347–75.

69. Carmines and Stimson, "On the Structure and Sequence of Issue Evolution."

70. Pomper, *Voters' Choice*, p. 168.

71. William Schneider, "1980 – A Watershed Year," *Politics Today* 7, no. 1 (January/February 1980): 30.

72. *Gallup Opinion Index*, Report #87 (April 1987), and Report #94 (November 1981).

73. Gant and Luttbeg, "The Cognitive Utility of Partisanship."

74. Philip E. Converse, "The Nature of Belief Systems in Mass Publics," in *Ideology and Discontent*, ed. David Apter (Glencoe, IL: Free Press, 1964).

75. Norman H. Nie with Kristi Anderson, "Mass Belief Systems Revisited: Political Change and Attitude Structure," *Journal of Politics*, 36 (August 1974): 540–91.

76. John L. Sullivan, James E. Pierson, and George E. Marcus, "Ideological Constraint in the Mass Public: A Methodological Critique and Some New Findings," *American Journal of Political Science* 22 (May 1978): 233–49; George F. Bishop, Alfred J. Tuchfarber, and Robert W. Oldendick, "Change in the Structure of American Political Attitudes: The

Nagging Question of Question Wording," *American Journal of Political Science* 22 (May 1978): 250–69; Philip E. Converse and Gregory B. Markus, "Plus Ca Change: The New CPS Election Study Panel," *American Political Science Review*, 73 (March 1979): 32–49.

77. Kathleen Knight, "Ideology in the 1980 Election: Ideological Sophistication Does Matter," *Journal of Politics*, 47 (August 1985): 828–53.

78. John Kessel, "Comment: The Issues in Issue Voting," *American Political Science Review*, 66 (June 1972): 459–65.

79. Michael M. Gant, "The Irrelevance of Abstract Conceptualization for Policy-Based Voting," *Polity*, 18 (Fall 1985): 149–60.

80. Ruth C. Hamill, Milton Lodge and Frederick Blake, "The Breadth, Depth and Utility of Class, Partisan and Ideological Schemata," *American Journal of Political Science*, 29 (November 1985): 850–70.

81. Mark A. Peffley and Jon Hurwitz, "A Hierarchical Model of Attitude Constraint," *American Journal of Political Science*, 29 (November 1985): 871–90.

82. Steven R. Brown, "Consistency and the Persistence of Ideology: Some Experimental Results," *Public Opinion Quarterly*, 34 (Spring 1970): 60–68.

83. Davis E. RePass, "Issue Salience and Party Choice," *American Political Science Review*, 65 (June 1971): 389–400.

84. Arthur H. Miller, Warren W. Miller, Alden S. Raine, and Thad A. Brown, "A Majority Party in Disarray: Policy Polarization in the 1972 Election," *American Political Science Review*, 70 (September 1976): 753–78.

85. Miller and Wattenberg, "Throwing the Rascals Out."

86. William Lyons and Michael M. Gant, "Non-Voting and Public Policy: The 1972–1984 Presidential Elections." Prepared for delivery at the Annual Meetings of the Midwest Political Science Association, Chicago, April 1989.

87. Jackson, "Issues, Party Choices, and Presidential Votes," p. 183.

88. Eugene DeClercq, Thomas L. Hurley, and Norman R. Luttbeg, "Voting in American Presidential Elections: 1956–1972," in *American Electoral Behavior: Change and Stability*, ed. Samuel A. Kirkpatrick (Beverly Hills, CA: Sage Publications, 1976), pp. 9–33.

89. Michael M. Gant and Dwight F. Davis, "Mental Economy and Voter Rationality: The Informed Citizen Problem in Voting Research," *Journal of Politics*, 46 (February 1984): 132–53.

90. This decision was made out of agreement with John Kessel's admonition that changes in issue voting in the American electorate can only be noted if the methodology for assessing such voting is held constant.

Otherwise, it may well be the methodology which causes the changes; see Kessel, "Comment: The Issues in Issue Voting." For various reasons scholars have focused on consistency in public attitudes on national issues as an indicator of the evaluative capabilities of the electorate. Unfortunately, there has not been a continuing and constant method of assessing these attitudes across the years. Thus, changes in consistency seem mainly the result of changing methodology rather than a changing electorate. Our earlier decision thus seems well justified. See Bishop et al. "Change in the Structure of American Political Attitudes" and Sullivan et al. "Ideological Constraint in the Mass Public."

91. Clubb *et al.*, "Partisan Realignment since 1960."

The Decline in Political

Participation

In this chapter we will analyze trends in political participation since *The American Voter*, as well as trends in voting turnout over a longer time span—beginning in the last century and continuing to the 1988 presidential election. Pre-1950s voting can be documented without opinion survey data using election statistics published by the Census Bureau and state governments, but these statistics do not provide adequate information as to *why* people vote. For recent elections, opinion survey data are available for interpreting the attitudinal correlates of voting and nonvoting.

In the latter part of this chapter we will look at political participation other than voting. While voting in presidential elections is the only participatory act engaged in by a majority of Americans, it is important to consider other types of participation to understand fully trends in political activism.

Most of this chapter is concerned with exploring those factors that are important in distinguishing between voters and nonvoters. In particular, we are concerned with factors contributing to the *decline* in voter turnout since 1960. Nonvoting, also referred to as abstention, has increased in elections at all levels of government (local, state, and national). Nonvoting in presidential elections has attracted the greatest attention, and it is in this context we will attempt to account for the decline in turnout.

Defining and Measuring Electoral Turnout

Voting turnout is a concept with a multitude of meanings and measurements. The first consideration in defining turnout involves identifying the potential electorate, which could be defined as all persons officially registered to vote.

However, in most instances in this book and others, the *potential electorate* includes all persons of voting age (now, at least eighteen) regardless of their registration status. Voting turnout is therefore usually defined as the proportion of persons of legal voting age who actually vote in a given election.

A second consideration in defining turnout is how it is measured. One way is to use official turnout counts reported by the government and media. This approach has one major drawback. If we want to understand *why* some people vote and others do not, we cannot simply rely on official vote tabulations. Instead, we must ask a sampling of persons whether they voted and then proceed to pose additional attitude questions to the same sample of people, to determine what attitudes and other attributes are related to nonvoting.

Thus far we have identified two methods for measuring turnout. The first method uses official counts. We will call this the *actual turnout*. A second method of measurement involves estimating turnout from a sample survey. This method results in what we will call *reported turnout*.

While reported turnout is invaluable to political scientists, it poses some very real problems as well. The primary problem is that reported turnout almost always exceeds actual turnout by a wide margin. For example, actual turnout for the 1988 presidential election shows that about 51 percent of the electorate voted. But the CPS sample survey of the electorate conducted after the 1988 election indicated that about 70 percent of the electorate had voted.

Figure 3-1 further illustrates this problem and gives actual turnout in the 1988 presidential election and several reported turnout figures taken from surveys conducted after the election. One can readily determine that reported turnout data are not terribly accurate. The census survey came closest to the actual figure, but it was still off by over 5 percentage points. The CPS survey was off by a full 19 percentage points. The primary explanation for inaccurate reported turnout is the tendency of many Americans to report having voted when, in actuality, they did not.

The rationale for persons overreporting their voting is complex. Some may not want to admit to interviewers that voting, an aspect of civic duty, was ignored or neglected. Another stimulus to overreporting occurs in Census Bureau surveys when one member of a household is asked to report on the voting behavior of an absent family member, such as a child at college. Thus a father, giving his son the benefit of any doubt, may tell the interviewer that a son away from home at college did vote in the last election when, in fact, the son did not vote at all.

There are several other important reasons for the lack of correspondence between actual turnout and reported turnout. First, surveys do not include persons who are permanent transients or are institutionalized. Because these persons would not normally vote, their exclusion from surveys can cause an

Figure 3-1

Actual and Reported Turnouts for the 1988 Presidential Election

| Actual Turnout | 51.4% |

| Census Survey | 57% |

| SRC/CPS Survey | 70% |

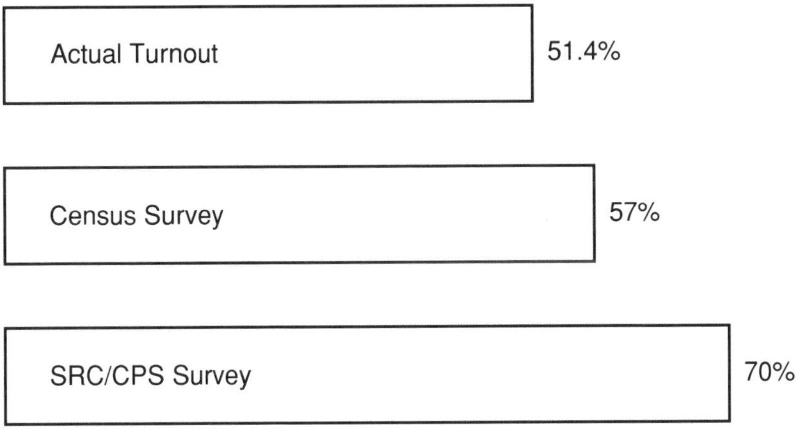

Source: Actual, 1988 *CQ Almanac,* and U.S. Bureau of the Census, *Current Population Reports,* Series P-20, No. 435; Census Survey, U.S. Bureau of the Census, *Current Population Reports,* Series P-20, No. 435; SRC/CPS Survey, 1988 CPS National Election Study.

overestimate of up to 5 percent in reported turnout, according to Louis Harris and Associates. Finally, in every election a large number of persons do vote only to have their votes later invalidated and excluded from the official count. Invalidation of votes results from improper voting practices such as voting for more than one candidate for the same office. According to Hugh Bone and Austin Ranney, "The Survey Research Center estimates that about 2 percent of the votes cast in presidential elections are regularly invalidated by election officials . . . ; in (presidential election years) a loss of nearly 3 million votes."[1]

One final explanation of the discrepancy between actual and reported turnout is that those persons interviewed for election studies or public opinion polls are somehow stimulated to vote, when otherwise they would not have done so. Alternatively, the interviewer may notify those interviewed, through the interview itself, that an election is imminent. While the latter possibility seems unlikely, given the hoopla surrounding presidential elections, it might be an important factor in elections at the subnational level. Aage Clausen, in ground breaking research, found that many had indeed voted as claimed.[2] Others have also found voters being stimulated by the interview, including one study which found a 30 percent increase in local participation among those interviewed.[3]

The Decline in Voter Turnout

In Figure 3-2 we present the trend in voter turnout in both presidential and congressional elections since 1932. As is evident, turnout in both elections has been decreasing since 1960. In particular, voting in presidential elections, in which higher rates of turnout are generally observed than for any other political office in this country, has decreased from 63 percent in 1960 to 51 percent in 1988, a decline of 12 percentage points or 19 percent. Not only has turnout been declining steadily over this time period, but turnout in the United

---

Figure 3-2

Trend in Voter Turnout: 1932–1988

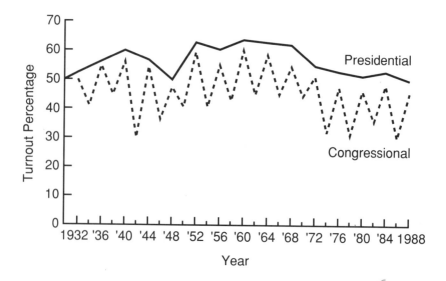

States also is far lower than in other industrialized democracies, which average about 80 percent turnout for national elections.[4] The relatively low turnout in the United States, and especially the downward trend in voting, has been a source of no small concern to political scientists and other analysts concerned about the quality of democracy in this country.

Why does such concern exist? From a purely philosophical perspective, increasing abstention is troublesome because it means fewer people are participating in the one process that influences the selection of government officials. And in a representative democracy, when abstention in elections for the highest office in government—the presidency—approaches 50 percent, a disturbing state of affairs exists.

More to the point, the decline merits concern because analysts are not sure what nonvoting means. Does the trend suggest that people are satisfied with what government is doing, and therefore see no reason to vote? If so, the decline may not be a source of concern. Does the decline mean that people are growing increasingly dissatisfied with their government? If so, is there a "critical threshold" of turnout, below which support for the system crumbles and chaos reigns? Or is declining turnout unrelated to these feelings, assuming they even exist? The cause for concern here is obvious.

These are complex questions, indeed, ones that we cannot pretend to answer in one chapter. But we can make a start, by sorting out the factors that appear to be related to turnout, and those that have contributed to the growth of abstention. It is to these factors we now turn.

Factors Which Influence Voter Participation

The list of factors thought to have some impact on voter turnout is almost endless. Influences on turnout are generally organized under three major headings: (1) legal factors, (2) psychological factors, and (3) personal or demographic factors. We will elaborate on specific aspects of each category and then analyze the comparative degree of influence each of these factors has exerted on turnout since 1952.

A word of caution to the reader: while the literature and data we cite in the ensuing pages make it appear we know a lot about the causes of abstention, in actuality we do not know that much. Part of this is due to the complexity of the factors involved; part of it is due to the fact that some of the factors may cancel each other out (for example, the decline of partisanship may be offset by the increase in education); and part of this is due to that fact that sometimes we are not sure of the meaning of the relationships we observe.

For example, we will present a fairly common finding—those who are interested in a campaign are much more likely to vote that those who are not interested. This is hardly a surprising conclusion, and one which immediately poses the question, "Why are some people interested, and others not?" And if we answer that question, still another poses itself. The reader should therefore keep in mind that while we know a great deal about what distinguishes voters from nonvoters, this does not mean that we understand *why* abstention occurs.

The Law and Voter Turnout

Legal factors have always played a significant role in determining who can or cannot vote as well as who votes once qualified. While some laws, especially at the state level, have been passed through the years to limit universal voter participation severely, the overall trend in legislation and court decisions has been to encourage voting. The changes since our nation's founding are astounding. It has been estimated that in 1789 "only about one of every thirty adult Americans (mostly propertied white males) were legally eligible to vote."[5] Today only a few adult Americans are legally barred from voting.

The remaining legal restrictions on universal suffrage are noncontroversial and unlikely to change. One exception is the requirement in many states that potential voters register in person, with the election rolls closing thirty days or more before a given election. Former President Jimmy Carter and others have advocated a national policy that allows registration up to and including the day of an election. Legal barriers to voting that are likely to remain unchanged include prohibitions on voting by convicted felons, inmates of correctional institutions, and persons adjudged mentally incompetent. There have been some publicized attempts by prison inmates to run for public office, but these have been more publicity seeking than philosophical in nature.

Certain changes in electoral laws have affected turnout. Historical data show that voter turnout reached an apex in the presidential election of 1876. In that election over 85 percent of the eligible electorate voted. Throughout the middle-to-late nineteenth century voter participation was high. But the election of 1896 marked a dramatic downturn in electoral participation.

Several legal developments are linked to this decline in turnout, from which the electorate has never fully recovered. Philip Converse, Jerrold Rusk, and to a lesser extent Walter Dean Burnham, have hypothesized that declining turnout was a result of the advent of voter registration laws enacted around the turn of the century.[6] Prior to such laws persons were allowed to vote, without registration, on their own pledge that they were residents of the community.

Most persons were readily recognizable in small communities, but as society became more urban and mobile, the lack of registration led to widespread voting fraud. There was nothing to prevent a voter from casting ballots at several polling places. The unfortunate results of efforts to fight such fraud was a downturn of "significant numbers of legitimate voters" at the polls.[7]

Another legal development that may have caused a decline in turnout was ratification of the Nineteenth Amendment to the Constitution in 1920. This amendment gave the vote to women, thereby doubling the electorate. Once given the vote, however, women were slow to use their new privilege. This is typical of any newly enfranchised group. A period of socialization must normally transpire before any new group's turnout equals that of the rest of the electorate. The difference between male and female turnout has disappeared in recent years. In fact, in 1988 the voting rate for women was slightly higher than that for men.

Poll Taxes and Literacy and Constitution Tests.   Laws having an impact on the turnout of black Americans have both aided and thwarted their participation in American elections. Blacks were first given the vote nationally with the passage of the Fifteenth Amendment to the Constitution in 1870, but as Reconstruction governments were dismantled in the South, Southern legislators moved to pass laws which discouraged or prohibited black voting. The exit of blacks from the electorate contributed to the post-1900 decline in voting.

State legislatures in the South employed a wide variety of legal limitations on black registration and voting. These included poll taxes, literacy tests, tests on understanding of the Constitution, and rigorous residency and registration requirements. The dominant Democratic party also excluded blacks from the political process through the use of its all white primary elections.

Poll taxes were small fees, usually one or two dollars, charged to voters in an election. While this practice discriminated against the generally impoverished black population, it also prohibited many poor whites from voting. Because of this, many states voluntarily eliminated the poll tax in favor of other restrictions on black voting. But, because of the persistence of the poll tax in five states, the Twenty-fourth Amendment was adopted in 1964. The amendment only affected national government elections, so in the 1965 Voting Rights Act Congress authorized a court test of poll taxes for state and local office elections. The Supreme Court declared *all* poll taxes unconstitutional in its subsequent 1966 judicial decision, *Harper v. Virginia State Board of Elections*.

Literacy tests and "understanding the Constitution" tests were also powerful tools used to disenfranchise blacks. These tests were very powerful, according to Jack Plano and Milton Greenberg, because:

> . . . examining officials have great discretion, especially when the tests are administered orally. In some southern states, for example, Negro college graduates were once disqualified because they failed to interpret constitutional passages to the satisfaction of a white board of examiners.[8]

The Voting Rights Act of 1965 also imposed a five-year suspension on the use of literacy tests. When this act was renewed in 1970, literacy tests were, in effect, permanently suspended in local, state, or national elections. The Supreme Court upheld the suspension in a 1970 decision, *Oregon v. Mitchell.*

For a time blacks were excluded from the Southern electorate because of "whites only" Democratic party primary elections. Democratic primaries were tantamount to general elections in the South because few, if any, Republicans were on the general election ballot. This prompted Democrats to declare their primary a private affair, one in which only whites could vote. But the Supreme Court held in *Smith v. Allwright* (1944) that to bar blacks from Democratic primaries in the South was in reality a violation of their right to vote guaranteed by the Fifteenth Amendment. Thus, the all white, private primary was thwarted.

Residence and Registration Requirements.   Blacks also were often kept from voting by the stringent residence and registration requirements of some states. But such requirements worked against others besides blacks. Young persons and other highly mobile groups, like migrant laborers, often could not meet residence requirements because of moves made for employment or schooling. Some critics have charged that elites conspired against such "undesirables" as students, blacks, and the working class because of fears of how these groups might vote if given the opportunity.

Reform of registration and residence requirements began with the Civil Rights Act of 1957 that authorized the attorney general to seek court injunctions against voting rights violations. More importantly, the act created a Civil Rights Commission to investigate voting rights violations and recommend appropriate legal remedies. The Civil Rights Act of 1960 went further and authorized courts to appoint referees to help blacks register to vote if the court found that discrimination was being practiced. This act also required that voting registrars keep records of voter registration applications.

Another major step was taken in 1965 when a voting rights act passed by Congress authorized the use of federal registrars in place of state officials where literacy tests had been used in the 1964 election and less than 50 percent of those eligible were registered or had voted in 1964. This act was renewed and expanded in the Voting Rights Acts of 1970 and 1975.

The Voting Rights Act of 1970 also dealt with the question of residency. It set a maximum residency requirement of thirty days for presidential elections. The Supreme Court's decision in *Dunn v. Blumstein* (1972) expanded the requirement for a "reasonable" registration deadline to all elections.

One problem created by the latter court verdict is the status of college students in a college community. While students can obviously meet the thirty-day residency requirement, some communities have balked at registering students, claiming they are not really residing in the community. The permanent residents obviously fear the election of students to important community government positions as has occurred in Ann Arbor, Michigan, and Berkeley, California, two university communities.

Other Barriers. The Voting Rights Acts of 1970, 1975, and 1982 eliminated two other subtle barriers to voting. The first act established uniform requirements for state laws which regulate absentee voting. This resulted in easier absentee balloting in many states. The 1975 act requires the use of bilingual ballots in areas of the country which have significant non-English-speaking populations. This increased turnout among Hispanic-Americans in particular. The 1982 act simplified the process of proving voting rights violations by stating that a law or election procedure that results in discrimination is illegal even if its intent is not to discriminate.

By 1970, the major remaining legal barriers to universal suffrage were laws in forty-six states prohibiting voting by persons under twenty-one years of age. In Alaska, Georgia, Hawaii, and Kentucky, eighteen- to twenty-year-olds were eligible to vote. Under a provision of the Voting Rights Act of 1970, Congress made all persons eighteen or older eligible to vote in local, state, and national elections. This action constituted the largest single expansion of the electorate since the women's suffrage amendment of 1920. This action of Congress was soon reversed by the courts, however. The Supreme Court held in *Oregon v. Mitchell* (1970) that Congress could not lower the voting age for state or local elections. So a constitutional amendment was passed in a matter of months that made eighteen the minimum voting age for *all* elections. This amendment, the Constitution's Twenty-sixth, was ratified in 1971, so the 1972 presidential contest could have involved up to twenty-five million new voters. Young Americans' response to this new opportunity, however, was less enthusiastic than anticipated.

Conclusion. We have shown that numerous laws and court decisions have been made with the specific intent of expanding the electorate and voter participation. These are summarized in Table 3-1. Despite their good intent, however, these laws and decisions have not restored turnout rates to the lofty heights achieved in the 1870s.

At least three institutional or structural factors appear to have contributed to the decline in turnout. First, voluntary registration laws in the United States

Table 3-1

Law and Voter Turnout: A Summary

Year	Action	Significance
1870	15th Amendment	Prohibited voter discrimination because of race
1920	19th Amendment	Prohibited voter discrimination because of sex
1944	*Smith v. Allwright*	Prohibited all white party primaries
1957	Civil Rights Act of 1957	Authorized Department of Justice to protect voting rights in the courts
1960	Civil Rights Act of 1960	Authorized courts to appoint referees to assist with voter registration
1961	23rd Amendment	Allowed District of Columbia residents to vote in presidential elections
1964	24th Amendment	Prohibited use of poll taxes in national elections
1965	Voting Rights Act of 1965	Suspended literacy tests; authorized federal voter registrars in 7 states
1966	*Harper v. Virginia State Board of Elections*	Prohibited poll taxes in any election
1970	Voting Rights Act of 1970	Lowered minimum voting age to 18 for federal elections; suspended state literacy tests; provided for uniform absentee voting rules
1971	26th Amendment	Lowered minimum voting age to 18 for all elections
1972	*Dunn v. Blumstein*	Shortened duration of residency requirements for voting
1975	Voting Rights Act of 1975	Extended more provisions of the 1970 Act; sent federal voter registrars to 10 additional states; provided for use of bilingual ballots
1982	Voting Rights Act of 1982	Extended provisions of the earlier 1970 and 1975 Acts; allowed private parties to prove a voting rights violation using a "results" test

appear to have depressed turnout. Voluntary registration simply means that citizens must take the initiative to register to vote; the actions required might be something as easy as filling out a card and mailing it in. Compare this system with *automatic* registration, the system many other democracies use in which all citizens are automatically registered to vote when they are the legal voting age. Understandably, such a system increases the *available* electorate — those who can actually vote in a given election. Since, as Robert Erikson points out, virtually everyone who registers also votes,[9] it is not surprising that voting rates in countries which use automatic registration are higher than in the United States. G. Bingham Powell estimates that voluntary registration reduces turnout in the United States by at least 10 percentage points, when compared to other democracies.[10]

Second, Richard Boyd has suggested that the sheer number of elections has decreased turnout observed in any particular election.[11] During especially active electoral years, (for example, presidential election years, in which a lot of other elections are held), voters may have the opportunity to go to the polls ten or more times. Citizens can therefore be fairly active in elections, that is, participation *overall* may be quite high, but turnout in any one election may still appear to be quite low. Moreover, it would seem that the likelihood of this phenomenon occurring would increase as an active election year comes to a close. Given that presidential elections occur in November, and are usually the last opportunity to go to the polls, Boyd's findings suggest that some people will not vote in presidential elections because they are "voted out."

Third, the changing age distribution of the American electorate cannot be ignored as we attempt to explain the decline in turnout. Part of this is directly related to the youthfulness of the electorate, brought about by the Twenty-sixth Amendment. Paradoxically, the electorate is also getting older, as life expectancies in the United States increase. Since age is a personal characteristic of voters, we will defer discussion of the impact of the changing age distribution of the electorate until our discussion of the impact of personal characteristics on turnout.

Psychology and Voter Turnout

As exemplified in the following statement, the authors of *The American Voter* demonstrated a strong link between psychology and turnout:

> We assume that the decision to vote, no less than the decision to vote for a given party, rests immediately on psychological forces. . . . Hence, our quest of understanding begins with an examination of motivational forces . . . and will describe a number of psychological influences that affect the likelihood the individual will vote.[12]

Psychological motivation was found, in *The American Voter*, to spring from several forces: intensity of partisanship, perceived closeness of an election, interest in the campaign, concern over the election outcome, sense of political efficacy, sense of personal efficacy, and sense of citizen duty. The general finding, therefore, was that intense psychological involvement in politics contributes to participation in elections. As data shown in Table 3-2 indicate, the relationship between one psychological factor, interest in the campaign, and participation in elections is as strong in recent years as it was in the 1950s.

Later research has shown that, as a general rule, turnout is linked to the salience which a particular election holds for the public. Important research on this theme was conducted by M. Kent Jennings and Harmon Zeigler. They found that national government affairs are more salient to most people than state or local government affairs.[13] This accounts for the persistent finding that turnout is higher in national elections than in either state or local elections. Of course the greater attention given by the news media to national elections and the more extensive use of the media in such campaigns may spur the greatest salience of national elections.

Another aspect of the influence of salience is evident in turnout for different types of national elections. As previously noted, presidential elections have the highest turnout. As was shown in Figure 3-2, turnout for presidential elections consistently exceeds turnout for nationwide congressional elections in off years (that is, when we are not electing a president). Going further in our comparison of presidential and congressional elections, we should point out that even in years when we elect a president, congressional election turnout

---

| | | | | | | | | | Table 3-2 |

Interest in Campaign and Voter Turnout, 1956–1988

Degree of Interest in the Campaign	1956	1960	1964	1968	1972	1976	1980	1984	1988
High	87%	90%	88%	88%	86%	84%	79%	89%	90%
Medium	72	76	78	76	76	72	64	70	72
Low	58	38	63	52	51	47	35	50	40

Note: Entries are the proportions of each category who indicated they voted in the election of that year.
Source: SRC/CPS Election Studies

is still lower. This phenomenon is known as *roll-off*. It occurs when people mark a ballot for a top office, like president, but do not bother to vote for lower offices such as congressional or state offices.

In Table 3-3 we present turnout rates in the 1988 presidential election for citizens with various psychological characteristics. Individuals who are very much interested in the campaign, who are concerned about the outcome of the presidential election, and who are strong partisans are much more likely to have reported voting than their attitudinal opposites. The hypothesis that those who think the election will be close are more likely to vote than those who do not is not supported by the results from 1988, a finding which is con-

Table 3-3

Psychological Factors and Voter Turnout, 1988

Attribute	Percent Voting
Very much interested in campaign	90%
Not much interested in campaign	40
Perceives race to be close	73
Does not perceive race to be close	66
Concerned about outcome of election	80
Not concerned about outcome of election	53
Strong partisan	84
Independent	50
People shouldn't vote if don't care*	63
People should vote anyway	83
Politics too complicated**	69
Politics not complicated	84
I don't have say***	69
I do have say	79
Public officials don't care****	63
Public officials do care	81

Note: Following are explanations of the questions: *"If people don't care how an election comes out, they shouldn't vote in it." **"Sometimes politics and government seem so complicated that a person like me can't really understand what's going on." ***"People like me don't have any say about what the government does." ****"I don't think public officials care much what people like me think."
Source: CPS Election Survey, 1988.

sistent with past research.[14] This proposition comes from rational choice theory, which we will discuss later in the chapter.

The final four sets of statements in Table 3-3 represent measures of political attitudes traditionally thought to have an impact on turnout. Citizens who feel they should vote even if they do not care how the election comes out are said to possess *civic duty*. The voting rates for such citizens are much higher than those without a sense of civic duty. Those who do not believe that politics and government are so complicated they cannot understand them are said to have *internal political efficacy*, a sense they can have an impact on government. These individuals are more likely to vote than those without such confidence.

The remaining two sets of statements measure what is called *external political efficacy*, the sense that government will respond to the individual. The difference in voting rates between those who do and do not feel that public officials "care much about what people like me think" is especially noticeable. As we shall see below, the decline in internal political efficacy, but not external efficacy, has contributed to the decline in turnout.

Psychological factors are also thought to account for the lower turnout of voters in party primaries than that in the general election. A longitudinal test of this hypothesis by Bone and Ranney, using data from 1962 and 1972, shows that "turnout in contested primary elections for governor and United States senator . . . was less than half as large as that in ensuing general elections."[15] Ranney also had shown previously that in presidential primaries turnout is generally about half to two thirds of that in the general election which follows.[16] Bone and Ranney believe that general elections inspire greater turnout because voters see candidates of their own party as the "good guys" doing battle with the "bad guys," nominees of the other party. Primaries lack such a stimulus and are therefore uninspiring, or maybe even confusing and ambiguous in the choices they offer.

At least four aspects of the relationship between psychology and turnout are not fully understood and pose dilemmas for researchers studying them. The first debate derives from the debate over the utility of voting. Rational choice theory, especially the work of Anthony Downs,[17] hypothesizes that citizens make a simple cost/benefit calculation in determining whether they will vote. The costs of voting include those associated with informing oneself of the candidates and issues, as well as taking the time and effort to go to the polls. The benefits of voting consist of two parts: First, it must make a difference to the voter which candidate wins the election, and the larger the difference, the greater the benefit to be derived from the election of that candidate. Second, the citizen's vote must contribute to realizing this benefit. If the individual's vote will potentially affect the outcome of the election, such as in a close contest (or one perceived to be close), then the citizen's vote has the potential (albeit quite small) to contribute to the benefit he/she will receive. If the election is not close, and the voter's preferred candidate will win, or lose, regardless of whether the individual votes, such a contribution would not exist.

The dilemma here is straightforward: given that so many people vote, especially in presidential elections, the probability that one vote will affect the outcome of an election is negligible. Thus, the benefits of voting are quite low and will never outweigh the costs of voting. Thus, the rational citizen should never vote. But many people *do* vote. This anomaly has been addressed by some scholars who point out that there are *psychological* rewards for voting (for example, voting contributes to feelings of self-worth and value as a citizen) and psychological costs to *not* voting (such as feeling guilty).[18] The dilemma is not easily resolved, and our own position is that the utility of rational choice theory in accounting for the increase in abstention is limited.

Another dilemma of political scientists studying turnout involves the relation of citizens' evaluations of government to the act of voting. For example, does a positive orientation toward government inspire one to vote or not? From one perspective, a satisfied citizen may believe it is unnecessary to vote because "things are already going so well" with government. But intuition and research tell us that a low turnout does not always mean that the citizenry is happy with government. In fact, low turnouts are often interpreted as symptomatic of deeply felt hostility toward or disappointment with government. The dilemma is whether apathy stems from satisfaction or dissatisfaction with government and whether political activism indicates pride in government or efforts to "throw the bums out." This is indeed an extremely complex research problem, one we will explore in the final two chapters.

The third dilemma concerns the effect of citizens' evaluations of the candidates on turnout. Specifically, does it matter that people are indifferent to the candidates, or like them equally, or dislike them equally? It would seem that those who are indifferent to the candidates, who do not care which candidate wins, would be the least likely to vote. This is supported by research conducted by Richard Brody and Benjamin Page.[19] On the other hand, Herbert Weisberg and Bernard Grofman have found that *satisfaction* depresses turnout; that is, those who like both candidates, according to their research, are the least likely to vote. Those who are alienated — who dislike both candidates — and those who are indifferent vote at higher rates than do those who are satisfied.[20] Again, the dilemma has not been resolved and will likely be the focus of much future research.

The final dilemma concerning psychology and turnout is primarily a theoretical issue. Is our system of government affected if people choose not to participate in elections? As we mentioned in Chapter 1, Bernard Berelson has expressed the sentiment that the system might collapse under pressure if everyone decided to become political activists.[21] Jack Walker, on the other hand, has countered that the system suffers if people stay away from the polls.[22] He claims that voting and other forms of participation integrate the participant into the system. While the argument may be valid that a voter cannot change the course of public affairs with one vote, continued voting over time can and does have a cumulative impact which benefits the voter, Walker argues.

These dilemmas illustrate a point we made at the beginning of this book: despite our extensive knowledge of electoral behavior, there are many important and interesting, but as yet unresolved, questions about it.

The Impact of Psychological Variables on Declining Turnout

Three psychological variables have contributed to the decline in voter turnout. According to Carol Cassel and David Hill, the proportion of people expressing concern over the outcome of a presidential campaign, as well as those claiming to be strong partisans, have declined over time, and these trends correspond to the decline in turnout.[23] They also note, however, that education has increased over time, as has interest in the campaign, and these increases apparently balance the decline in concern with party identification.

Paul Abramson and John Aldrich focus on two psychological variables in their attempt to explain increasing abstention: decreases in strength of partisanship and declining internal political efficacy.[24] According to their research, almost 70 percent of the decline in turnout in presidential elections can be attributed to the decline in these two characteristics. If these results can be taken at face value, the "puzzle" of declining turnout would be largely resolved. But an analysis by Carol Cassel and Robert Luskin suggests that Abramson and Aldrich have attributed too much importance to party identification and internal political efficacy.[25]

Cassel and Luskin assume that if one wants to explain the decline in turnout over time, it is necessary to take into account *all* variables that are related to voting and have changed over time. Failure to do so will result in ascribing too much importance to the variables one does include. For example, they argue that Abramson and Aldrich are mistaken in their research because they ignored the effects of education, which has a strong impact on turnout (see ignored the effects of education, which has a strong impact on turnout (see next section), but which has *increased* over time. When education is taken into account, only about one quarter, not 70 percent, of the decline in turnout can be explained by Abramson and Aldrich's model, since increasing education should have increased turnout. It would appear the decline in turnout cannot be explained solely in terms of psychological variables.

Personal Characteristics and Turnout

The authors of *The American Voter* established strong links between certain demographic characteristics and electoral turnout. And most of these links continue to exist, even if not as strongly, down to the present time, as Table 3-4 shows. The characteristics listed in the table should only be viewed as a rough guide to some personal factors that affect turnout.

Some of these characteristics should not be viewed as causally related to turnout. For example, Republicans are more likely to vote than Democrats not because they are Republicans, but rather because Republicans tend to be disproportionately drawn from high turnout groups like college graduates and high income persons. The same logic may apply to other categories like religion and race.

Research since *The American Voter* shows interesting changes in the voting habits of three groups: blacks, women, and the young.

Turnout among Blacks. There are two facets of change worth noting in blacks' voting turnout before 1982. First, as shown in Table 3-5, in the North and West black electoral participation declined dramatically between 1964 and 1976 before leveling out in 1988 at 56 percent. In the South, there was an upward spurt in black voting in 1968, 1970, and 1984. However, between 1970 and 1982, voting turnout among Southern blacks declined, hovering several points below 50 percent in presidential elections. Given that the up-

---

Table 3-4

Personal Characteristics and Voter Turnout

Higher Turnout	Lower Turnout
Strong partisans	Weak partisans and independents
Republicans	Democrats
College graduates	Less than high school
Annual income above $25,000	Annual income below $10,000
Professional and technical workers	Unskilled laborers and unemployed
Persons 45–70 years old	Persons 18–24 years old
White persons	Nonwhite persons
Non-Southerners	Southerners
Jews and Catholics	Protestants

	Table 3-5

Reported Voter Turnout Among Blacks, by Region, 1964–1988

	North and West		South	
	Presidential	Congressional	Presidential	Congressional
1964	72%		44%	
1966		52%		33%
1968	65		52	
1970		51		37
1972	57		48	
1974		38		30
1976	52		46	
1978		41		33
1980	53		48	
1982		48		38
1984	59		53	
1986		44		42
1988	56		48	

Source: U.S. Bureau of the Census, *Current Population Reports,* Series P-20, No. 435.

tick to 53 percent in 1984 was most likely due to the successful efforts of the Reverend Jesse Jackson to register new black voters, the 48 percent figure observed in 1980 and 1984 is probably the "normal" black turnout in the South for presidential elections.

A second and perhaps more important observation about longitudinal change in black turnout can be made by comparing black and white turnout over the past two decades. As shown in Table 3-6, the gap between black and white voting, while marginally smaller than it was in 1964, persisted at a surprisingly high level, about 10 percent until 1982. The gap in turnout between blacks and whites has narrowed somewhat, achieving a low of less than 5 percentage points in 1986. In turn, the difference between black and white registration rates has declined as well, such that in 1988, the difference was less than 3.5 percentage points.[26] The relative increase in black electoral participation has been attributed to increases in education levels among blacks, relative to whites, and increasing feelings of political efficacy.[27]

Further evidence of increases in black political participation is the dramatic increase in the numbers of black elected officials. Harold Stanley and Richard

Table 3-6

Reported Voter Turnout, by Race, 1964–1988

Year	Black Turnout	White Turnout	Difference
1964	58.5%	70.7%	12.2%
1966	41.7	57.0	15.3
1968	57.6	69.1	11.5
1970	43.5	56.0	12.5
1972	52.1	64.5	12.4
1974	33.8	46.3	12.5
1976	48.7	60.9	12.2
1978	37.2	47.3	10.1
1980	50.5	60.9	10.4
1982	43.0	49.9	6.9
1984	55.8	61.4	5.6
1986	43.2	47.0	4.8
1988	51.5	59.1	7.6

Source: U.S. Bureau of the Census, *Current Population Reports,* Series P-20, No. 435.

Niemi report that in 1970, there were 1,469 black elected officials in the United States. By 1988, this figure had grown to 6,829, an increase of over 350 percent.[28] And perhaps more encouraging was the sudden increase in black turnout in the 1982 congressional elections and several 1983 mayoral contests. As shown in Tables 3-6, black turnout in 1982 and 1986 jumped to 43 percent, nearly 6 percent higher than black turnout in the 1978 congressional election and less than 4 percentage points lower than white turnout in 1986. Considering that black turnout had always been 10 points lower than white turnout prior to 1982, the events of that year were very significant. Table 3-5 shows that black turnout in 1982 and 1984 increased in the South and the rest of the nation. Whether this surge in turnout will continue remains to be seen.

Turnout among Women.   The trend in turnout among women exhibits more significant change. The turnout rate among women, once well below that of men, is now higher than that of males (see Table 3-7). This should not be taken to mean that the early lag in turnout among women, attributed to non-transmission of the norm of voting to women, has completely disappeared.

Table 3-7

Reported Voter Turnout, by Sex, 1964–1988

Year	Males	Females	Difference
1964	71.9%	67.0%	4.9%
1966	58.2	53.0	5.2
1968	69.8	66.0	3.8
1970	56.8	52.7	4.1
1972	64.1	62.0	2.1
1974	46.2	43.4	2.8
1976	59.6	58.8	0.8
1978	46.6	45.3	1.3
1980	59.1	59.4	0.3
1982	48.7	48.4	0.3
1984	59.0	60.8	1.8
1986	45.8	46.1	0.3
1988	56.4	58.3	1.9

Source: U.S. Bureau of the Census, *Current Population Reports*, Series P-20, Nos. 143, 174, 192, 228, 253, 293, 332, 370, and 435.

Women vote at a higher rate today than men *not* because they are voting in greater numbers than before, but because the turnout rate among females has declined at a slower rate than among males. There are no good *theoretical* reasons to suggest that males and females will vote at different rates in the future. However, if current trends continue, women will constitute a permanent majority of the American electorate.

Age-related Turnout.   Philip Converse, one of the authors of *The American Voter*, analyzed the Michigan studies of the 1952 and 1956 elections to determine the impact of age on turnout. He noted the existence of a *political life cycle* in which persons turn out more frequently for elections as they get older. This increase stops at about age sixty to sixty-five, at which point turnout decreases.[29] This cycle is illustrated in Figure 3-3, using 1980 data.

Converse's life cycle notion, and his explanation for it, have been widely accepted. Persons in their middle years, the years in which they are most affected by society and politics, are most likely to vote. Young persons may not vote because of an absence of social responsibilities or because of apathy. Old persons may be physically infirm and unable to vote or live alone and/or do not receive social reinforcement from friends or family to vote. If there is a problem with Converse's explanation, it lies in the fact that the trend appears to have been reversed. In 1988, those 65 years of age and older had a *higher* turnout rate than any other age group. This suggests that the factors which depressed turnout among those in this age group are no longer applicable.

Some studies indicate that young persons who entered the electorate in the late 1960s and 1970s may not be participating according to the pattern that past experience would suggest. V. Lance Tarrance notes a "pattern of decreasing turnout among successively younger birth cohorts." Further, he states the following:

> The major conclusion is that younger age cohorts have matured in a period of lowered partisan intensity and reduced community pressures to engage in political activity, and that "cohort effects of historical periods are now known to be important sources of variation in the voting decision."[30]

Such a trend—declining youth turnout with continued nonparticipation after aging—was not expected by those who campaigned so hard for the Twenty-sixth Amendment. This trend seemed to continue into 1988, when only 36 percent of all persons eighteen to twenty-four years old voted, compared with 41 percent in 1984. And in 1972, the first presidential election after ratification of the Twenty-sixth Amendment, turnout among those eighteen to twenty-four years of age was about 50 percent. Turnout among older age cohorts declined much less dramatically.[31] It would appear that the trend identified

Figure 3-3

Vote Turnout in 1980 Presidential Election, by Age

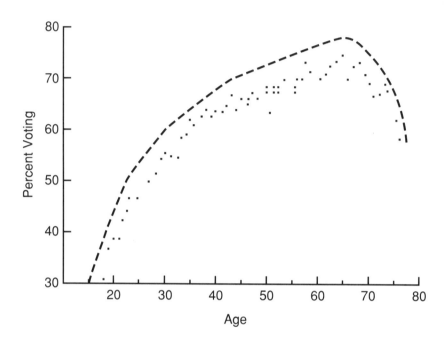

Source: U.S. Bureau of the Census, *Current Population Reports,* Series P-20, No. 370.

by Tarrance may be picking up momentum. If so, continued future declines in turnout are to be expected.

The Impact of Personal Factors on the Decline in Turnout

Four personal characteristics of citizens—education, gender, race, and age— are related to turnout, and should help us in accounting for the decline in turnout. We will discuss each of these in turn.

Education: Education has increased dramatically since 1952. In that year, only 15 percent of the respondents to the SRC/CPS survey had at least one year of college; in 1988, the figure had risen to 41 percent. And education is still strongly related to turnout. In 1988, about one half of those with less than a high school education reported voting, compared with 85 percent among those with at least one year of college. Despite these trends, however, turnout has decreased. More than anything else, the absence of a noticeable impact of rising education levels on turnout contributes to the riddle of increasing abstention.

Race: As noted earlier, the gap between black and white voting has decreased in recent years because black turnout has decreased at a slower rate than has white turnout. Nevertheless, turnout has declined among both groups, while the composition of the electorate with respect to blacks and whites has remained relatively stable. Racial differences cannot account for the overall decline in turnout.

Gender: Neither can turnout trends among males and females account for the increase in abstention. Turnout among both males and females has declined since the 1950s but at a slower rate for women. Moreover, there are now more women in the potential electorate than males. With respect to gender, the riddle of declining turnout remains unresolved.

Age: The changing age distribution of the electorate does help account for at least some of the decline in turnout, according to research by Richard Boyd.[32] Boyd notes that historically the age groups with the lowest levels of turnout are the very young and the very old. The influx of the "baby-boom" generation, coupled with increases in life expectancies, have expanded the relative sizes of these cohorts. As a consequence, turnout has declined. However, "baby-boomers" are now in their thirties and forties, and those citizens age sixty-five and older now vote at higher rates than other age groupings. At the very least, the aging of the electorate may not be relevant to the puzzle of declining turnout.

But we cannot ignore the impact of younger cohorts on the turnout rate, given that the eighteen-to-twenty-four age group votes at far lower rates than in the 1970s and at far lower rates than any other cohort (all others are above 50 percent turnout). We feel confident that lower participation rates among new entrants into the electorate has contributed, at least partially, to the decline in turnout.

Factors Affecting Turnout: A Summary

Critics of the American electorate are often vocal in berating citizens for not voting in greater numbers than we have found. They point out that citizens of European democracies have much greater turnout rates than is the case in America.

Some political scientists have countered that when certain factors are taken into account, turnout in American elections does not look so bad. For example, one innovative and creative study of the 1960 presidential election concludes that "80 to 85 percent of those legally eligible and physically able to vote did so."[33] The only problem in applying that study to the 1970s is that a greater proportion of the electorate is now legally eligible to vote. When the few remaining legal and physical considerations are taken into account, Bone and Ranney find that only about 66 percent of the citizenry voted in 1972.[34] So we must conclude that turnout among those legally and physically eligible to vote has declined even more than is evident in reported turnout figures available from the Census Bureau and SRC/CPS.

As we have noted, the reasons behind the overall downward trend of American turnout rates are not easily determined. Converse notes that "all attitudinal factors for nonvoting were less frequent than legal (nonregistration) or personal (ill health, flat tire, etc.) reasons" during the 1950s.[35] For example, over twice as many persons cited personal rather than attitudinal reasons for not voting in the 1952 and 1956 elections, a trend which continued at least through 1980. People still report more often than any other reason that they simply cannot get to the polls because of health, transportation, or other problems. Of course, these responses may be *post hoc* excuses which belie apathy or lack of concern about politics, but we cannot be sure.

Data reported on reasons for nonregistration[36] also reveal excuses for nonparticipation. From 1970 to 1980 there was a drop in the frequency of cases in which persons blame their actions on residency requirements. This makes sense when one considers the reform in residency requirements over the same period. The interesting increase over this period appears in the numbers of persons having vague reasons or no reasons for not being registered. Of course, rational justifications are difficult to come by in our reasonably open registration system.

But perhaps our system of voting and registration should be made even more open. Many have called for the elimination of all laws which require citizens to register before election day. Under such a proposal voters could register when they voted. Such reform has been tried in some states, and it seems to be helpful in increasing turnout.[37] And if Powell's conclusions are correct, such reforms should substantially increase turnout.[38]

Finally, some observers still contend that turnout would be improved if the electorate had a better attitude toward government and elections. This consideration will be broached in chapters 4 and 6.

Other Forms of Participation

While voting is probably the easiest, and therefore the most common, form of political participation, citizens have available to them a wide variety of alternative forms of political activity. These range from writing to a government official about some particular problem or issue, to contributing money to a political party, to running for public office.

There are two alternative definitions of *political participation*. One, primarily identified with Lester Milbraith's research, suggests that participation is cumulative and that different forms of participation can be ranked according to difficulty.[39] For example, voting is relatively easy to do when compared with attending a campaign rally. Thus, persons who attend a rally could also be expected to vote.

A second concept of participation is associated with the work of Sidney Verba and Norman Nie, who conclude that citizens have certain participation specialties.[40] For example, some people do not vote but instead seek to contact public officials in person or with letters. Other persons concentrate on group activities, like party work. Some persons may have several specialties, but many have only one—voting. Verba and Nie estimate that about 21 percent of the populace limits its participation to the simple act of voting. More importantly, they found that 22 percent of the electorate specializes in doing absolutely nothing. These are the "inactives."

Americans, like other citizens of developed democracies, engage in few acts of political participation other than voting. This has been shown repeatedly in the CPS's reports of public participation in such acts as going to a political rally or meeting, working for a party or candidate, wearing a campaign button or putting a campaign sticker on one's car, belonging to a political club, or contributing money to a party or candidate. Table 3-8 shows that none of these acts involves more than one in five Americans. While no trend of decreasing participation is evident in these less common forms of participation, presidential voting turnouts have been falling since 1964, when reported turnout was 79 percent (actual turnout in 1964 was 62 percent), to 1988, when reported turnout was 70 percent (actual turnout was 51 percent). These data also provide support for the cumulative *and* specialization theories of individual political participation as discussed earlier.

There is some evidence that levels of participation in political acts other than voting have increased over the past two decades. Norman Nie, Sidney Verba, and their associates conducted extensive studies of political participation by Americans in 1967 and 1987.[41] As with all other studies, they found that turnout has declined. Virtually all other acts of participation, however, have either remained constant or *increased* in frequency. The incidence of such political activities as working for a political party or candidate; giving money to a party or candidate; contacting government officials about specific policies; and persuading other people how to vote has increased substantially since the late 1960s. The proportion of citizens who report regularly engaging in four or more political acts rose from 22 percent in 1967 to 31 percent in 1987. Finally, out of thirteen possible acts of political participation (excluding voting),

Table 3-8

Political Participation, 1952–1988

Political Activity	1952	1956	1960	1964	1968	1972	1976	1980	1984	1988
Worked for party or candidate	3%	3%	6%	5%	6%	5%	4%	4%	4%	3%
Attended rallies or meetings	7	7	8	9	9	9	6	8	8	7
Tried to persuade others how to vote	27	28	33	32	33	32	37	36	32	29
Wore campaign button or displayed bumper sticker	—	16	21	16	15	14	8	7	9	8
Belonged to political club or organization	2	3	3	4	3	—	—	3	—	—
Contributed money to campaign	4	10	12	11	9	10	9	6	13	6
Voted, reported	73	73	74	79	76	73	72	71	74	70
Number responding	1742	1762	1829	1450	1351	2285	2868	1407	2257	2040

Source: National Election Studies, 1952–1988.

the average number of activities per citizen rose about 25 percent, from 2.05 in 1967 to 2.53 in 1987.

Turnout in Subnational Elections

There is often the temptation, for purposes of brevity and simplicity, to discuss only the national scope of declining participation in presidential elections. And, furthermore, we often overlook related trends in voting for state and local offices. Such oversights can be explained in part by the fact that national opinion surveys produce samples that usually are too small to say much about regional or state differences in any of the patterns we have been discussing.

We do, however, have election turnout data for each of the states across time. These data include turnout figures for presidential elections, off year congressional elections that fall in even numbered years when presidents are not elected, and gubernatorial elections, some of which are held in even years and some of which are held in odd numbered years when we are electing neither a president nor a Congress.

Turnout trends for each of these types of elections are depicted in Figure 3-4. (The percentages reported in the figure represent actual turnout and were calculated by dividing the total number of votes cast in all states holding each respective type of election by the total number of eligible voters in those states.) We can see that there has been a steady decline in turnout across all types of elections, except for the relatively few gubernatorial elections which are held in odd numbered years, which in turn have reflected remarkable volatility in turnout. Overall, turnout has declined for all elections – gubernatorial, congressional and presidential.[42]

A Trend Assessment: Political Participation

In this analysis we will consider trends in political participation as a variable in the changing nature of the American voter. Specifically, we will seek to assess whether some eligible voters do not participate in the political life of our nation because they are disenchanted by the options afforded by the two major political parties or, alternatively, because they are increasingly sophisticated in the evaluation of candidates and find no one espousing the issues or

Figure 3-4

Turnout in Presidential, Congressional, and Gubernatorial Elections, 1960–1988

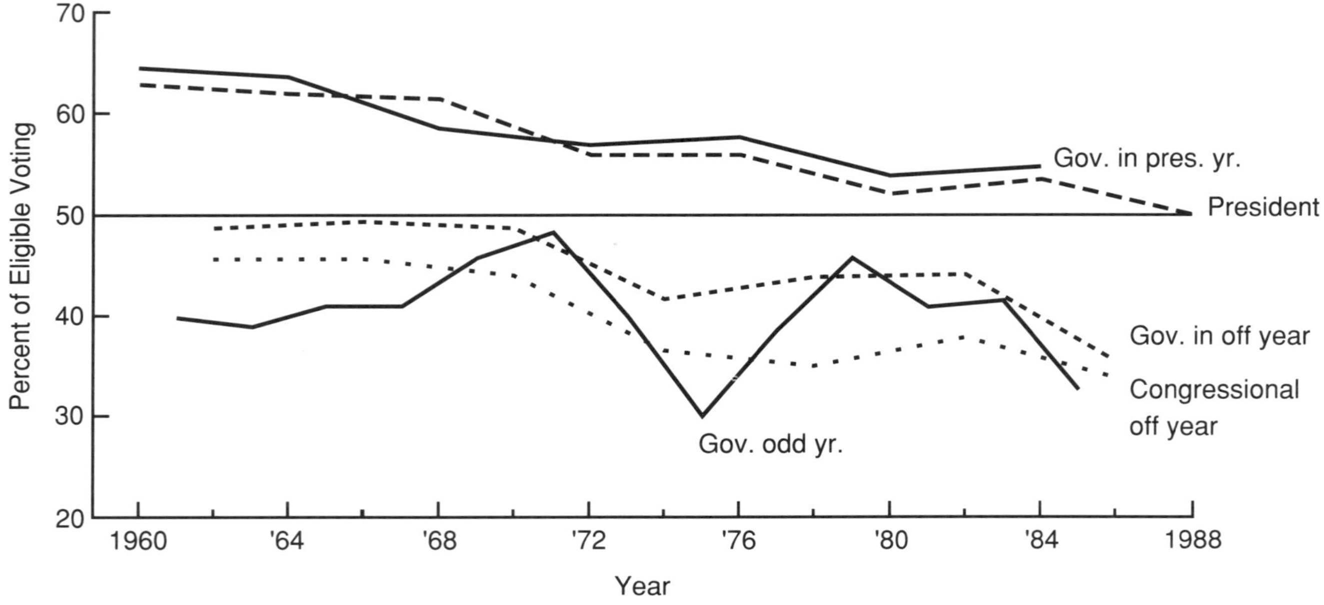

ideological positions they favor. But before we consider such relationships and whether there has been a change over time, we must consider how to measure political participation.

As we have noted, few Americans engage in political activity other than voting, even in the peak periods of presidential election years. It has been an issue of mild concern in political science whether those who engage in the more unusual forms of political participation also participate in the more common forms, such as voting.[43] Because we believed it would be more informative to have a measure of political participation that did more than divide people as to whether or not they voted, we attempted to include in our measure whether the person also contributed money to a candidate, attended political rallies or meetings, wore a campaign button, or belonged to a political club.

Our effort to analyze a broader measure of political participation was unsuccessful. Some of the SRC/CPS surveys on which we based our analysis omitted some questions on participation; others found one or more acts of participation unrelated to other acts; and, probably most important, most people fell either within the "voted-only" category or the "did not participate at all" category. The measure of political participation used in this section is therefore a simple dichotomy of those who voted for president in a specific election versus those who did not.

Typically about one American in four reports that he or she did not vote for president. Nonparticipation has varied little, according to the reports of the SRC/CPS surveys. (See Table 3-8.) While the peak of participation was the 1964 election, when 78 percent of those interviewed reported they voted for president, the elections in the 1950s and those in the 1970s still show nearly identical rates of participation. The small increase in participation until 1964, as well as the subsequent decline, closely parallel the voting turnout reported by the Census Bureau, but at a somewhat higher level of voting. This may be overreporting, perhaps due to simple misrepresentation in order to impress the interviewer, or it may be a real increase in participation by those who were stimulated to vote by having been interviewed during the campaign.[44]

Table 3-9 shows the percentage of participants (voters) who have achieved the six different levels of sophistication in candidate evaluations (as explained in Chapter 2). In 1952, only 17 percent of all participants achieved an issue oriented level of candidate evaluation, while 68 percent of all participants expressed an image based evaluation of the candidates. By contrast, since 1980 at least one half of all voters have expressed issue based evaluations, with an astounding 71 percent mentioning issues in their evaluations of the candidates in 1984. The low point of the less sophisticated image evaluation was observed in 1984, when less than one voter in five differentiated between the candidates solely in terms of superficial image differences, such as "I like him" or

Table 3-9

Trend in Quality of Candidate Evaluations among Voters, 1952–1988

Year	Ideologue	Issue Oriented	Group Benefit	Partisan	Image	No Content	N
		Percent of Respondents Using Various Types of Candidate Evaluations					
1952	1	17	4	1	68	10	1704
1956	1	19	6	—	68	6	1761
1960	2	22	5	—	65	7	1103
1964	6	37	4	—	47	6	1440
1968	4	24	4	20	39	9	1319
1972	9	48	6	5	28	5	1118
1976	8	38	9	14	26	3	1600
1980	13	50	3	6	19	9	1407
1984	7	71	4	5	7	5	2257
1988	10	53	5	12	12	7	1773

Source: National Election Studies, 1952–1988.

"I like his smile." Certainly, participants in presidential elections show a marked improvement in their evaluation of the presidential candidates.

Table 3-10 presents the same data but from a different perspective. The percentage of each type of candidate evaluator who voted is shown for each election. Some minor changes are evident across the years. Ideological evaluators, those using concepts such as liberal or conservative, consistently prove to be the most likely to vote of all citizens. Those with no content evaluations, which means they had nothing to say in evaluating either candidate, prove least likely to participate; further, except for 1980, the turnout rate for these individuals has declined steadily since 1952. Every group shows a high point of participation in the early 1960s but returns to 1950 levels or lower in the 1970s. The only exceptions are the candidate image evaluators whose turnout rate has declined substantially since 1960.

Our main concern is with the issue oriented evaluators. Since issue oriented evaluation has become increasingly common among voters (Table 3-9), and since issue oriented evaluators show no change in participation which is not also notable among other evaluators (Table 3-10), it appears that there are proportionally more issue oriented evaluators, and that this change is unrelated to the act of voting. It may be that participation has been declining since the 1960s, and that issues play an increasingly important part in the candidate evaluations given by the general public, but these same issue evaluations are not contributing to the decline of political participation. If anything, these trends can be explained by the very real possibility that low quality evaluators are dropping out of the electorate, leaving a higher proportion of high quality evaluators, without increasing the actual number of high quality evaluators.

Partisanship and Participation

Inasmuch as somewhat fewer persons are now identifying with one of the major political parties, and voting has declined in presidential elections since the 1960s by more than 10 percent, could it be the independents who are increasingly choosing not to vote? As we have seen, the independent in early studies of voting proved marginally less interested in the campaign and marginally less likely to vote. Figure 3-5 confirms this pattern of lower turnout by independents across all presidential elections since 1952.

A nearly consistent pattern is evident, as the strong partisans prove most participant, followed by the weak partisans (including those independents who admit to be leaning toward one of the parties), and finally the independents. But the pattern has been one of sharply declining participation by independents (except for a small rebound in 1980), mild decline among weak

Table 3-10

Voting by Persons with Differing Qualities of Candidate Evaluations, 1952–1988

Year	Ideologue	Issue Oriented	Group Benefit	Partisan	Image	No Content	N
		Percent of Respondents Using Various Types of Candidate Evaluations					
1952	87%	76%	63%	71%	79%	48%	1704
1956	87	72	73	—	78	42	1761
1960	100	87	84	—	85	50	1103
1964	81	80	69	75	81	51	1440
1968	93	79	64	77	79	54	1319
1972	87	73	79	61	72	43	1118
1976	77	74	70	72	67	33	1600
1980	87	74	60	80	68	53	1407
1984	88	76	73	77	70	45	1464
1988	92	75	75	76	67	35	1773

Source: National Election Studies, 1952–1988.

Figure 3-5

Turnout and Partisanship, 1952–1988

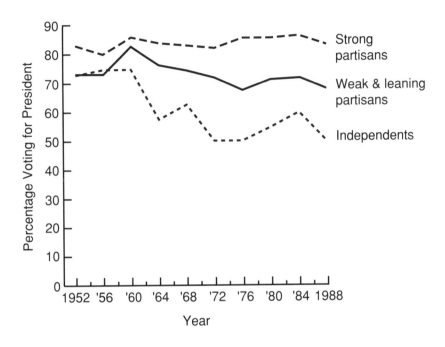

Source: SRC/CPS National Election Studies, 1952–1988.

partisans evident only in 1976, and little change among strong partisans. While in the 1950s strong partisans were marginally more likely to vote, and weak partisans and independents differed little in their voting turnout, the pattern since 1960 is one of sharply declining participation as the comparison moves from strong partisans to weak partisans to independents.

The significance of nonparticipation by independents should not be exaggerated. Pure independents, even in 1988, constituted only a small percentage of the total electorate (11 percent). More significant is the fact that about 83 percent of all citizens who failed to vote for president in 1988 were partisans. Nonvoting among partisans affects more people and thus demands more attention.

Conclusion

Independents increasingly fail to vote. Those evaluating candidates in terms of issues and ideological concepts persist in being the most likely to vote. Thus increasing independence from political parties has contributed to declining participation, but the improvement in candidate evaluation within the electorate has had no effect, neither increasing nor decreasing participation. As we have pointed out previously, numerous researchers have suggested that the quality of candidate evaluations plays a crucial role in the effort to tie together the various trends we have introduced thus far in our explanation of American political behavior. The fact that we have found no significant relationship between public evaluation of presidential candidates and trends in partisanship, defection from party, and political participation suggests that new explanations of American voting behavior are in order. But before suggesting our own alternative considerations on behavior of the electorate, we should add the facts on the relationships between the four variables thus far considered—defection from party identification, nature of independency, quality of candidate evaluation, and participation—and the subject of the next chapter, political distrust and alienation.

Notes

1. Hugh A. Bone and Austin Ranney, *Politics and Voters*, fourth ed. (New York: McGraw-Hill, 1976), p. 35. For further discussion of misreporting of voting see Michael W. Traugott and John P. Katosh, "Response Validity in Surveys of Voting Behavior," *Public Opinion Quarterly*, 45 (Winter, 1981).
2. Aage R. Clausen, "Response Validity: Vote Report," *Public Opinion Quarterly*, 32 (Winter 1968–69): 588–606.
3. Michael W. Traugott and John R. Katosh, "Response Validity in Surveys of Voting Behavior," *Public Opinion Quarterly*, 43 (Fall 1979): 359–77; Norman R. Luttbeg, "Voter Interview Stimulation in the Multiple Sample NES 1980 Study." Presented at the Annual Meetings of the Midwest Political Science Association, 1982; and, Robert E. Kraut and John B. McConahay, "How Being Interviewed Affects Voting: An Experiment," *Public Opinion Quarterly*, 37 (Fall 1973): 398–406. The latter in a local election study.
4. G. Bingham Powell, "American Voter Turnout in Comparative Perspective," *American Political Science Review*, 80 (March 1986): 17–43.
5. Bone and Ranney, *Politics and Voters*, p. 4.

6. Philip E. Converse, "Change in the American Electorate," in *The Human Meaning of Social Change*, eds. Angus Campbell and Philip E. Converse (New York: Russell Sage Foundation, 1972): Jerrold D. Rusk, "The Effect of the Australian Ballot Reform on Split Ticket Voting: 1876–1908," *American Political Science Review*, 64 (December 1970); Walter Dean Burnham, "The Changing Shape of the American Political Universe," *American Political Science Review*, 59 (March 1965).

7. Converse, "Change in American Electorate," p. 281 ff.

8. Jack C. Plano and Milton Greenberg, *The American Political Dictionary* (Hinsdale, IL: Dryden Press, 1976), p. 125.

9. Robert S. Erikson, "Why Do People Vote? Because They are Registered," *American Politics Quarterly*, 9 (July 1981): 259–76.

10. Powell, "American Voter Turnout in Comparative Perspective." Currently, 49 states (all but North Dakota) and the District of Columbia have some sort of voter registration system. Thirty-one states also impose a minimum residency requirement for registration, ranging from 1 to 50 days. The most common residency requirement is 30 days. See Harold W. Stanley and Richard G. Niemi, *Vital Statistics on American Politics*, second ed. (Washington, D.C.: CQ Press, 1990), pp. 35–37.

11. Richard W. Boyd, "Decline of U.S. Voter Turnout: Structural Explanations," *American Politics Quarterly*, 9 (April 1981): 133–59.

12. Angus Campbell, Philip E. Converse, Warren E. Miller, and Donald E. Stokes, *The American Voter* (Chicago: University of Chicago Press, 1960), p. 90.

13. M. Kent Jennings and Harmon Zeigler, "The Salience of American State Politics," *American Political Science Review*, 64 (June 1970): 523–35.

14. Carrol B. Foster, "The Performance of Rational Choice Voter Models in Recent Presidential Elections," *American Political Science Review*, 78 (June 1984): 678–90.

15. Bone and Ranney, *Politics and Voters*, pp. 32–33.

16. Austin Ranney, "Turnout and Representation in Presidential Primary Elections," *American Political Science Review*, 66 (March 1972).

17. Anthony Downs, *An Economic Theory of Democracy* (New York: Harper, 1957).

18. William H. Riker and Peter C. Ordeshook, "A Theory of the Calculus of Voting," *American Political Science Review*, 62 (March 1968): 25–42; Richard G. Niemi and Herbert F. Weisberg, *Controversies in*

American Voting Behavior (San Francisco: W. H. Freeman, 1976), p. 27.

19. Richard A. Brody and Benjamin I. Page, "Indifference, Alienation and Rational Decisions: The Effects of Candidate Evaluation on Turnout and the Vote," *Public Choice*, 15 (Summer 1973): 1–17.

20. Herbert F. Weisberg and Bernard Grofman, "Candidate Evaluations and Turnout," *American Politics Quarterly*, 9 (April 1981): 197–219.

21. Bernard R. Berelson, Paul F. Lazarsfeld, and William N. McPhee, *Voting* (Chicago: University of Chicago Press, 1954), Chap. 14.

22. Jack L. Walker, "A Critique of the Elitist Theory of Democracy," *American Political Science Review*, 60 (June 1966): 285–95.

23. Carol A. Cassel and David B. Hill, "Explanations of Turnout Decline: A Multivariate Test," *American Politics Quarterly*, 9 (April 1981): 181–95.

24. Paul R. Abramson and John H. Aldrich, "The Decline of Electoral Participation in America," *American Political Science Review*, 76 (June 1982): 502–21.

25. Carol A. Cassel and Robert C. Luskin, "Simple Explanations of Turnout Decline," *American Political Science Review*, 82 (December 1988): 1321–30.

26. Bureau of the Census, *Current Population Reports*, Series P-20, No. 435 (February 1989): p. 3.

27. Graham R. Ramsden, "A Partial Explanation for Black Turnout Patterns: 1952–1980." Prepared for delivery at the Annual Meetings of the Midwest Political Science Association, Chicago, April, 1988.

28. Stanley and Niemi, *Vital Statistics on American Politics*, p. 365.

29. Philip E. Converse with Richard Niemi, "Nonvoting among Young Adults in the United States," in *Political Parties and Political Behavior* second ed., ed. William J. Crotty, D. M. Freeman, and D. S. Gatlin (Boston: Allyn & Bacon, 1971), pp. 443–66.

30. V. Lance Tarrance, "The Vanishing Voter: A Look at Non-Voting as a Purposive Act," in *Voters, Primaries and Parties*, eds. Jonathan Moore and Albert C. Pierce (Cambridge, MA: Harvard University Institute of Politics, 1976), p. 12.

31. Census Bureau, *Current Population Reports*, p. 1.

32. Boyd, "Decline of U.S. Voter Turnout."

33. William G. Andrews, "American Voting Participation," *The Western Political Quarterly*, 19 (1966): 630–39.

34. Bone and Ranney, *Politics and Voters*, p. 36.

35. Converse with Niemi, "Nonvoting among Young Adults," p. 455.

36. David B. Hill and Norman R. Luttbeg, *Trends in American Electoral Behavior*, second ed. (Itasca, IL: F.E. Peacock, 1983): p. 97.

37. Stanley Kelley, Jr., Richard E. Ayres, and William G. Bowen, "Registration and Voting: Putting First Things First," *American Political Science Review*, 61 (June 1967): 359–77; Raymond E. Wolfinger and Steven J. Rosenstone, *Who Votes?* (New Haven: Yale, 1980).

38. Powell, "American Voter Turnout in Comparative Perspective."

39. Lester W. Milbraith and M. L. Goel, *Political Participation*, second ed. (Chicago: Rand McNally, 1977).

40. Sidney Verba and Norman H. Nie, *Participation in America* (New York: Harper & Row, 1972).

41. Norman H. Nie, Sidney Verba, Henry C. Brady, Kay Lehman Schlozman and Jane Junn, "Participation in America: Continuity and Change." Prepared for delivery at the Annual Meetings of the Midwest Political Science Association, Chicago, April, 1989.

42. There are substantial differences among the states in how turnout for both state and national office elections have changed since 1960. See Norman R. Luttbeg, "Differential Voting Decline in the American States, 1960–1982," *Social Science Quarterly*, (March 1984): 60–73; and, Norman R. Luttbeg, "Attitudinal Components of Turnout Decline," *Social Science Quarterly*, (June 1985): 435–43.

43. For a brief description of these issues, see Milbraith and Goel, *Political Participation*, p. 12.

44. Traugott and Katosh, "Response Validity in Surveys."

The Decline in Political Trust

Political scientists have seen Americans move from an attitude of benign affection for government during the 1950s and early 1960s to a state of apparent distrust, lack of confidence, and alienation in the 1970s and early 1980s. *The American Voter*, dating from the period of trust in government, gave scant attention to distrust, protests, or any form of violent political behavior. Many contemporary observers see the growth of distrust as a refutation of *The American Voter* model introduced in Chapter 1.

In order to evaluate this trend, we must consider the historical context of declining trust or increasing alienation. The Korean War and the tumultuous McCarthy hearings on communists in America had largely faded in the public's memory at the time of the 1956 presidential election. Our nation was at peace with the world, and the Cold War had not begun to heat up as it eventually did in the 1960s. Because of the relative calm of this period, Americans probably gave less thought to government and political issues. And those thoughts they did maintain were essentially positive. The notion of an alienated, politically estranged citizenry was so remote that it was not until the 1958 election survey that Michigan's Survey Research Center asked respondents to express positive or negative statements about government officials. Nowhere in *The American Voter*, that period's most comprehensive document on American political behavior, was there mention of any negative sentiment about government among the masses.

Early studies of political socialization discovered that children, like adults, were happy with government and politics during the late 1950s and early 1960s. It was difficult during this period to find a child or adolescent who would express any doubt about the goodness or greatness of the president. One study demonstrated that American children thought that leaders were more trustworthy and better people than their own parents.[1]

Perhaps one of the most important outgrowths of these early studies of children's behavior was a theory of political support. David Easton developed a *systems theory* of political life in which he hypothesized that Americans give two types of support to their government.[2] The first type of support is based on evaluations of political authorities and the policies they advance and is called *specific support* for the political system. Easton suggested that there is also a second type of support that he called *diffuse support*. This second type has little to do with the actions of specific political authorities, but focuses on the acceptance or rejection of the basic aspects of the entire political system. Easton differentiates the concepts of diffuse and specific support by stating that the former "represents more enduring bonds and thereby makes it possible for members to oppose the incumbents of offices and yet retain respect for the offices themselves, for the way in which they are ordered, and for the community of which they are a part." Specific support is "directed to the perceived decisions, policies, actions, utterances or the general style of . . . authorities."[3]

While Easton considered the maintenance of specific support important, he considered the existence of diffuse support absolutely necessary. The consequences of a failure to generate diffuse support are catastrophic, according to Easton, because if "the input of support falls below minimum, the persistence of any kind of system will be endangered. A system will finally succumb unless it adopts measures to cope with the stress."[4]

Easton and other scholars agree on the potential impact of low levels of support and concomitant high levels of alienation. As William Flanigan and Nancy Zingale have stated, "at a minimum, demands for social and political change will be widespread."[5] Edward Muller suggests more directly that when low levels of political trust combine with a high degree of belief in effectiveness of violent protests, political violence may well occur.[6]

Perhaps Arthur Miller best sums up the concerns about trust in government with these words:

> A democratic political system cannot survive for long without the support of a majority of its citizens. When such support wanes, underlying discontent is the necessary result and the potential for revolutionary alteration of the political and social system is enhanced . . . when dissatisfaction with the existing situation leads to pervasive distrust of government . . . flexibility [of the system] is greatly curtailed, thereby increasing the potential for radical change.[7]

With this basis of understanding for the theoretical implications of political support, we will examine carefully the meaning of terms which have been used to describe various dimensions of political support. Before we proceed further, however, a word of explanation is in order.

In Chapter 3, which dealt with political participation, and especially the decline in voter turnout, we noted that turnout began to decline after the 1960 presidential election. Moreover, we noted that some who have studied this decline suggest that one factor contributing to this decrease in voter participation was decreasing feelings of political efficacy.

As we discuss below, political efficacy is one way in which support for the political system is manifested. Thus, as support declines, so does participation. But this is but one way in which declining system support can affect the system. Ultimately the stability, if not the existence, of the political system may be placed in jeopardy.

Our concern with declining trust and support, then, is twofold. At one level, this phenomenon should help us understand not only declining turnout, but other aspects of political behavior as well. At another level, decreasing support has serious implications for the health of the political system. Because of its importance, therefore, we feel it necessary to explore, at some length, the meanings and implications of declining political trust. In the final section of this chapter, we will more explicitly determine to what extent declining trust helps us make sense of other trends in political behavior.

The Meaning of Alienation

Political alienation and *malaise* were perhaps two of the most overworked terms in political science and political news coverage during the 1970s. Public opinion polls indicated that Americans were alienated from their leaders. Indeed, as we will show in this chapter, there is evidence that alienation from government and other social institutions had become one of the most significant changes among Americans during that time period. But before looking at the substance of change in the realm of political alienation, we must precisely define the term as it is used by political scientists.

While the word *alienation* has taken on numerous meanings throughout history, it has usually implied that there is a separation between two things. The term was probably first used by Christian philosophers to indicate a separation between humankind and God. Philosophers like Jean-Jacques Rousseau and Karl Marx took the concept of alienation into other realms. For example, Rousseau used the concept to describe what he saw as a separation between mankind and the "natural state." Karl Marx came to believe that alienation "meant the separation of man from his humanness and from his natural social development." Both Rousseau and Marx, like other philosophers who have examined the concept of alienation, believed that humans' separation from something else was prompted by conditions in society.

Some students of philosophy argue that social scientists have overused the term *alienation* and have applied it in some instances inappropriately. Almost all scholars agree, however, that there are numerous acceptable meanings of the term. We will say, therefore, that alienation is a *multidimensional concept*. The multidimensionality of alienation comes from defining the nature of the separation that is being described. Alienation also takes on a multidimensional character in that humans' separation may be from any of a multiplicity of objects, like society, self, or government. Thus, to understand alienation fully, we must identify both the type of separation *and* the object or objects from which this separation is experienced.

Types of Alienation

There are several distinct conceptions of alienation that are used by political scientists, although sociologists make much greater and broader use of the term.

The first type of alienation is referred to as *powerlessness*. Melvin Seeman explains that powerlessness is "the expectancy or probability held by the individual that his own behavior cannot determine . . . the outcomes . . . he seeks."[8] The opposite of powerlessness is *efficacy*. Citizens who are efficacious believe their behavior can affect the outcomes of government. Powerlessness can have multiple dimensions, just as the concept of alienation does.

In one sense, powerlessness means that the individual believes that he cannot affect government in its decisions because of some fault of the government. He feels that the government is somehow not responsive because of its own faults. Individuals who believe that government *is* responsive are said to have *external efficacy*. Conversely, an individual may believe that he/she cannot affect government simply because of his or her own inadequacies. In this instance the government is not perceived as faulty, instead, fault rests on the individual. Those who do *not* perceive themselves as inadequate are said to possess *internal efficacy*. In either case, the absence of efficacy will cause the individual to feel separated from the government.

A second form of alienation is called *anomie*. This particular type of alienation may also be conceived of as *normlessness, distrust,* or *cynicism*, though these three terms are not always used interchangeably. Anomie occurs when an individual thinks that the performance of government and its leadership is inappropriate and violates widely accepted norms. A state of anomie occurs when an individual has high expectations for government and leaders performing in an acceptable manner. It is the failure to live up to these high expectations that results in the anomic state. Thus, anomie constitutes a much more generalized and deep-seated separation from government than does a lack of political efficacy.

A third type of political alienation involves *meaninglessness*. When experiencing this condition, the individual believes that there is no discernible pattern to political decision making. It has been observed that "this feeling is illustrated by an individual's inability to distinguish any meaningful political choices, and the sense that political choices are themselves meaningless, because one cannot predict their probable outcomes nor, consequently, use them to change social conditions."[9] Here, the political world simply does not make sense to the individual.

A fourth type of political alienation centers on the notion of *isolation*. This particular type of alienation is activated by an individual's belief that the norms and goals of government and its leaders are "unfair, loaded, illegitimate."[10] This form differs from anomie in that anomie suggests that an individual perceives that others are violating norms which he accepts. But in the case of political isolation, an individual rejects the norms themselves and is not concerned with whether leaders are adhering to them or not.

While the distinctions between the different types of alienation cited above have theoretical importance, it is another thing to find these distinctions made consistently in practical research applications. Survey questions often seem to overlap several different types of alienation or even to constitute an entirely new concept. Like other researchers, we must be flexible in our use and definition of survey items designed to measure the concept of political alienation.

Trends in Political Alienation

A significant change in political alienation began in the mid-1960s. Most nationwide surveys of public opinion showed that positive evaluations of government and society had declined precipitously after 1964.[11] That the current crisis of confidence began in 1964 is important. Too often journalists and other political observers suggest that public disaffection was a function of Watergate and its related events. But as Table 4-1 shows, Americans had begun to doubt their leaders long before Richard Nixon was elected president in 1968. There can be little doubt that the events of Watergate stimulated and accelerated the trend toward a cynical public, but all of the blame cannot be attributed to Watergate.

The questions presented in Table 4-1 are taken from the SRC/CPS's quadrennial studies of political attitudes. The decline in political trust is best captured in the first SRC/CPS question, which asks persons to rate how much of the time they think they can trust the government in Washington to do what is right. As Table 4-1 indicates, in 1964, 76 percent of those surveyed thought they could trust the government in Washington always or most of the time to do what is right. By 1980, this figure had declined to 25 percent. In a relatively brief period of time the American public made a substantial reassessment of its orientations toward the trustworthiness of Washington.

Interestingly, trust in government had rebounded in 1984 to 44 percent, a level last achieved prior to Watergate in the early 1970s. By 1988, the level of trust had slipped back to 40 percent, still substantially higher than the figures observed for the time period of 1976–1980. And yet, the proportion of the electorate believing they can "always" trust the government is less than one third of what it was in 1952. The upsurge in 1984 may very well have been a residual effect of the Reagan presidency that by 1988 had already begun to wane. In general, it appears the decline in political trust may have reversed itself in the mid- to late-1980s, but distrust is still far higher than it was in the halcyon days of the Eisenhower era.

But government is not the only institution singled out for public criticism. The second item in Table 4-1 suggests that Americans grew increasingly distrustful of "big interests" during the years between 1964 and 1980. Only 29 percent believed that government was run by a few big interests in 1964. By 1980 more than twice that number, 70 percent, believed that government was run by a few "big interests" looking out for themselves. The third question in the table demonstrates tremendous growth of the belief that there are crooks in government. This may stem from concern about the growing power of "special interests."

The patterns of responses to these two questions mirror that of responses to the political trust measure. Specifically, the proportion of individuals who believe the government is run by a few "big interests" declined to pre-1974 levels in 1984 but increased somewhat in 1988. Further, those who expressed the view that "quite a few" people in government are "a little crooked" declined in 1984 to pre-1972 levels, but again an increase is noted in 1988.

The last item in Table 4-1 deals with political efficacy or a persons' belief that he or she can influence government. It is clear that there has been an increase in the belief that we cannot have much say about what the government does. This trend is not as consistent and the change has not been as spectacular as for political trust. But the decline, unlike that for the other measures, has been constant through 1988. The proportion of respondents in 1988 who believe they don't have any say about what the government does, 45 percent, was as high as it has ever been (matching the figure observed in 1978). Clearly, Americans in 1980 were less likely to feel politically efficacious than was the populace in the 1960s.

The SRC/CPS data suggest that political alienation increased after 1964 on almost every dimension which was discussed earlier in this chapter. Next, we will examine questions regarding the objects of this change in political alienation. We will attempt to see whether alienation is directed toward our system of government or more narrowly toward the incumbent officeholders during this era of change.

Objects of Political Alienation

The decline in political trust has caused considerable debate among political scientists. This debate involves questions about attitude objects and centers on the nature of contemporary mass disaffection. Briefly stated, one of the two opposing points of view claims that recent declines in traditional support indicators, such as those we have just discussed, portend great danger for the American system of government. As David Easton has noted, these political scientists believe the United States "is now suffering a 'crisis of regime.' "[12] Juxtaposed to this view is one which holds that Americans are not so much alienated from the system (or the regime, to use Easton's terminology) as they are from incumbent officeholders.

This debate about the nature of declining affection for things political was best captured in a September 1974 exchange between Arthur H. Miller and Jack Citrin in the *American Political Science Review*.[13] Miller and Citrin were commenting on decline in political trust from 1964 to 1972 as measured by the SRC/CPS items discussed earlier. Despite use of the same data, Miller and Citrin offer different interpretive approaches. Miller sees declining trust as quite serious and an indication that "the whole system of government is threatened." He concludes from his examination of the data that increased "distrust of government was partially related to the changing attitudes on the issues of racial integration and U.S. involvement in the Vietnam War." Miller implies further that public malaise over the failure of leaders in institutions to implement satisfactory policies might be generalized into a broader dissatisfaction with the system in general.[14]

Citrin, to the contrary, believes that mistrust, such as that recorded in the SRC/CPS measures, is largely opposition to incumbents that would not be readily translated into a more general kind of dissatisfaction with the "system." Citrin considers it extremely important that distrusting respondents are no differ-

Table 4-1

National Election Studies Measures of Trust and Efficacy, 1964–1988

Trust: How much of the time do you think you can trust the government in Washington to do what is right—just about always, most of the time, or only some of the time?

	1964	1968	1972	1974	1976	1978	1980	1984	1988
Always	14%	8%	7%	3%	3%	3%	2%	4%	4%
Most of the time	62	53	45	33	29	26	23	40	36
Some of the time/None of the time	22	37	45	61	62	67	73	54	58
Don't know/Not ascertained	2	2	3	3	1	4	2	2	2
	100%	100%	100%	100%	100%	100%	100%	100%	100%

"Big Interests": Would you say the government is pretty much run by a few "big interests" looking out for themselves or that it is run for the benefit of all the people?

	1964	1968	1972	1974	1976	1978	1980	1984	1988
For the benefit of all	64%	52%	43%	24%	24%	24%	21%	39%	31%
Few "big interests"	29	39	48	65	66	65	70	55	63
Other/Depends/Both	4	5	3	3	2	1	—	—	—
Don't know/Not ascertained	3	4	6	8	8	10	9	6	6
	100%	100%	100%	100%	100%	100%	100%	100%	100%

Honesty: Do you think that quite a few of the people running the government are a little crooked, not very many people are, or hardly any of them are crooked at all?

	1964	1968	1972	1974	1976	1978	1980	1984	1988
Hardly any	18%	18%	16%	10%	13%	12%	9%	14%	11%
Not many	48	49	46	41	40	41	41	50	44
Quite a few	29	25	34	45	41	39	46	32	40
Don't know/Not ascertained	5	8	4	4	6	8	4	4	5
	100%	100%	100%	100%	100%	100%	100%	100%	100%

External Efficacy: People like me don't have any say about what the government does.

	1964	1968	1972	1974	1976	1978	1980	1984	1988
Agree	29%	41%	36%	40%	41%	45%	39%	42%	45%
Disagree	69	58	63	57	56	52	59	56	54
Don't know/Not ascertained	2	1	1	3	3	3	2	2	1
	100%	100%	100%	100%	100%	100%	100%	100%	100%

Source: National Election Studies, 1964–1988.

ent in their political behavior than their trusting counterparts. As he states, the politically cynical "were as likely as those expressing trust in government to be eligible for good citizenship awards."[15]

This finding, plus the belief that many respondents give distrustful answers because they are "fashionable," led Citrin to see declining trust as considerably less threatening than Miller does. Citrin agrees that many Americans think times are bad, but these individuals are not ready to repudiate the American form of government. To make his point, Citrin used the following analogy:

> . . . political systems, like baseball teams, have slumps and winning streaks. Having recently endured a succession of losing seasons, Americans boo the home team when it takes the field. But fans are often fickle; victories quickly elicit cheers. And to most fans what matters is whether the home team wins or loses, not how it plays the game.[16]

According to this analysis a modest "winning streak" and perhaps some new names in the lineup may be sufficient to raise the level of trust in government.

Since the exchange between Citrin and Miller, there have been several new names in the government lineup including three new presidents, Jimmy Carter, Ronald Reagan, and George Bush. Carter seemed to be especially sensitive to what he called the public malaise, prompting him to work aggressively to restore the American people's sense of trust in their government. In his 1976 inaugural he specifically promised a government for America that is "as good and as competent as its people." Despite the efforts of Carter and other public officials, the public was not convinced; the decline of trust persisted through 1980. However, the rather substantial reversal of the decline in distrust observed in 1984 suggests that a president *can* generate more positive evaluations of the political system. In turn, this suggests that Citrin's interpretation of distrust may be more valid than Miller's.

The persistence of political alienation in the late 1980s still does not tell us whether Miller's argument for distrust of the system or Citrin's argument for distrust of incumbents is more accurate. Only a succession of the lineup changes prescribed by Citrin and continued changes in Americans' attitudes is likely to increase dramatically our understanding of the precise meaning of this trend.

Who Is Alienated?

Flanigan and Zingale wrote in 1975 that decreasing levels of political trust in "the last decade or so" focused upon the following three important population subgroups:

... blacks who became discouraged by the failure of government programs to promote social and economic progress; people, particularly young people, who became frustrated at their failure to reverse the policy of military involvement in Southeast Asia; and a third group of people who became increasingly alarmed over the unwillingness of the government to deal firmly with the other two groups.[17]

Trends in the alienation of each of these groups will be considered next. After these discussions, we will examine levels of political distrust and alienation for a variety of social groups, using the measures described in Table 4-1, for 1988.

Black Political Cynicism

Studies of political cynicism or distrust frequently focus on the attitudes of black Americans. Political distrust by blacks is not particularly surprising when much of the political attitude literature links negativism with social and economic deprivation. What has surprised some observers, though, is that SRC/CPS studies of trust in government show that blacks were more trusting than whites from 1964 to 1968.[18] This tide of black trust undoubtedly sprang from an acknowledgment by blacks that government, at least the federal government, was making serious attempts to improve the economic, social, and political condition of America's black people. Miller has specifically linked black satisfaction to passage of the 1964 Civil Rights Act.[19]

Whatever the cause of black trust in the early to mid-1960s, the precipitous drop in black political trust to below that of whites in every SRC/CPS survey after 1966 prompts more difficult questions of causality. Miller has hypothesized that advances brought about in the early and mid-1960s by the civil rights movement created expectations among blacks that could not be fulfilled in the latter part of the 1960s. Miller also presents data suggesting that while the Vietnam involvement caused distrust of government among both blacks and whites, it had an earlier and more profound impact on black attitudes. This could be explained, perhaps, by the fact that the black community was more "personally" involved in the Vietnam War, blacks having served in disproportionate numbers in the armed forces. Miller's thesis, we conclude, is that political cynicism is greater among blacks than whites primarily because of blacks' less favorable evaluations of policies of the federal level of government.[20]

We do not wholeheartedly agree with Miller. We believe that analysis of the origins of post-1966 political cynicism should take into account blacks' evaluations of state and local governments as well as their evaluation of the federal government. Our reasoning is based on data presented in Table 4-2

	Table 4-2

Expression of Greater Confidence in National Than State or Local Government, by Race

	Percentage of Respondents Expressing More Confidence in National Government	
	White	Black
1968	43%	59%
1972	42	51
1974	29	38
1976	29	29

Note: Question not asked in surveys after 1976.
Source: SRC/CPS Election Studies, 1968–1976.

(SRC/CPS data) which show that, at least prior to 1976, blacks were less cynical than whites in their attitudes toward the federal government. Furthermore, the data demonstrate that prior to 1976 blacks' confidence in the federal government always exceeded that of whites. Taken together, these findings suggest strongly that early declines in black trust in government were prompted by unfavorable evaluations by blacks of the policies of state and local governments. More recently, however, blacks' confidence in the federal government has fallen to the level of whites while blacks' general political trust lags well behind that of whites.

Age and Political Alienation

The second group of disaffected Americans identified by Flanigan and Zingale were the young and others "who became frustrated at their failure to reverse the policy of military involvement in Southeast Asia."[21] Youthful alienation was new to Americans. In 1975 Flanigan and Zingale made the following observation:

> . . . over the last fifteen years [before Vietnam, etc.] the youngest voters have typically been the most trusting of government, even as general levels of trust have declined, a tendency one would expect given their recent exposure to the educational process that at least in part sees itself as building support for the system.[22]

Flanigan and Zingale suggest that the socialization process may not have provided youth of the 1960s and 1970s with a deep enough reservoir of support to mediate their indignation toward the Vietnam conflict and fear of the draft. Flanigan and Zingale also imply that youth were more affected by Vietnam and early Watergate revelations because they had the "least firmly established attitudes" before such events.[23]

But whatever the cause and magnitude of youthful negativism in the 1960s and 1970s, the most severely alienated group of Americans in recent years is persons sixty-five and older. The alienation of the aged has gone largely without notice by the media, probably because the "meager outcries (of the aged) have been constantly upstaged by the dramatic indignation of youth."[24]

Gilmour and Lamb have used SRC/CPS data collected from 1960 to 1972 to analyze age and its relationship to what they call "extreme alienation." This attitude structure is defined as a combination of three distinct feelings: "distrust of government and politicians, a sense of meaninglessness of . . . political choices, and personal powerlessness to influence . . ." American politics. Gilmour and Lamb show that "in 1968 and again in 1972, extreme alienation was the response of nearly 30 percent of Americans over age sixty-five." Youthful alienation was far below this figure in 1968 and 1972. Gilmour and Lamb have concluded from extensive interviewing that "the elderly have been inescapably buffeted by long lifetimes of unprecedented change" and are frequently "cast aside by family and friends to the isolation of institutional 'homes' and retirement communities, caught in the squeeze between stagnant social security benefits and double-digit inflation."[25]

During the 1960s and 1970s, trust was lowest among the youngest and oldest age groups in the electorate. But with the end of the Vietnam War, and the waning resentment over Watergate, young Americans are once again relatively more trusting as they were before these traumatic events. In the meantime, older Americans remain more alienated. We will discuss this further in our consideration of political alienation in 1988.

The Newly Alienated

Flanigan and Zingale have identified the third major group of disaffected Americans as those who became alarmed over the government's response (or lack of response) to civil rights and Vietnam protest. Miller has characterized these Americans as "cynics of the right."[26] Former Vice President Spiro Agnew dubbed these Americans "the silent majority." He and other conservative politicians said that this group of disaffected Americans had been silent and ignored for far too long in American politics.

Richard Dawson has argued that skilled laborers like construction workers are typical of the silent majority Agnew sought to represent. Regarding their attitudes, Dawson states that "skilled workers have the highest incidence of negative attitudes." He also notes the following:

> The skilled worker tends to see the government supporting or engaging in programs and actions designed to aid the very poor. Rightly or wrongly, he often perceives these efforts as operating at his expense rather than for his benefit. He sees the sons and daughters of the privileged engaging in riots, demonstrations, and other behavior generally considered immoral or illegal, for which they receive little or no punishment. He sees the young flouting the values of hard work, patriotism, and respect for law and authority, which he was taught must be abided by and believed in for acceptance and success. He sees a government that seems responsive not to his interests and needs, but instead to those of others, many of whom he sees as less deserving.[27]

While Dawson's analysis has focused on skilled workers, there is some speculation that similar discontent has spread to other middle-class, even white-collar, occupational groups. James Q. Wilson, referring to Arthur Miller's analysis of SRC/CPS data, notes that the most extensive decline in public confidence from 1958 to 1972 occurred among those persons earning middle range incomes. Middle income blacks and whites lost more ground in confidence than lower and higher income persons of either race. Wilson contends that middle-class discontent springs from the "rise of problems deeply affecting the middle class which the government would like to solve but cannot."[28] He cites crime and other issues related to public order as examples of unsolvable problems. Miller similarly states that his "cynics of the right" have a fixation on social control issues.[29]

Disaffection in 1988

With the turbulence of the civil rights movement, the war in Vietnam, and the Watergate scandals behind us, it may be that alienation from and distrust of the political and social systems have declined. Indeed, the data in Table 4-1 suggest that, in general, this is the case. What Table 4-1 does not address are the relative levels of disaffection among various social groups in the American electorate. The preceding discussions suggest that some groups, such as blacks and the working class, are more likely to be alienated and distrustful than are others. In this section we examine the distribution of a variety of measures of distrust and alienation for several social groups in the United States in 1988.

Political Alienation in 1988

In Table 4-3 we present levels of *political alienation* for several groups in 1988. Alienation is measured through the use of the following two questions from the 1988 CPS election study:

1. I don't think public officials care much about what people like me think.
2. People like me don't have any say about what government does.

Respondents could agree or disagree with these statements. Those agreeing with *both* statements are classified as *alienated*. All others are classified as *less alienated*.

As our previous discussion suggests, blacks, older Americans, and blue collar workers were more likely to be alienated from the political system than were whites, younger citizens, and nonworking-class individuals. Moreover, alienation decreases as both education and income increase. These data indicate that alienation is a function of one's relative position in the social system. As people improve their positions in the system, they become less alienated. They feel more a part of government.

Trust and Efficacy in 1988

In Tables 4-4 through 4-7 we present the distributions of these same subgroups for the four measures of political trust and political efficacy described in Table 4-1. We will discuss each in turn.

Political Trust: As with alienation, political distrust decreases as education and income increase. Blacks are substantially less trustful of government than whites, while women are only slightly more distrustful than men. Blue collar workers are more likely than other occupational groupings to express feelings of distrust. Finally, older and younger citizens do not differ on this dimension. In general, distrust, like alienation, appears to be a function of social position: the higher the position, the greater the trust.

	Table 4-3

Political Alienation for Various Socioeconomic Groups, 1988

Education	Proportion
Less than high school	38.1
High school	29.4
Some college	23.3
College degree or more	15.4

Race	
White	25.6
Black	36.4

Gender	
Male	27.2
Female	27.2

Age	
18–29	22.8
30–49	26.4
50 or older	30.6

Income	
Less than $10,000	35.7
$10–25,000	31.5
More than $25,000	21.3

Occupation	
Blue-collar	34.6
Clerical/Sales	25.5
Professional	25.1
Managerial	18.6

Note: Proportions are listed for those who are alienated. See text for further explanation of index.
Source: CPS National Election Studies, 1988.

Table 4-4

Distrust of Government for Various
Socioeconomic Groups, 1988

Education	Proportion
Less than high school	68.0
High school	57.6
Some college	57.1
College degree or more	53.7

Race	
White	56.1
Black	74.4

Gender	
Male	56.8
Female	60.4

Age	
18–29	59.8
30–49	58.7
50 or older	58.2

Income	
Less than $10,000	69.2
$10–25,000	61.6
More than $25,000	52.6

Occupation	
Blue-collar	63.0
Clerical/Sales	55.4
Professional	59.7
Managerial	54.0

Note: Proportions are listed for those responding "Only some of the time," or "None of the time" to the question, "How much of the time do you think you can trust the government in Washington to do what is right?"
Source: CPS National Election Studies, 1988.

Table 4-5

Government as Captive of Big Interests
for Various Socioeconomic Groups, 1988

Education	Proportion
Less than high school	72.8
High school	69.5
Some college	64.7
College degree or more	61.7

Race	
White	66.0
Black	73.3

Gender	
Male	65.9
Female	68.3

Age	
18–29	58.5
30–49	71.8
50 or older	67.2

Income	
Less than $10,000	73.8
$10–25,000	72.2
More than $25,000	62.3

Occupation	
Blue-collar	71.5
Clerical/Sales	68.2
Professional	66.6
Managerial	62.9

Note: Proportions are listed for those responding "For a few big interests," to the question, "Would you say the government is run by a few big interests looking out for themselves or that it is run for the benefit of all the people?"
Source: CPS National Election Studies, 1986.

"Big Interests":   Not surprisingly, the perception that government is run "for a few big interests" is also a function of social position. The likelihood of expressing this sentiment decreases as education, income, and occupational status rise. Further, blacks are more likely to view government in this fashion, as are women (although not by much). In terms of age, younger people are the least likely to view government as a captive of "big interests," with little difference between middle-aged and older Americans.

Dishonesty in Government: As education, income, and occupational status increase, the tendency to view government officials as dishonest decreases. Whites are much less likely to express the view that "quite a few" people in government are "a little crooked" than are blacks, just as males are less likely to express that view when compared to females (although the latter difference is not substantial). Finally, perceptions of dishonestly increase with age, with older citizens the most likely group to perceive a lack of integrity among government officials.

External Efficacy: The same pattern as above emerges with reference to the statement, "People like me don't have any say about what the government does" (which is also a component of our index of political alienation). Efficacy increases with higher levels of education and income and with increased occupational status. Whites are substantially more efficacious than blacks. Women and older citizens are less likely to express efficacy than are men and the young, but the differences here are not very large.

Summary: Disaffection in the United States

Tables 4-3 through 4-7 present some disturbing findings, in that support for the political system is not especially widespread. In particular, those relatively disadvantaged in the sociopolitical system—blue-collar workers, blacks, and those with lower levels of education and income—are decidedly less supportive of the political system than are other Americans.

As with any data, these findings are open to interpretation. Specifically, are the disaffected *cynics* or *realists?* It can be argued that these individuals are cynics. Having failed to achieve a desirable position in the system, such individuals project blame onto the system, rather than accept their failure as a product of their own shortcomings and lack of effort. The benefits of living in the United States are open to all, so the argument goes, and those who do not partake of them fail to do so only because of their own inadequacies and not because of any problems inherent in the system. But the lower echelons refuse to accept this and cynically blame the system for their lack of success.

Table 4-6

**Perceptions of Dishonesty in Government
for Various Socioeconomic Groups, 1988**

Education	Proportion
Less than high school	51.4
High school	44.1
Some college	39.0
College degree or more	31.4

Race	
White	39.8
Black	54.8

Gender	
Male	38.1
Female	44.6

Age	
18–29	36.0
30–49	41.4
50 or older	45.2

Income	
Less than $10,000	51.9
$10–25,000	45.6
More than $25,000	35.5

Occupation	
Blue-collar	46.1
Clerical/Sales	38.8
Professional	42.4
Managerial	35.4

Note: Proportions are listed for those responding "Quite a few" to the question,
"Do you think that quite a few of the people running the government are a little
crooked, not very many people, or hardly any of them are crooked at all?"
Source: CPS National Election Studies, 1988.

Table 4-7

Lack of External Efficacy
for Various Socioeconomic Groups, 1988

Education	Proportion
Less than high school	56.5
High school	47.2
Some college	33.7
College degree or more	25.3

Race	
White	39.4
Black	56.1

Gender	
Male	39.6
Female	43.1

Age	
18–29	39.0
30–49	40.1
50 or older	44.7

Income	
Less than $10,000	52.4
$10–25,000	47.5
More than $25,000	33.6

Occupation	
Blue-collar	50.1
Clerical/Sales	39.5
Professional	38.5
Managerial	30.2

Note: Proportions are listed for those agreeing with the statement, "People like me don't have any say about what the government does."
Source: CPS National Election Studies, 1988.

On the other hand, it can be argued that those in a relatively deprived position are *realists*. In an economic and social system such as in the United States, there will always be individuals who are worse off than others. This is not to suggest, necessarily, that "the poor will always be with us" (although if poverty is defined as having substantially less than others, the poor *will* always be with us). Rather, unless wages and salaries are somehow equalized through governmental action, there will always be disparities in education, income, occupations, and the like. Individuals on the lower rungs of the ladder may realize this and will naturally be less supportive of the political and economic system than those who have achieved relatively greater success.

The question is a complex one, and cannot be definitively answered, with these or any other data. Our own feeling, however, is that while those at the lower end of the sociopolitical spectrum may at times be unduly cynical, it is realistic for them to think the government pays no attention to them or to be distrustful of government. Only the naive would seriously argue that government pays equal attention to all citizens. The lower class probably does not have the impact on government that the middle and upper classes do. It is therefore unfair to expect the disaffected to be anything but alienated and distrustful.

Alienation and Contact with Government

In explaining the origins of political alienation in the United States as people's responses to unpopular policies, our premise has been that alienation from government is a shared response to policies which disadvantage a class of persons. While alienation may be propagated among some Americans in this fashion, for many others the road to alienation may be an individual rather than group experience. Some political journalists and political scientists have suggested that alienation may have its origins in an unsatisfactory personal experience with government officials.

Personal experiences with government and government officials may take several forms. A relatively small segment of the population has engaged in self-initiated contact with government. Surveys conducted on national and local levels have consistently shown only about 20 percent of Americans have contacted government officials.[30] Many more Americans come into contact with government officials without initiating the contact. They may be compelled to appear before government officials for routine matters such as renewal of a driver's license, obtaining a permit to fish in public waters, or registering to vote. In such matters an individual problem or complaint is seldom involved, the contact is engaged in by most Americans, and is usually initiated by a government agency rather than by the individual.

Whether contact is initiated by government or coincidental, research by Herbert Jacob, Robert Weissberg, and a Survey Research Center team directed by Daniel Katz has indicated that unsatisfactory experiences with government officials are not generalized into more comprehensive forms of alienation.[31] But a different pattern emerges when contact is self-initiated. Ryles finds that citizens who have contacted a government official and judged that contact to be unsuccessful are likely to experience lower levels of political trust and efficacy.[32] Moreover, as Louis Harris stated before Congress, only one in twenty Americans has had a *highly* satisfying encounter with an official of our national government.[33] Thus there is reason to study citizen-government interaction carefully if alienation continues to increase.

A Trend Assessment: Alienation

The definitions and measures of distrust and alienation discussed in this chapter are subject to disagreement among scholars. There is agreement, however, that it is of little constructive benefit to a society for its citizens to distrust its officials. It may be that political distrust is an innocuous and isolated belief which is increasingly held by the general public but is unrelated to any disruptive or threatening political action or inaction by citizens. At best, however, no social benefit can be found in increasing public alienation.

In our assessment of this trend we will examine the political behavior of those who find their public officials unresponsive. We might expect, for example, that those who are distrustful or alienated are less inclined to vote. Thus, the decline in turnout might be explained by the increase of alienation within the public. Defection and independence from political parties might be the result of the alienation felt by issue oriented voters who see little choice among the candidates nominated by the major political parties. For the first time, then, we can combine assessments of the trends discussed in this book.

Are declining public participation, a growth in independency, and more frequent deviating elections the result of an issue responsive public growing increasingly distrustful of its public officials? Or are these trends unrelated to one another? To answer this we offer an assessment of the relationship between alienation and the previously developed measure of defections, independency, participation, and quality of candidate evaluation.

Before we can assess these trends, we must first examine the trends in political alienation and political distrust. Table 4-8 shows the proportions of citizens who we classify as alienated since 1952 and as distrustful (see Table 4-1) since 1964. Both attitudes have increased dramatically over time. Alienation increased from 16 percent of the population in 1960 to 36 percent in 1976, before set-

Table 4-8

Alienation and Distrust, 1952–1988

	Alienation	Distrust
1952	20%	*
1956	16	*
1960	16	*
1964	21	22%
1968	35	37
1972	31	45
1976	36	62
1980	26	73
1984	26	54
1988	27	58

*Question not asked prior to 1964.
Source: SRC/CPS election studies, 1952–1988.

tling in at the 26–27 percent range in the 1980s. The increase in distrust has been even more dramatic, almost tripling from 1964 to 1980. The 58 percent of the electorate in 1988 who were distrustful of government is more than two and one-half times the proportion observed in 1964. Clearly, dissatisfaction with the political system has increased over the past three decades. But is this pattern of growth connected to the other trends we have identified in previous chapters?

The growth of issue oriented evaluation of the presidential candidates appears unrelated to changing levels of alienation in the electorate. Figure 4-1 shows that both the best (issue and ideologue) and the worst (image and no-content) of the evaluations of the candidates have been similarly affected by changing patterns of political alienation since 1960. Ideological, issue oriented, and image evaluators have differed little in the extent of their alienation, although ideologues are the least likely to be alienated. By 1988, the difference in levels of alienation between even the ideologues and those classified as "no-content" had decreased substantially.

Those respondents unable to describe any difference between the candidates that would cause them to vote for one rather than the other, those we have classed as no-content evaluators, have proven consistently to be the most alienated. Even in the 1950s their alienation was at levels not reached by those more capable of evaluating the candidates until the 1970s. Issue oriented candidate evaluators have not been exceptional in their contribution to the aliena-

Figure 4-1

Relationship Between Presidential Candidate Evaluation and Alienation, 1952–1988

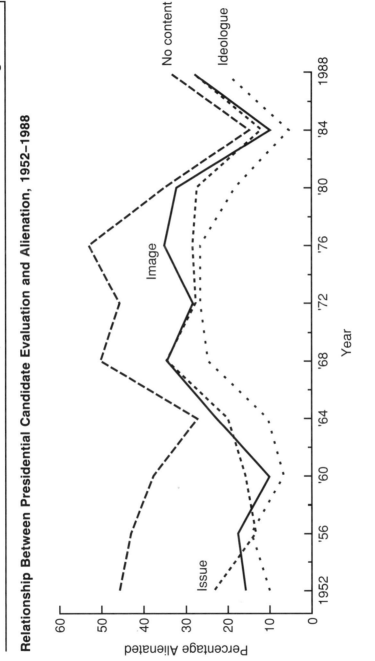

Source: NES Election Studies, 1952–1988.

tion of the American electorate. Rather it is those unaffected by the increasing sophistication of the electorate that continue to be alienated. In short, the increasing alienation of the electorate cannot be attributed to the increasing issue orientation of the electorate.

The relationship between alienation and party identification depicted in Figure 4-2 varies greatly between elections. At various times independents, Republicans, and Democrats have each been the most alienated, but all three seem to have been similarly affected by the increase of alienation affecting the country at large. In 1976 and 1980 independents were more alienated than Democrats and Democrats more alienated than Republicans, a pattern that is not unlike

---

Figure 4-2

Relationship Between Political Party Identification and Alienation, 1952–1988

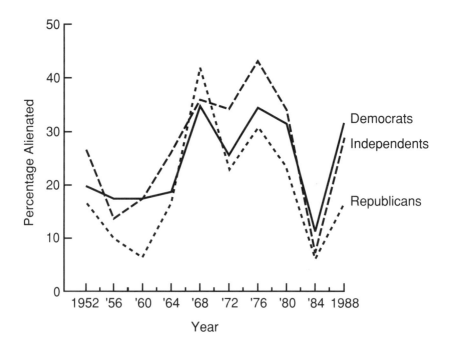

Source: NES Election Studies, 1952–1988.

that noted in 1952 at a somewhat lower overall level of alienation. In 1988 Democrats were slightly more alienated than were independents, with Republicans by far the least alienated. Given these trends, we cannot conclude that the growth in independency results from increases in political alienation.

Defection from one's political party is related to political alienation as shown in Figure 4-3. In 1968, 1980, and 1984, little difference in alienation was notable between those who defected in at least one vote for president, senator, or representative and those who were loyal in their votes. But between 1968 and 1976, defectors were somewhat more alienated, although this difference was only 7 percentage points in 1976.

Figure 4-3

Relationship Between Defection from Political Party and Alienation, 1952–1988

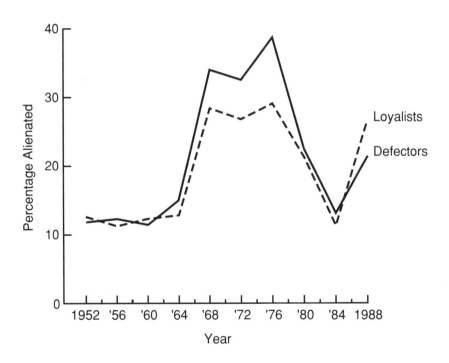

Source: NES Election Studies, 1952–1988.

In 1988 the pattern reversed, with loyalists slightly more likely to be classified as alienated than defectors. Prior to 1988 the pattern suggests that some citizens perceived the opposition party as an alternative source of leadership to which they could turn. The data for 1988, however, indicate that the alienated are less likely to seek out such alternatives, suggesting that defection and alienation are independent phenomena. More importantly, these data suggest that those who are alienated are not abandoning the political parties for their failure to offer choices to the electorate.

Participation shows no consistent relationship to alienation over time. Until 1968, quite contrary to expectations, the alienated were increasingly likely to participate, at least to the extent of voting in presidential elections, as the following figures show: in 1952, 58 percent of the alienated voted; 1956, 58 percent; 1960, 64 percent; 1964, 73 percent; 1968, 71 percent. But in 1972 the proportion of alienated citizens who reported voting suddenly dropped back to 58 percent, the same level observed in the 1950s. Since 1972 the proportion of alienated citizens who report voting in presidential elections has been either 57 or 58 percent. Still, better than half of those who are alienated nevertheless vote for president. This, of course, is substantially short of the 75 percent turnout typically achieved by the less alienated.

These figures mean that the alienated are less likely to vote than the non-alienated. But as alienation increased, the alienated actually voted more, becoming a larger group within the voting part of the electorate (in the 1950s about one voter in six was alienated, while in 1988 about one in four were alienated). Both the likelihood of the alienated to vote and their share of all voters peaked in 1968. These findings do not form the foundations for any definitive conclusions about alienation and voting. Nevertheless, we believe it is most important to remember that a majority of the alienated continue to express some hope for and faith in our system of government by turning out to vote in presidential elections.

Conclusion

Not unlike other variables we have considered in the two preceding chapters, political alienation does not appear to play a central role in unraveling the mysteries of American electoral behavior. It explains neither why people are less likely to vote today than two decades ago nor what factors are more likely to influence the candidate choice of those who do vote. The slight decline of political alienation in 1988 reinforces our conclusion that this phenomenon is not responsible for some of the other trends we have observed. In the face of declining alienation, defections from political parties soared, participation continued to decline (although not sharply so), and the quality of candidate evaluations improved. If alienation were central for accounting for the other trends in electoral behavior, we would have expected the opposite result in terms of the defection rate, turnout, and candidate evaluation. Indeed, in looking closely at the relationships between alienation and our other trends, we find a weakened relationship in the late 1980s in almost every instance.

Taken together, our findings about change in political trust and alienation do not absolutely refute the notion that contemporary disaffection might render serious damage to our republic. We generally agree with theorists who stress the philosophy that a government needs the support of its citizenry in order to function satisfactorily. But, as we have demonstrated in this chapter, the fact that many Americans are reluctant to give their unqualified support to the government does not signal the undoing of our party and electoral systems. Therefore, while we urge continued research into the causes and effects of alienation among the masses, we do not believe that alienation currently represents a force that threatens the stability of the American electorate or system of government.

Notes

1. David Easton and Jack Dennis found that children believe the president is more persistent, diligent, and likely to keep promises than their own fathers. *Children in the Political System* (New York: McGraw-Hill, 1969), pp. 249–72.
2. David Easton, *A Systems Analysis of Political Life* (New York: John Wiley & Sons, 1965).
3. The definitions of type of political support cited here are from David Easton's latest restatement of his concepts: "A Re-Assessment of the Concept of Political Support," *British Journal of Political Science*, 5 (October 1975): 435–57.
4. Easton, *Systems Analysis of Political Life*, p. 220.
5. William H. Flanigan and Nancy H. Zingale, *Political Behavior of the American Electorate*, third ed. (Boston: Allyn and Bacon, 1975), p. 183.
6. Edward N. Muller, "A Test of a Partial Theory of Potential for Political Violence," *American Political Science Review*, 66 (September 1972): 954.
7. Arthur H. Miller, "Political Issues and Trust in Government: 1964–1970," *American Political Science Review*, 68 (September 1974): 951.

8. Melvin Seeman, "On the Meaning of Alienation," *American Sociological Review*, 24 (December 1959): 783–91.

9. Ada Finifter, "Dimensions of Political Alienation," *American Political Science Review*, 64 (June 1970): 390.

10. *Ibid.*, p. 391.

11. Miller, "Political Issues and Trust in Government."

12. Easton, "Re-Assessment of Concept of Political Support," p. 435.

13. Miller, "Political Issues and Trust in Government;" Jack Citrin, "Comment: The Political Relevance of Trust in Government," *American Political Science Review*, 68 (September 1974): 973–88; Arthur H. Miller, "Rejoinder to 'Comment' by Jack Citrin: Political Discontent or Ritualism?" *American Political Science Review*, 68 (September 1974): 989–1001.

14. Miller, "A Rejoinder to 'Comment' by Jack Citrin."

15. Citrin, "Comment," p. 984.

16. *Ibid.*, p. 987.

17. Flanigan and Zingale, *Political Behavior of American Electorate*, p. 183.

18. Miller, "Political Issues and Trust in Government," p. 955.

19. *Ibid.*

20. Miller, "Rejoinder to 'Comment' by Jack Citrin," p. 990, states that on a "practical, operational level, political trust may be treated as an affective orientation toward the 'government in Washington' – the most salient level of government in the United States."

21. Flanigan and Zingale, *Political Behavior of American Electorate*, p. 183.

22. *Ibid.*, pp. 181–82.

23. *Ibid.*, p. 182.

24. Robert S. Gilmour and Robert B. Lamb, *Political Alienation in Contemporary America* (New York: St. Martin's Press, 1975), p. 63.

25. *Ibid.*, p. 67.

26. Miller, "Political Issues and Trust in Government," p. 962.

27. Richard E. Dawson, *Public Opinion and Contemporary Disarray* (New York: Harper & Row, 1973), p. 102.

28. James Q. Wilson, "The Riddle of the Middle Class," *The Public Interest*, 39 (Spring 1975): 125–29.

29. Miller, "Political Issues and Trust in Government," p. 962.

30. Sidney Verba and Norman H. Nie, *Participation in America* (New York: Harper & Row, 1972), p. 31; Tim Ryles, "The Processing of Citizen Complaints in Local Government" (Paper presented at the Southern Political Science Association meeting, Atlanta 1974; Peter K.

Eisinger, "The Pattern of Citizen Contacts with Public Officials," in *People and Politics in Urban Society*, ed. Harlan Hahn (Beverly Hills: Sage Publications, 1971), pp. 43–69.

31. Herbert Jacob, "Contact with Government Agencies: A Preliminary Analysis of the Distribution of Government Services," *Midwest Journal of Political Science*, 16 (1972): 123–46; Robert Weissberg, "Adolescent Experiences with Political Authorities," *Journal of Politics*, 34 (1972): 797–824; Daniel Katz, Barbara A. Gutek, Robert L. Kahn and Eugenia Barton, *Bureaucratic Encounters* (Ann Arbor, MI: Institute for Social Research, 1975).

32. Ryles, "The Processing of Citizen Complaints in Local Governments."

33. U.S. Congress, Senate, Committee on Government Operations, Subcommittee on Intergovernmental Relations, *Confidence and Concern: Citizens View American Government*, Committee Print, 93rd Congress, 1st Session, 1973, Part I, p. 115.

5

Incumbency and Partisanship

in Congressional Elections

In the preceding chapters we have considered how Americans vote in the quadrennial presidential elections. While these contests have been the focus of electoral research, in many ways they are quite unusual when compared with other elections. The presidency is undoubtedly the most important political office in this country, but it is only one of about one-half million elective offices. The number of elective offices in this country is truly staggering, if one considers elections for the Senate and the House of Representatives at the national level; elections for governors and legislative and judicial seats at the state level; and elections for such local governing bodies as city councils, school boards, and county commissions.

Why, then, are presidential elections the focus not only of scholarly inquiry but of public attention as well? A variety of forces serve to produce this inordinate attention, the most important of which are the following:

1. Turnout in presidential elections, while lower in comparison with other industrial democracies, is higher than voting rates observed in virtually any other election in the United States.
2. The major party candidates receive many millions of dollars in public funding for their campaigns, much of which is spent on media advertisements that in turn generate additional interest among the electorate.
3. The national television networks devote a great deal of time in news and special program coverage to presidential elections.

4. While there have been weak presidential candidates fielded by both of the two major parties, in general the contests are usually competitive. The office is only won with a real contest between two or more candidates. In turn, this competitiveness generates interest and attention.

5. Because of the money spent by the candidates and the coverage by the mass media, almost all Americans are familiar with the major parties' candidates for the presidency, while this is not true in most other elections.

6. No individual can be elected to more than two terms to the presidency, while most other elective offices have unlimited eligibility for re-election. Limited eligibility ensures that the incumbent president will not have a perpetual electoral advantage beyond the second full term in office.

Despite its uniqueness and importance, the presidency does not by itself constitute the federal government. In this chapter, we will examine how Americans vote in one additional type of election, that for the United States House of Representatives. While the United States Senate is an equal partner with the House in the enactment of legislation, the bulk of research in congressional elections has focused on the House. There are at least three reasons for this. First, there are more House elections, 435, than Senate elections, 100, to study; there is, therefore, a larger data base for students of congressional elections to use in their research. Second, members of the House serve two-year terms, while Senators serve six-year terms; therefore, all seats in the House are up for election every two years, while only one third of the seats in the Senate are filled in the same time period. Again, this means there is a larger data base for scholars to exploit.

Finally, the House of Representatives is generally considered the more "representative" house of Congress. This is so because in the original Constitution Senators were chosen by state legislatures, while members of the House were chosen in popular elections. If one is interested in how well the government reflects the will of the public, then, House elections are simply more interesting. While we will have occasion to comment on Senate elections, by and large we will confine ourselves to elections for the House of Representatives. As will become clear, the most important difference between presidential and congressional elections is the extraordinarily high re-election rate of incumbents in congressional elections.

Members of the House of Representatives, also referred to as members of Congress, serve two-year terms. All are elected from geographically determined, single-member districts, and with few exceptions these are *local* districts, in the sense that they contain portions of large cities, or encompass all of medium-sized cities, and are typically less than one hundred square miles in size.

The typical congressional district consists of approximately 550,000 people. Depending on the district, this usually translates into an eligible electorate of between 350,000 and 400,000. While this may appear to be a large number of individuals, they are sufficiently concentrated that they are equally affected by local events, such as drought, flood, or economic boom or bust. As noted above, unlike the president, members of Congress can serve as many terms as they or their constituents wish. For example, Representative Sidney Yates, a Democrat from Illinois, has served in the House of Representatives since 1948.

Rich sources of data are readily available for students of these contests. Data are generated by the outcomes of congressional elections themselves. Surveys are conducted by the Center for Political Studies at the University of Michigan every two years (for both presidential and midterm election years). Research on congressional elections has focused on such questions as the following:

1. To what extent are the outcomes of congressional elections the result of *national* forces, such as rising inflation rates or increasing levels of unemployment, as opposed to *local* forces, such as candidate and voter characteristics?
2. To what extent is voting in congressional elections a function of the same forces affecting presidential voting, specifically, party identification, issues of public policy, and the candidates' personal characteristics?
3. To what extent does the advantage of incumbents in congressional elections supercede the impact of party identification, issues, and the like?
4. To what extent are congressional elections competitive? Have they grown more or less competitive over time? What are the factors that might account for the rise or fall in competitiveness?

In this chapter we will briefly explore the literature pertaining to congressional elections, focusing on two broad themes. First, what are the characteristics of the outcomes of congressional elections? Second, what are the factors that influence how people vote in congressional elections?

Characteristics of Congressional Elections

We begin with a discussion of the outcomes of congressional elections. We are concerned with describing characteristics such as how many people vote in congressional elections; the roles of partisanship and incumbency in shaping the results of these contests; and to what extent congressional election outcomes are shaped by what we have described as national or local forces. We will conclude this section with some specific evidence from the 1988 elections for the House of Representatives.

Turnout

As we noted in Chapter 3, fewer Americans vote in the off year congressional elections than in presidential election years. The Census Bureau reports that for 1986, turnout in all congressional contests totaled only one third (33.4 percent) of the voting age population.[1] Even in presidential election years, the vote for members of Congress totals about 10 percentage points less than turnout for the presidency; in 1988 the relevant figures were 50.1 percent voting for president and 44.7 percent voting for Congress. Also, as we noted earlier, turnout in congressional elections has declined relatively steadily since the high point observed in 1960.

There are several reasons turnout in congressional elections is lower than that observed in presidential contests. Perhaps the most important reason is that congressional elections are not national elections. They feature local issues and local candidates appealing to a relatively small group of voters. As a consequence, most House races receive no attention from the national news media. Citizens are not as often exposed to information about the election and, as a result, are not as likely to participate in the election.

Second, many contests for seats in the House of Representatives are non-competitive; moreover, the level of competitiveness has declined in recent years. As we will note in greater detail more and more congressional districts can be characterized as "safe" for one party or the other; that is, the incumbent, or the incumbent's party's candidate, regularly wins at least 60 percent of the vote. In the absence of competitiveness turnout declines. Many people will not vote if they perceive the election will not be close and that their vote is unlikely to have any impact on the outcome of the election.

Partisan Success

In previous chapters, we noted that while a majority of Americans identify with the Democratic party, the presidency is usually captured by the candidates of the Republican party. Since 1952, the Republicans have won seven of the ten presidential elections. Despite this success at the national level, however, Republicans do not fare nearly as well in congressional elections. The last time the Republican party won a majority of seats in the House of Representatives was 1952. Typically, Democrats win between 55 and 60 percent of seats in the House of Representatives.[2] In 1988, Democrats captured 59.8 percent of the seats. Given the stability of this pattern since the 1950s, it is safe to suggest that in the near future the Democratic party will control the House of Representatives.

Democrats usually control the Senate as well. With the exception of a brief period during Eisenhower's presidency, and Ronald Reagan's first term, the Democratic party has likewise controlled the Senate. The normal state of affairs, then, is for the Republican dominance of the presidency to be at least partially offset by the Democratic control of Congress.

Split Outcomes and Partisan Defections

Another feature of congressional elections closely related to these patterns of partisan outcomes is the widespread occurrence of split outcomes and partisan defection. A *split outcome* occurs when the presidential candidate of one political party, such as George Bush in 1988, wins a majority of the vote in a congressional district, while the congressional candidate of the other party wins the House seat. In 1988, 148 of the 435 congressional district elections resulted in split outcomes, with most of these consisting of a Bush victory coupled with a Democratic winner in the House contest.[3] While the pattern of split outcomes has been quite erratic, peaking at 45 percent in 1984, generally they are increasing.

For a split outcome to occur, many voters are voting for a Democrat for one office and a Republican for the other. These voters engage in *partisan defection* — voting for the candidate other than that of one's own party — in one of the two elections. Of course, voters considering themselves independent cannot engage in partisan defection; rather, they would merely split their votes. The question is in which election, the presidential or congressional contest, are partisans more likely to defect.

As we noted in an earlier chapter, in 1988 only 13 percent of voters defected from their party identification in voting for president, according to the National Election Study of that year. In that same election, 22 percent defected in Senatorial voting, while 21 percent defected in voting for the House of Representatives. We can, therefore, conclude that voters are more loyal to their partisanship in presidential than in congressional balloting. In turn, while the pattern of partisan defection in presidential elections has been quite erratic, the pattern in congressional elections has reflected an increasing trend since the early 1970s.[4] In all likelihood, many Republicans are voting loyally for their party's presidential candidate and defecting to vote for incumbent Democrats as their member of Congress.[5] As we will note more fully below, 96 percent of all Republicans who defected in casting their congressional votes did so by voting for an incumbent of the Democratic party, a pattern that will almost guarantee split results.

Competition for Congressional Seats

If one candidate wins an election with approximately 55 percent of the vote in that district, the seat for that district is called a *safe*, or noncompetitive, seat. Contests in which the winner receives less than 55 percent of the vote are called *marginal*, or competitive, seats.[6] In the midterm elections of 1986, 80 percent of congressional elections were won with at least 60 percent of the vote going to the victor.[7] Since at least 1970, when approximately 72 percent of all seats were so easily won, this pattern has been increasing.

Congressional elections, then, are becoming less competitive in that more and more seats can be classified as safe. When we consider the success of incumbents in winning re-election, the reasons for this become clear. In 1988, 94 percent of all incumbent members of Congress ran for re-election, and 98.5 percent of them won.[8] Thus, 92.6 percent of the One Hundredth Congress were carryovers from the Ninety-ninth Congress. In contrast, 91 percent of incumbents ran for re-election in 1946, with 82.4 percent winning, for a carryover rate of just 75 percent.[9]

As in most elected parliaments and legislatures, incumbent members of Congress have a tremendous electoral advantage. Should an incumbent choose to seek re-election, he or she almost always wins. On the other hand, members of the United States Senate do not enjoy quite the advantage of their counterparts in the House. In the last three Senatorial elections (only a third of the Senate is elected every two years) 84 percent of all incumbents sought re-election, and 83.3 percent won. This produces a carryover rate of approximately 70 percent, which is substantially lower than that observed in the House of Representatives.

The Electoral Advantages of Incumbency

There is little question that the primary focus of those interested in congressional elections has been the increasing success of incumbents in achieving re-election. A variety of explanations have been offered to account for this phenomenon. First, members of Congress, especially those in the House of

Representatives, devote a great deal of time (both their own and their staff's) to constituency service. These activities include such things as answering letters from constituents, welcoming and meeting with constituents when they visit Washington, and helping constituents deal with a rather cumbersome government bureaucracy. These activities help build loyalty to, or at the very least positive feelings toward, the incumbent.[10]

Second, members of Congress are able to influence government decisions about construction projects and other types of expenditures by the federal government. When such projects are to take place in the incumbent's district, he or she is quick to claim credit for these projects, since they involve an obvious economic benefit to the district. Engaging in "pork barrel politics," as the dividing up of government construction dollars is sometimes called, is a common device used by incumbents to increase their chances of re-election.[11]

Third, members of Congress grow increasingly adept at presenting themselves favorably to constituents, often at the expense of Congress. Each member develops his or her own "home style," emphasizing their concern for and responsiveness to his or her constituents.[12] Again, this generates positive evaluations of the incumbent on the part of constituents, such that they become more predisposed to vote for the incumbent at the next available opportunity.

A fourth possible explanation for incumbency advantage involves campaign expenditures. The amount of money available to incumbents to run for re-election is not only much greater than that available to challengers but has grown at a faster rate as well. In 1974, the average incumbent spent $56,539 on his or her campaign, 41 percent more than the $40,015 spent by the average challenger. In 1988, incumbents spent on average $378,316, which was 218 percent more than the average challenger expenditure of $118,877.[13] With such huge war chests, incumbents can not only overwhelm their challengers during a campaign but can discourage prospective challengers from even trying to compete for the seat at all.[14]

All of these factors add up to an extraordinary advantage for the incumbent member of Congress in seeking re-election. Constituency service, the pork barrel, the member's personal style, and the tremendous advantage with respect to campaign funding leads to greater name recognition and more positive evaluations. In short, incumbent members of Congress win re-election because they are better known, and more highly thought of, than their challengers.[15]

Finally, the incumbency advantage is so strong, it can even negate the impact of party identification on voting decisions in congressional elections. Mann and Wolfinger suggest that well over one half of all defections from one's party are to the incumbent.[16] Data from the 1988 National Election Study suggest an even stronger pull of incumbency. Of those Democrats who defected (that is, voted for the Republican candidate) in their vote for the House of Representatives, 87 percent voted for the incumbent running in that election. Of those Republicans who defected, almost all—96 percent—defected to the Democratic incumbent member of Congress. Incumbency, then, can help us understand why people abandon the relatively straightforward cue of partisanship in voting for members of Congress.

Congressional Elections: National or Local Events?

Since 1930 all off year, or midterm, congressional elections have resulted in the incumbent president's loss of party seats in Congress, especially in the House of Representatives. For example, from 1946 to 1982, the incumbent president's party lost, on average, about twenty-five seats in the House. The trend abated substantially in the 1980s; for example, in 1986 the Republicans lost but five seats in the House. But the overall pattern has sparked interest in accounting for the apparently unavoidable loss of seats by the president's party.

One answer provided by students of congressional elections is that these contests, especially those held at the midpoint of a president's term, are national events, in that they are determined primarily by national forces. In the absence of a national election, that is, for the presidency, voters use their congressional votes to express their sentiments concerning such national concerns as the economy, foreign affairs, the performance of the president, and so forth.[17] Congressional elections, in this view, are essentially national referenda on the performance of the national government, especially the presidency. The opposing argument is that congressional elections are local events, in that the outcomes are largely determined by local citizen concerns and evaluations of the incumbent and the challenger.

Most of our discussion has implicitly assumed that congressional elections are local events, in that we have emphasized the roles of party identification (of the voter and the candidates) and incumbency, which is a characteristic of one of the candidates. In turn, when we discuss citizens' behavior and evaluations, we will likewise focus on the candidates and voters and not national forces. In this section, however, we will discuss in some detail the argument that congressional elections, especially at midterm, are national referenda and we will present some empirical evidence from the 1988 NES relating to this thesis.

A classic statement of the argument that midterm elections are national events is Tufte's analysis of presidential party decline in midterm elections.[18] Edward Tufte argued that the president's party loses seats in the House in midterm elections due to changes in economic conditions and changes in the president's popularity. To the extent that both decline, the president's party loses seats. Given that one or the other, or both, almost always decline, the seat loss is easily explained.

Specifically, Tufte examined midterm elections from 1938 to 1970. In his empirical analysis, Tufte was able to account for over 90 percent of the variation in the loss of votes experienced by the president's party. Although the correspondence between the share of the vote received by a party and the number of seats in the House of Representatives won by that party is not exact, the model sufficiently accounts for the presidential party's seat loss in midterm elections. In turn, Tufte's argument and analysis clearly support the proposition that midterm elections are national referenda.

There is some evidence, however, that in the 1980s this role of midterm elections as referenda on the national political scene has diminished. Specifically, the Republican party should have lost far more seats in the House of Representatives in 1982 and 1986 than they actually did. For example, Tufte's model would predict a loss of about fifty-eight seats for the Republicans in 1982, when in actuality they lost only twenty-six seats—less than half of what was predicted.[19] According to Gary Jacobson and Samuel Kernell, the Republican party was able to offset some of the traditional loss at midterm through superior organizational and fundraising activities.[20]

Evidence from 1988

While the thesis that congressional elections are national events was designed to account for the outcomes of midterm elections, it may be instructive to examine some components of it in the context of the 1988 election. Respondents to the NES of that year were asked, among other things, for whom they voted for the House of Representatives; whether they approved or disapproved of the way Reagan had performed as president; and whether they felt the economy had done well or not in the past year. These questions can be used to assess the impact of presidential approval and perceptions of the economy on congressional voting.[21]

In Table 5-1 we present the relationship between assessments of Reagan's performance in office and whether people voted for the Democratic or Republican candidate for the House of Representatives. The top part of the table displays this relationship for all voters. Clearly, assessments of Reagan have a strong effect on congressional voting; 82 percent of those who disapproved of Reagan's performance voted for the Democratic House candidate, while only 44 percent of those who approved of Reagan voted for the Democratic candidate for Congress.

	Table 5-1

Congressional Voting and Approval of Reagan, 1988

All Voters		
Voted For	Approve	Disapprove
Democrat	44%	82%
Republican	56	18

Democrats Only		
Voted For	Approve	Disapprove
Democrat	79%	89%
Republican	21	11

Republicans Only		
Voted For	Approve	Disapprove
Democrat	28%	34%
Republican	72	66

Note: Approval was measured with the question, "Do you approve or disapprove of the way Ronald Reagan is handling his job as President?" "Voted for" indicates whether respondent chose the Democratic and Republican House candidate. **Source:** National Election Study, 1988.

One of the things about party identification that is relevant to the relationship just described is that it affects how people evaluate political figures and events, as well as serving as a guide to voting. Indeed, this appears to be operating in Table 5-1. If we look at just Democrats, and then Republicans, much of the impact of presidential approval on congressional vote choice disappears. For all voters, the difference in the proportions voting for the Democratic candidate between those who approve and disapprove of Reagan in 1988 is 38 percentage points. Among Democrats only, the difference drops to a mere 10 percentage points. Among Republicans, the difference is even less, only 6 percentage points. While evaluations of Reagan did somewhat affect how people decided between congressional candidates in 1988, it is clear that these evaluations were not nearly as strong as party identification in the minds of voters.

The same picture emerges when we examine the impact of perceptions of the economy on congressional voting. Table 5-2 presents the proportions voting for the Democratic and Republican House candidates by those who thought the economy over the past year had gotten better, stayed about the same, or had gotten worse. As in Table 5-1, we present the relationship for all voters and for Democrats and Republicans separately. Among all voters, the proportion of those who thought the economy had improved and who voted for the Democratic House candidate in their district was only 41 percent, while the support for the Democrat among those who thought the economy had gotten worse was 71 percent, a difference of 30 percentage points. Perceptions of the economy do appear to have a substantial impact on congressional voting.

| | | Table 5-2 |

Congressional Voting and Perceptions of the Economy, 1988

All Voters

Voted For	Better	Same	Worse
Democrat	41%	61%	71%
Republican	59	39	29

Democrats Only

Voted For	Better	Same	Worse
Democrat	80%	87%	87%
Republican	20	13	13

Republicans Only

Voted For	Better	Same	Worse
Democrat	26%	31%	30%
Republican	74	69	70

Note: Perceptions of the economy were measured with the question, "Would you say that over the past year the nation's economy has gotten better, stayed about the same, or gotten worse?"
Source: National Election Study, 1988.

As before, however, most of this effect is due to party identification. Among Democrats, the difference in support for the Democratic House candidate between those who felt the economy had gotten better and those who felt it had grown worse was only 7 percentage points. Among Republicans, the difference was negligible—only 4 percentage points. Again, party identification, not a national force such as the economy, predominated in congressional voting decisions.

While the evidence is certainly not conclusive, it is reasonable to suggest that elections for Congress, at least in 1988, are not primarily influenced by national forces. This suggests, in turn, that other forces affect how people vote in congressional elections. In the next section, we examine the impact of individual-level forces on congressional voting.

How Americans Vote in Congressional Elections

In the previous section we examined the broad contours of congressional elections, to describe the most important characteristics of these contests. In this section we turn to a discussion of the factors that influence whether, and how, individuals vote in elections for the House of Representatives. We begin our discussion of how well the model of voting described in *The American Voter* fits voting in congressional elections. We then turn to factors such as issues and incumbency, and conclude, as before, with evidence from the 1988 congressional elections.

The American Voter Model and Congressional Voting

Since 1958, national samples of prospective voters in congressional elections have been surveyed, using similar concepts and questions as those used in studying presidential elections. In the original study of 1958, just over 11 percent of all voters defected from their party identification if voting for members of Congress, compared to 21 percent in 1988.[22] Turnout was highest among those with strong partisan loyalties, and issues played little role in decisions concerning candidate choice. For example, respondents were asked whether they knew which political party controlled Congress, if they thought Congress was the most effective branch of the federal government, and whether domestic affairs had gone well or gone badly. It was also determined which party's candidate for Congress respondents supported. If domestic policy and government performance have any impact on voting, we would expect to find different rates of defection among partisans who felt things had gone badly while their own party controlled Congress and among partisans who felt things had gone well while the other party controlled Congress.

As the data in Table 5-3 show, only the latter expectation was met. Twenty-two percent of those who believed things had gone well while the other party controlled Congress defected in 1958 to the other party. Among those who thought things had gone badly, no real difference in defection rates existed between those whose party controlled, and did not control, Congress. Surprisingly, the defection rate among those who felt things had gone well while their own party controlled Congress (Cell I) was 16 percent, higher than for those who thought things had gone badly. It is difficult to argue that issues played much of a role in 1958 in voters' decisions when, according to these data, people were least likely to switch to the other party when things were going badly.

In 1958 the most powerful voting cue was party identification. Studies of that election indicate very low levels of information, such that the most common single piece of information held by voters was their party's candidate. If this was all they knew about the election and the candidates, voters defected at a rate of only 2 percent.[23] In the unlikely occurrence that the only piece

---

Table 5-3

Percentage of Party Identifiers Defecting in Their Vote for U.S. House of Representatives

Thought That Domestic Affairs	Thought That More Effective Branch of Government Was Controlled by	
	Own Party	Other Party
	I	II
Had gone well	16%	22%
	N = 43	N = 46
	III	IV
Had gone badly	14	13
	N = 152	N = 122

Source: Stokes, Donald E. and Warren E. Miller, "Party Government and the Saliency of Congress," *Public Opinion Quarterly,* (Winter, 1962): 531–46.

of information they held was the name of opposition party's candidate, the observed defection rate was 40 percent. Note that this means that 60 percent of these voters cast their ballots for someone whose *name they did not know*—the candidate of their party. Finally, as we noted previously defections were rather rare in 1958, a pattern that continued in later midterm elections.[24] While the defection rate in 1988 was almost double that observed in 1958 (21 percent versus 11 percent), the comparison is not totally valid, given the presence of presidential candidates in 1988, which were lacking in the 1958 midterm election.

Issue Voting in Congressional Elections

Early efforts to detect the impact of issues on congressional vote choices were rather unsophisticated, and one might suspect that the reason these efforts were unsuccessful was the naive procedures used. For example, issue voting is generally conceived as voting for the candidate closest to one on the issues, a concept that is measured easily through the use of seven-point issue scales. But later attempts to discover a link between issue positions and votes for congressional candidates, some of which relied on seven-point issue scales, were only partially successful. In fact, respondents were not even given the opportunity in the 1988 NES to place candidates for the House of Representatives on seven-point scales, perhaps because of this lack of success.

Apparently the basic problem is not with the techniques used to measure issue voting but with citizens themselves. Specifically, the available evidence suggests that citizens have little interest in congressional elections, especially when it comes to discovering the issue positions of the candidates. The data in Table 5-4 are ample demonstration of this proposition. In this table, "Vietnam" refers to a scale whose endpoints represent the positions of immediate withdrawal and winning at any cost. The other two scales, "Welfare" and "Liberalism/Conservatism," have standard liberal and conservative endpoints. Even on so salient and divisive an issue as the Vietnam War, no more than 40 percent of the respondents could venture an opinion as to the candidates' positions on the issue. In the absence of such basic information, issue voting in congressional elections is impossible for large segments of the electorate.

Evidence from the 1978 National Election Study also casts doubt on the ability of the electorate to engage in issue voting in congressional elections. In their analysis of data from this study, Hurley and Hill confined their attention to those issues the respondents identified as important and determined what proportion of respondents could assign a position to the incumbent member of Congress. On the issue of the federal government guaranteeing women's

Table 5-4

Percentage Answering "Don't Know" When Asked to Place Candidates and Parties in 1972

	Self	Party		Presidential Candidates		Congressional Candidates	
		Dem.	Rep.	Dem.	Rep.	Dem.	Rep.
Vietnam	4	12	11	10	9	59	60
Welfare	3	16	14	13	11	60	59
Liberalism/ Conservatism	7	17	16	18	17	58	56

Note: Percentage who could not place on a seven-point issue scale in a Wisconsin sample of 841 prior to 1972 elections.
Source: Hinckley, Barbara, "Issues, Information Costs, and Congressional Elections," *American Politics Quarterly,* (April, 1976): 131–52.

rights, only 45 percent could assign a position to the incumbent, and only 15 percent could do so for the challenger. Also, of those who did offer an opinion of the incumbent's position, only 40 percent named a position consistent with how the Representative had actually voted on a roll call vote.[25] Again, issue voting cannot be expected under these circumstances.

Invisible Opponents?

In our earlier discussion of incumbency we noted that, on balance, incumbents enjoy overwhelming rates of re-election because they are better known, and better liked, than their challengers. The data in Table 5-5, taken from the 1988 NES, demonstrate this point, especially for elections for the House of Representatives. In this table, to "recall" a name is to volunteer it in response to a question; to "recognize" is to pick the name from a list provided by the interviewer. Note that only 10 percent of respondents could recall the name of the challenger in House elections, and less than two thirds (58 percent) could even recognize the name. On the other hand, 90 percent of the respondents could recognize the incumbent's name. Incumbent Senators enjoy a similar, although not as dramatic, advantage over their challengers. Incumbents win because to many citizens their challengers are invisible.

Table 5-5

Recall and Recognition of Candidates in 1988

	House Incumb.	House Chall.	Senate Incumb.	Senate Chall.	House Open	Senate Open	Senator Not Up for Elect.
Percent recalling	26	10	35	23	25	34	22
Percent recognizing	90	58	95	80	79	88	92

Source: Alford, John R. and John R. Hibbing, "The Disparate Electoral Security of House and Senate Incumbents," a paper presented at the Annual Meetings of the American Political Science Association, 1989. National Election Studies data, 1988.

Evidence from the 1988 Elections

In this final section we present some findings of relevance to our previous discussions of congressional elections, based on data from the 1988 National Election Study. We begin with Table 5-6, which presents some descriptive characteristics of the 1988 congressional elections.

Several of the items in Table 5-6 are self-explanatory or have been previously discussed, but some bear examination. First, as in most surveys, the reported turnout rate of 62 percent is highly inflated, and need not concern us further, although we shall return shortly to the topic of turnout. With respect to vote choice, substantial majorities reported voting for the Democratic candidate, and for the incumbent, which is expected given the outcome of the election. In fact, over one half (54 percent) of all votes were cast for Democratic incumbents. Note also that almost twice as many respondents reported voting for the Republican challenger than for the Democratic challenger; this result most likely can be attributed to the greater number of Republican challengers for whom to vote.

The data indicate that incumbent members of Congress are held in higher esteem than is Congress as an institution, with approval ratings of 66 percent and 52 percent, respectively. It is surprising that a lower proportion of respondents rated the incumbent than rated Congress; 28 percent could not assess the performance of the incumbent, while only 14 percent could not rate Con-

Table 5-6

Characteristics of Congressional Voting and Evaluation, 1988

Percentage Who:	
Voted	62
Voted for the Democratic candidate +	59
Voted for the incumbent +	83
Defected from partisanship +	21
Approved of the incumbent	66
Could not rate the incumbent	28
Approved of Congress	52
Could not rate Congress	14
Voted for the Democratic incumbent +	54
Voted for the Democratic challenger +	6
Voted for the Republican incumbent +	29
Voted for the Republican challenger +	11
Were contacted by the incumbent	79

Note: The approval questions were: "In general, do you approve or disapprove of the way Representative _____ has been handling (his/her) job?" and "In general, do you approve or disapprove of the way the U.S. Congress has been handling its job?"
+ Proportion of those who reported voting. Proportion is those of the two-party vote.
Source: National Election Study, 1988. All data are self-reports.

gress. If we eliminate from consideration those who did not offer an assessment of the incumbent, or Congress, the approval ratings jump to 92 percent for incumbents, but only 60 percent for Congress, a quite substantial difference. The fact that 79 percent of all respondents reported having been contacted in some way by their Representative may help explain this high level of incumbent approval, as well as the gap betwen the personal and institutional ratings.

Table 5-7 shows the reported turnout rates for various subgroups within the 1988 NES sample. Most of the findings are fully consistent with those presented in the context of presidential turnout. For instance, we find that as strength of partisanship, education, and interest in the campaign all increase, so, too, does the likelihood of an individual voting in the House of Representatives election. In turn, the difference in turnout between males and females is quite

Table 5-7

Correlates of Congressional Election Turnout, 1988

Group	Percentage Voting
Strong partisans	76
Weak partisans	60
Independent leaners	58
Independents	41
Male	64
Female	60
Less than high school	43
High school	56
Some college	69
College	83
Incumbent contact	70
No incumbent contact	30
High interest	82
Low interest	53
Black	49
White	65

Source: National Election Study, 1988. Entries are proportions of groups who reported voting.

small, while the difference in turnout between blacks and whites is more substantial.

The one finding with respect to turnout that is unique to congressional elections is the impact of incumbent contact on reported turnout. Citizens can be contacted in a variety of ways — in person, through a personal letter, through a mass mailing newsletter, and so forth. Regardless of the type of contact, those whose Representative has been in touch with them are far more likely to vote — 40 percentage points more likely — than are those who have not been contacted. At least one activity of members of Congress that is related to their own self-interest, that is, getting re-elected, also apparently serves democracy, in that it stimulates voter turnout.

Tables 5-8 and 5-9 represent factors associated with vote choice. We have noted that the two most important determinants of vote choice in congressional elections are partisanship and whether one of the candidates is an incumbent. The data in Table 5-8 are not surprising, in that they indicate that the more closely one identifies with the Democratic party, the more likely one is to have

Table 5-8

Party Identification and Congressional Voting, 1988

Party Identification	Percentage Voting for Democratic Candidate
Strong Democrat	88
Weak Democrat	82
Independent/Leaning Democrat	87
Independent	67
Independent/Leaning Republican	36
Weak Republican	30
Strong Republican	23

Source: National Election Study, 1988. All proportions are of two-party vote.

reported voting for the Democratic candidate for the House of Representatives. The converse is also true: the greater the affinity for the Republican party, the greater the likelihood of voting for that party's House candidate.

Of greater interest, perhaps, are the data presented in Table 5-9. Here, we present several correlates of voting for the incumbent in congressional elections. The percentage entries in the table are the proportions of those individuals who voted for the incumbent. For example, 90 percent of those who approved of how the incumbent was handling the job reported having voted for the incumbent, as opposed to only 31 percent of those who disapproved. This result is not terribly surprising. Note, however, that approval of Congress as an institution has virtually no impact on incumbent support. Voters apparently evaluate the person, not the institution, when deciding how to vote in congressional elections. And, as we have seen, people like the incumbent.

This raises the question of the joint impact of ratings of the incumbent and Congress on decisions to vote for the incumbent. The last four rows in Table 5-9 address this question. Note that those approving of both the incumbent and Congress vote for the incumbent at a rate of 92 percent, only two percentage points higher than the rate for those approving of the incumbent, irrespective of the rating of Congress. And, if respondents approved of the incumbent, but *disapproved* of Congress as an institution, the support for the incumbent drops only 4 percentage points, to 86 percent. When respondents disapprove of the incumbent, however, the voting rate drops to around 30 percent, depending on whether the Congress is viewed as having done a good job. Clearly, in deciding whether to vote for the incumbent, the voter's view of Congress as an institution is virtually irrelevant.

| Table 5-9 |

Incumbent Support, 1988

Group	Support (Percentage Points)
Approved of incumbent	90
Disapproved of incumbent	31
Approved of Congress	88
Disapproved of Congress	76
Contacted by incumbent	84
Not contacted by incumbent	77
Approved of incumbent and Congress	92
Approved of incumbent, but not Congress	86
Disapproved of incumbent, approved of Congress	31
Disapproved of incumbent and Congress	28

Source: National Election Study, 1988. Entries are proportions of groups who voted for the incumbent, if running.

Finally, note that whether or not the voter was contacted by the incumbent had little effect on whether the voter supported him or her. This may be surprising, until one takes into account the proportion of voters who supported the incumbent, 83 percent and the proportion of all respondents who were contacted by the incumbent, 79 percent. Given these overwhelming majorities, it is hardly surprising to find that incumbent contacts only marginally increase support for the incumbent.

Conclusion

Earlier in this chapter we presented four questions concerning the forces that impact the outcomes of congressional elections, as well as the voting decisions made by citizens. Let us summarize our findings with respect to these questions.

Question #1: To what extent are the outcomes of congressional elections the result of *national* forces, such as the state of the economy, as opposed to *local* forces, such as candidate and voter characteristics?

The evidence prior to 1980 suggests that congressional elections, especially midterm elections, were influenced primarily by national forces, specifically the incumbent president's popularity and the state of the economy. Since 1980, however, this explanation has weakened considerably due, perhaps, to the superior organizational and fundraising abilities of the Republican party. In turn, we examined the impact of approval of Reagan, and the way voters viewed the economy, on congressional vote choices. We found that most of the impact of presidential approval and perceptions of the economy on vote choices were due primarily to party identification, in that Democrats viewed Reagan with disapproval, and saw the economy as not doing well, and voted for the Democratic candidate. We would conclude that national forces do have some impact, although in 1988 the outcome of the congressional elections was determined largely by local forces, that is, characteristics of the candidates and voters.

Question #2: To what extent is voting in congressional elections a function of the same forces affecting presidential voting, specifically, party identification, issues of public policy, and the candidates' personal characteristics?

Party identification is probably the most important determinant of vote choices in presidential elections, and is likewise of paramount importance (along with incumbency) in congressional elections. While evidence exists of the role of issues in presidential elections, little evidence of policy voting in congressional elections exists, largely because citizens are unaware of the issue positions of the candidates. Personal characteristics of presidential candidates also affect vote choices, but in congressional elections, the impact is much less, again because so little is known about the candidates, especially the challenger.

Question #3: To what extent does the advantage of incumbents in congressional elections supercede the impact of party identification, issues, and the like?

By far the most important factor affecting congressional voting is whether an incumbent is running. If so, he or she will almost always be re-elected. The incumbency factor supercedes party identification, in that almost all partisan defectors, that is, those who vote for the opposition party's candidate, vote for an incumbent. Given that incumbency appears to be more important than party identification, and the latter is more important than any other factor, it follows that incumbency also supercedes issue concerns, personal characteristics of the candidates, and the like.

Question #4: To what extent are congressional elections competitive? Have they grown more or less competitive over time? What are the factors that might account for the rise or fall in competitiveness?

Over the years, congressional elections have declined in competitiveness. The average victory margin has increased, as shown by the decreasing number of marginal elections—those in which the winner captures less than 55 percent of the vote. In turn, this trend appears linked to the increase in the re-election advantage of incumbents, and much of the decline in competitiveness can be attributed to the same factors that contribute to the incumbent's electoral advantage: constituency service, the incumbent's "home style," pork barrel politics, and the tremendous advantage of incumbents with respect to campaign finances. The advantage of incumbents is so great, and elections involving an incumbent are so little in doubt, that incumbent members of Congress, especially members of the House of Representatives, might as well be running against "invisible opponents."

Discussion

Given that the Congress, especially the House of Representatives, is the "representative" body of the federal government, as well as an equal partner with the president in the formulation of public policy, it is appropriate to conclude this chapter by considering the implications of the findings presented here for Congress as an institution. We shall briefly examine two functions of Congress: as an institution which represents the policy preferences of citizens and as an institution which acts as a counterbalance to the power of the presidency.

In the original Constitution, the House of Representatives was to be the "representative" body of the federal government, in that it was the only body to be elected directly by the citizenry.[26] In turn, it is clear that at least one of the functions of the House was to represent the interests of citizens in the formation of public policy. The purpose of this, according to Madison in *The Federalist* Number Ten, was "to refine and enlarge the public views, by passing them through the medium of a chosen body of citizens . . ."[27] By "public views," Madison meant the selfish interests of citizens; citizens would incorporate these views in their vote choices, and elected Representatives would "refine" these views into the best possible public policy.

This process depends, of course, on citizens voting on the basis of policy concerns. But in contemporary congressional elections, this does not happen. Voters cannot, with any consistency, attribute to incumbents' policy positions and have virtually no ability to express the views of challengers. If citizens do not know the policy positions of the candidates, they cannot vote on the basis of policy. Rather, they vote for the incumbent, or the candidate of their party (unless the incumbent is of the other party, in which case citizens usually defect). We must conclude that the Congress, especially the House of Representatives, does not function as Madison hoped it would, to represent the policy views of constituents in the policy making process.

We have noted substantial evidence of the existence of partisan defection, one of the results of which is split outcomes. In turn, one of the results of split outcomes, at least in contemporary American politics, is control of the Congress by the Democratic party, and control of the presidency by the Republican party. We would argue that this result is perfectly consistent with the doctrine of separation of powers, which divides governmental authority between co-equal branches of government.

One important aspect of the separation of powers is that the two elected branches of government, the Congress and the presidency, are given different constituencies, that is, they are elected by, and therefore responsible to, different groups of people. If two groups of elected officials must be elected by different groups of people, they must make different appeals to these groups. As a consequence, they would be much less likely to act together to thwart the will of the people.

The purpose of this whole scheme of separation of powers, according to Madison, in *The Federalist* Number 47, was to prevent tyranny, which he defined as "the accumulation of all powers, legislative, executive, and judiciary, in the same hands, whether of one, a few, or many. . . ."[28] We would argue that the scheme works well. Not only are the powers of the federal government divided between three branches, but the two elected branches are controlled by different parties. And, in the absence of some future events that would radically change the party system in this country, this is likely to continue. If nothing else, the forces that shape the outcomes of congressional elections in the late twentieth century contribute to the prevention of tyranny by the federal government.

What we have, then, is a trade-off between policy representation and the control of tyranny. There is no logical reason congressional elections, and for that matter presidential elections, could not be decided by policy concerns and split results to occur as well. But that is not what happens. Members of Congress, especially the House of Representatives, do not represent the policy views of constituents. On the other hand, the Congress and the presidency are usually controlled by different parties, thus preventing the Madisonian version of tyranny. We would not presume to suggest that the trade-off is worthwhile, only that citizens should be aware of it and to decide for themselves. We hope this chapter will have cause the reader to do just that.

Notes

1.   The accuracy of this estimate of the eligible voting population has been the target of a substantial amount of criticism. In many other countries registration procedures require that *all* eligible individuals be registered; there is, therefore, no "estimate" of the eligible electorate needed. In the United States, those in prison, in mental institutions and legal

aliens are included in the estimate of eligible voters, although they cannot vote (except for legal aliens in some states), while illegal aliens are excluded from the estimate, even though in some states they can vote.

2. Ornstein, Norman J., Thomas E. Mann, and Michael J. Malbin, *Vital Statistics on Congress, 1989–1990* (Washington: American Enterprise Institute, 1990), p. 59.

3. *Ibid.*, p. 62.

4. This increase is about 28 percent. See Ornstein, et al., p. 65.

5. Eubank, Robert B., "Incumbent Effects on Individual-Level Voting Behavior in Congressional Elections: A Decade of Exaggeration," *Journal of Politics*, (August, 1985); 58–67.

6. Mayhew, David, "Congressional Elections: The Case of the Vanishing Marginals," *Polity*, (Spring, 1974): 295–317.

7. *Statistical Abstract of the United States, 1989* (Washington: Census Bureau, 1989), p. 249.

8. Ornstein, *et al.*, p. 56.

9. *Ibid.*, p. 57.

10. Fiorina, Morris, "The Case of the Vanishing Marginals: The Bureaucracy Did It," *American Political Science Review*, (March, 1977): 177–81.

11. Mayhew, David, *Congress: The Electoral Connection* (New Haven: Yale University Press, 1974).

12. Fenno, Richard, *Home Style* (Boston: Little, Brown, 1978).

13. Jacobson, Gary C., *Money in Congressional Elections* (New Haven: Yale University Press, 1980); and Jacobson, Gary C., *The Politics of Congressional Elections* (Boston: Little, Brown, 1987).

14. Goldenberg, Edie N., and Michael W. Traugott, *Campaigning for Congress* (Washington: CQ Press, 1984), pp. 92–95; and, Bond, Jon R., Cary Covington, and Richard Fleisher, "Explaining Challenger Quality in Congressional Elections," *Journal of Politics*, (May, 1985): 510–29.

15. Mann, Thomas E., and Raymond E. Wolfinger, "Candidates and Parties in Congressional Elections," in *Controversies in Voting Behavior*, eds. Richard G. Niemi and Herbert F. Weisberg second ed. (Washington: CQ Press, 1984): pp. 269–91.

16. *Ibid.*, pp. 272–75.

17. See Niemi and Weisberg, pp. 199–203.

18. Tufte, Edward R., "Determinants of the Outcomes of Midterm Congressional Elections," *American Political Science Review*, (September, 1975): 812–26. See also Kernell, Samuel, "Presidential Popularity and

Negative Voting: An Alternative Explanation of the Midterm Congressional Decline of the President's Party," *American Political Sciennce Review*, (March, 1977): 44–65.

19. Jacobson, Gary C., and Samuel Kernell, "Strategy and Choice in the 1982 Congressional Elections," in *Controversies in Voting Behavior*, second ed., eds. Richard G. Niemi and Herbert F. Weisberg (Washington: CQ Press, 1984): pp. 239–50.

20. *Ibid.*, pp. 244–46.

21. Using these questions is an indirect test, at best, of Tufte's model. Tufte was interested in the share of the vote received nationwide by the president's party, not how individuals vote. In turn, to measure economic performance, Tufte used changes in real disposable income per capita, not perceptions of how the economy is doing. Still, the results prove interesting, in that little support for Tufte's thesis is found at the individual level.

22. Stokes, Donald E., and Warren E. Miller, "Party Government and the Saliency of Congress," *Public Opinion Quarterly*, (Winter, 1962): 531–46.

23. *Ibid.*, p. 541.

24. Freedman, Stanley R., "Salience of Party and Candidate in Congressional Elections: A Comparison of 1958 and 1970," in *Public Opinion and Public Policy*, third ed., ed. Norman R. Luttbeg (Itasca, IL: Peacock, 1981), pp. 118–22.

25. Hurley, Patricia A., and Kim Quaile Hill, "The Prospects for Issue Voting in Contemporary Congressional Elections: An Assessment of Citizen Awareness and Representation," in *Public Opinion and Public Policy*, third ed., ed. Norman R. Luttbeg (Itasca, IL: Peacock, 1981), pp. 163–77.

26. Under the terms of the original Constitution, Senators were selected by state legislatures, not through popular vote. Of course, the president is technically chosen by the Electoral College, although seldom has the popular vote and the Electoral College vote differed.

27. Madison, James, *"The Federalist* Number 10," in *The Federalist Papers*, ed. Andrew Hacker (New York: Washington Square Press), p. 21.

28. Madison, James, *"The Federalist* Number 47," in *The Federalist Papers*, ed. Andrew Hacker (New York: Washington Square Press), pp. 103–04.

6

The Meaning of Change

in American Electoral Behavior

As we reflect on trends in American electoral behavior, it is clear that the electorate of the 1980s is different from those studied in the 1940s and 1950s. There are fewer ardent partisans now than then. Issues play a more important role in voters' evaluations of candidates. Americans are increasingly inclined to avoid the polls on election days, and while not as pervasive as in the 1970s, distrust and alienation are still substantially higher than in the 1950s and 1960s. With respect to congressional elections, the incumbency advantage is stronger than ever.

But despite the obvious fact that the electorate has changed in some regards, we have cautioned throughout this book that the magnitude of change in these trends should not be exaggerated. We are a different electorate today but not greatly different in most respects.

The Pattern of Change in the Electorate

Despite the absence of sweeping change in American electoral behavior, some political scientists persist in their concern about many of the trends we have examined in this book. As we have noted, this concern stems from a belief that certain trends may be the harbinger of an era of social and political upheaval. A rather substantial body of political theory supports this belief by arguing, for example, that a government cannot remain stable without the trust and confidence of its citizens. Furthermore, professional interest in the patterns of change in American electoral behavior points to possible interrelationships between several trends, interrelationships that might accelerate or render

179

irreversible the most feared trends. In this book we have examined interrelationships among five of these trends in an effort to determine whether they individually or collectively merit our continued concern. We have analyzed the following trends:

1. Declining partisanship
2. Increased defection from party voting
3. Increased concern with issues
4. Declining voter turnout
5. Increasing political distrust and alienation

Our reasons for examining relationships among these trends are several. If declining turnout, increased defection, increased independency, and declining trust are the common result of a frustrated electorate that is not satisfied with the alternatives afforded by the major political parties, we cannot be optimistic about America's future. Some voters may become receptive to demagogues offering quick solutions to our nation's problems. Others could come to violate the laws and norms of our society as their disenchantment grows.

If there is an ever-increasing number of Americans impatient with government's failure to adopt certain solutions to the problems faced by our society, and if this impatience makes them less disposed to accept government policy decisions, government may be burdened with higher costs to gain public compliance. Furthermore, these citizens may become receptive to substantial changes in the political process that could disrupt the stability we have enjoyed for over 200 years. Such voters, for example, may press to make political parties illegal or circumscribe sharply what government can do by supporting legislation like California's tax-cutting Proposition 13.

This book has sought to determine whether there is evidence of a substantial group of issue oriented, less partisan, distrusting citizens refusing to participate in the existing political process. Our analysis has turned on an assessment of the five changes in the electorate noted above and their possible interrelation. We have used what we think are the best measures available, National Election Studies survey questions asked in conjunction with each presidential election since 1952. We think each group of questions straightforwardly and validly assesses relevant attributes of the electorate.

The importance of using identical measures to assess trends and change cannot be overstated. As some of the studies cited herein have demonstrated, different data can result in different conclusions. Had we used different questions in different years, the wording of the questions, instead of actual changes, could very well have produced the results we would have observed. Certainly, even minor changes in the wording of survey questions can alter the response patterns of respondents.

We have measured partisanship and independence from political parties with survey questions in which respondents were asked to express their willingness to identify with a political party or even to admit leaning toward one. Defection was measured by simply comparing survey respondents' votes with their political party identification; defectors do not vote for the candidates of their party. Issue voting was appraised by survey respondents' statements about what would cause them to vote for or against the major political parties' presidential candidates. We have demonstrated that the candidate evaluations of some people reflect more concern with issues and ideology, causing us to label them ideological or issue oriented evaluators. Others' judgments are less sophisticated. We have called these voters group-benefit, partisan, image, or no-content evaluators based on their particular responses to the candidates. Voting has been measured by self-reports of respondents. And finally, political alienation has been measured by two survey questions that assess beliefs about individual influence on government and perceptions of the responsiveness of public officials.

These measures confirm many of the trends, although there have been some discontinuities and even reversals in certain trends. Independents have become more numerous, comprising 11 percent of the electorate in 1988 versus 5 percent in 1952, and 8 percent in 1956. Alienation has also increased, with 36 percent of the SRC/CPS sample classified as alienated in 1976 versus 20 percent in 1952. The trend reversed in 1980, however, when only 26 percent of those interviewed could be classified as alienated, and the percentage has remained at this level since. The quality of candidate evaluations has changed, too. Low quality evaluations based solely on candidate image have declined from 62 percent in 1952 to only 8 percent in 1984, with a small increase noted in 1988. Issue oriented evaluations and defection have fluctuated over the last ten elections. Voting turnout has dropped in a steady fashion since 1960, but we observed that current turnout levels are not much worse than those which occurred in the 1940s and 1950s.

Our analysis of the interrelationships among the five trend variables yields little support for concern that they are related and comprise a potential danger for our society. The quality of a respondent's candidate evaluations does relate to participation and to alienation, but not in a way consistent with what we might expect. Instead of the issue oriented evaluators being less participant and more alienated, it is the no-content evaluators that prove distinctive. Typically, less than half of those saying nothing in evaluating presidential candidates vote in presidential contests. No-content evaluators also have been consistently the most alienated group of citizens.

The quality of the electorate's evaluation of presidential candidates is often at the root of explanations of how the trends in participation, partisan voting, and alienation are related. This explanation does not appear to be adequate because while improvements in candidate evaluations can be noted, relationships with participation, partisan voting, and alienation are weak or nonexistent. The pattern of relationships we have found is compatible with the depiction in *The American Voter* of those marginally involved in politics as being uninformed, nonparticipant, and least likely to identify strongly with a political party or to vote consistently with party identification.

While independents did not prove to be distinctive in terms of candidate evaluations, they are somewhat more numerous in contemporary society and less likely to vote than before. In 1952 only 6 percent of all nonvoters were independents, but in 1988 they comprised 17 percent. But independents prove to be no more alienated than either strong or weak partisans. Issues are no more pivotal to the candidate assessments of independents than they are to those of partisans, and the declining participation of independents is unrelated to their greater alienation. So neither issue orientation nor alienation accounts for the declining participation of independents.

By defining the alienated as those respondents believing that "officials do not care what people like me think," and that they personally have "no say in what government does," we found some ties with other political behavior but no consistent patterns. Based on 1988 data that compare alienated and nonalienated Americans, the alienated are less likely to vote for president but are slightly less likely to defect from the political party with which they identify to vote for the opposition party's candidate. Further, alienation is not related to issue or ideological evaluation of a candidate or to independency.

Thus we end up with three clusters of atypical types of citizens: (1) those who have nothing to say when evaluating the candidates, who consistently fail to participate, and who are alienated, (2) the increasingly nonparticipant independents, and (3) the alienated who are consistently less participant and more likely to defect. Each of these groups is a minority when contrasted with the largest group of citizens—the trusting, partisan voters.

Other Changes in the Electorate

Two other changes can be noted in the American electorate since the 1950s, in addition to the trends discussed previously. Both of these changes involve significant demographic changes in the electorate. First, Americans are increasingly better educated. Census Bureau figures indicate that the median school years completed for the adult population (twenty-five years of age and older) increased from 10.6 years in 1960 to 12.5 in 1980. There has been an even greater increase in the percentage of the population attending college. In 1960, only 16 percent of the adult population had completed one year or more of college. By 1988, nearly 40 percent had completed one or more years of college. Thus, the exposure of the electorate to college has more than doubled in just two decades.

Second, changes in the birth rate since 1940 have had and will continue to have an impact on the age distribution of the electorate. The first major change in the birth rate occurred after World War II when veterans, in particular, married in extraordinary numbers and produced what is now known as the "baby boom" generation. Great numbers of these post-World War II babies became eighteen during the 1970s. Their entrance into the electorate was hastened by the Twenty-sixth Amendment to the U.S. Constitution, enacted in 1971, which lowered the minimum voting age from twenty-one to eighteen years of age. The net result of these events was a lowering of the median age of the electorate. The baby boom cohort will continue to influence the age distribution of the electorate by increasing the median age as its members pass into their middle and elderly years. This is because the birth rate has dropped almost every year since 1960, meaning new voters will comprise a smaller and smaller percentage of the electorate for several years to come, while the baby boom generation will comprise a larger and larger percentage.

Why are these demographic trends—increased education and a declining birth rate—so important? They are important because education and age are possibly related to some of the other major trends we have discussed. What is confusing, however, is that some political attitudes and behaviors have not moved in the direction that we would expect, given the simultaneous changes in demographics. Changes in voter turnout illustrate this puzzle. As we have observed, turnout has declined steadily since the early 1960s. The change in turnout is perfectly consistent with the change in the age distribution of the electorate. Young citizens vote less frequently than their elders, and given that young people have made up an increasingly greater percentage of the voting age population since 1960, we would expect turnout to decline. Educated citizens, however, are more likely to vote than the less educated; as we have a better educated populace now, turnout should have increased. But it has not, constituting a rather intriguing puzzle.

In order to assess the relationship between these two demographic trends and the other trends analyzed in this book, we have divided age and education into three and four categories, respectively. The analysis of age divides the population into three groups: those eighteen to twenty-nine years of age in 1988, those thirty to forty-nine, and those fifty and over. The analysis of education divides persons into four categories: less than high school education, high school, some college, and college degree or more.

Our analysis of data collected in 1988 confirms much that we learned in previous elections about the relationships between these demographic variables and electoral behavior. In 1988, those between eighteen and twenty-nine years of age constituted only 22 percent of the electorate but represented 29 percent of all "pure" independents, 26 percent of leaning independents, and 35 percent of nonvoters. The relationship is strongest between age and nonvoting as 49 percent of respondents between eighteen and twenty-nine reported not voting in 1988, compared with about 30 percent for the CPS sample as a whole. When one combines the impact of youth and nonpartisanship, the effect on abstention is heightened: only 26 percent of young (eighteen to twenty-nine years old) independents reported voting in 1988.

Our youngest category of potential voters, those between eighteen and twenty-nine years of age, also proved modestly different than other age groups on other measures in 1988. While 55 percent of this group gave issue based or ideological evaluations of the presidential candidates, as compared to 58 percent of those between 30 and 49 years old, and 52 percent of the oldest members of the electorate, the youngest voters led all age groups in having nothing to say about the candidates (23 percent no-content, versus 14 percent of the middle-aged group and 12 percent of the oldest segment). The youngest age cohort is the most likely to defect from partisan voting but is less likely to be alienated than those over 30 years of age.

Our analysis of the relationship between education and electoral behavior suggests that all but one of the trends we have discussed have been affected by the increased education of the electorate. The lone exception is the trend in partisan defection. We find that in 1988 the educated tended to be slightly more partisan, equally likely to defect, considerably more likely to have reported voting, less alienated, and more likely to use issues and ideology in evaluating candidates. Persons in the college-educated sector of society are less likely to call themselves independents (6 percent among the college educated versus 12 percent among others). Thus, without increasing education, independents would be slightly more common.

The impact of education on partisan defection at the ballot box reveals very little difference in defection rates among the various education categories. Differences were apparent for political alienation, however, as only 20 percent of those with some college education were alienated in 1988 compared with 33 percent of the other respondents. It seems that political alienation would be less common if the public were better educated. In truth, however, education can scarcely account for the changes in alienation, inasmuch as the educational level of Americans has not changed to the same degree, nor in the same fashion, as has alienation over the last three decades.

The college educated are also more likely to have reported voting; 85 percent of the college educated voted in 1988, compared with 58 percent of those with less education. Thus the decline in turnout has been retarded by education. Finally, education has affected candidate evaluations. In their evaluations of Bush and Dukakis, the college educated were clearly more likely to use ideology and issues than were those with no college education. Twenty-eight percent of the less-than-high-school education category used image or no-content evaluations of Bush and Dukakis, compared to 17 percent of those with at least one year of college. Thus, at least some of the increase in issue oriented evaluations noted earlier can be explained by the improving education of the American electorate.

In conclusion, we can say that education has *inhibited* certain politically relevant changes in American society. Were American society to be no better educated today than was the case in the 1950s, participation and partisanship would probably be lower, and alienation and image oriented evaluations of political candidates would be more common.

Conclusion

At this point it is fair to ask whether any substantial conclusions can be noted about the changes in the American electorate. We believe that four conclusions are justified. The first conclusion is that, overall, stability rather than change best characterizes the American electorate over the period 1952–1988. While the American electorate is changing, for example becoming more likely to evaluate presidential candidates in terms of issues, this evolution is quite gradual at best and erratic and patternless at worst. In many ways the 1988 election was more like elections in the 1950s than any election in the interim. If one were forced to pick between the polar adjectives, *changed* and *unchanged*, the electorate seems unchanged.

This lack of change is most apparent in the impact of partisanship on voting: party identification remains highly predictive as to how people will vote. While the number of independents has more than doubled since 1952, 89 percent of the electorate still identifies with a political party, and 85 percent of these voted for their party's nominee in 1988, rather than defecting. Thus, at least three quarters of all votes for major party candidates for president in 1988 can be explained by partisanship in the electorate, whatever the source of partisanship might be.

The impact of party identification on voting in congressional elections is attenuated somewhat by the effects of incumbency. Higher rates of partisan defection are observed in elections for the House of Representatives than for the presidency, with most defectors voting for the incumbent. This helps us understand why the Democratic party has such a strong hold on the House. Republicans are loyal in presidential voting but often vote for the incumbent in House contests. Given that the incumbent is most likely to be a Democrat, partisan defection and continued Democratic control of the House of Representatives result.

Second, even today there remains a very substantial minority of persons so peripherally involved in politics that even the noisy trappings of the presidential campaign gives them nothing to say about the candidates. Such persons also typically fail to vote. It is far more common today, as it was in the 1950s, for nonvoters to be passive bystanders of the political scene rather than zealous proponents or opponents of policy who failed to find a choice among the presidential candidates. Nonparticipant bystanders, rather than nonparticipant zealots, while equally unfortunate for the goal of participatory democracy, are probably less threatening to the smooth performance of democracy.

Third, verbal assurances of trust for the political system and officials within it, which were common in the 1950s, do not appear as essential as suggested by David Easton and others. We have seen substantial distrust and alienation in the 1970s and 1980s among voters and nonvoters, defectors and partisan loyalists, issue evaluators and those unable to articulate any candidate attributes, and among independents and strong partisans. However, the alienated are much less likely to vote than are the non-alienated, suggesting that the increase in disaffection since 1964 has partially contributed to the decline in voter participation.

Fourth and finally, the forces affecting the electorate over time are not as simple as some theories would suggest. It is not sufficient to tie trends together, based on perceptions of an increasingly issue oriented electorate that sees little choice among the major political parties and is therefore rebelling into independency, nonvoting, and alienation. No doubt there are Americans who do follow this dynamic pattern, but our analysis suggests this simple theory does not account for the patterns of stability and change that are most notable within the electorate.

Despite these conclusions, there have been limits to our analyses. In our assessment of trends in the American electorate, we have used data from large national samples. This has necessarily meant that we are assessing the impact of national trends rather than more limited regional patterns of change. We have also limited our primary analysis to patterns of presidential and congressional voting. There is no systematic assessment of statewide elected office voting comparable to the National Election Studies we have used here. There is research, which must still be judged as tentative, that suggests that state- and local-level voting differ somewhat from the patterns found here.

It is beyond the scope of our effort to deal with these differences. The reader should be aware, however, that media coverage, public familiarity with the candidates, and participation are all less in such subnational elections. In most respects, presidential voting affords the electorate the greatest opportunity for obtaining information on the candidates and issues associated with an election. This greater, more dynamic, flow of information in presidential campaigns would seem to foretell greater change in future presidential elections than subnational contests.

Similarly, the reader should note that our assessment is limited to ten presidential elections. We cannot say with confidence which outcomes were the result of long-term changes in the behavior of the electorate and which were the one-of-a-kind results of unique combinations of presidential candidates. If we had data on many more presidential elections, we might be able to say something definitive about what happens when Democrats nominate a Southerner and the Republicans a Midwesterner, or when the Democrats nominate a liberal candidate rather than a moderate, or when Republicans nominate a conservative. Many of our figures show erratic changes over the ten elections. Were we to have many more elections, we might be better able to see underlying long-term changes that transcend these erratic short-term changes. In many ways our speculation, indeed anyone's speculation, about changes in the American electorate is like predicting whether a baseball team will have a good season after having watched its first ten games.

The presidential election of 1984 serves as a good example of the dangers associated with trying to use one election's results to predict future trends. Of course, in 1984 the minority party won the presidential election. This has been the rule during the time period we have studied. In fact, only in 1960, 1964, and 1976 has the majority party won the presidency. Many political observers interpreted Reagan's 1980 victory, given his ideological orientations, as a conservative mandate that continued and was reinforced in 1984 and 1988. Voters in the 1980s were seen by some as taking a new, more conservative, direction. We would urge caution in such an interpretation, especially given the lessons of the past. For example, Eisenhower's victory in 1952 and Nixon's in 1968 were also interpreted as signaling a dramatic restructuring of American politics, but these restructurings did not occur. More importantly, most public opinion polls in the late 1980s, including election studies, continue to show the American public to hold moderate, not conservative, policy positions.

As we have seen in the case of increasing alienation among Americans in the 1960s and 1970s, the limited perspective of even several presidential elections can be in error. Carter's victory in 1976, as well as Reagan's in 1980, can be interpreted as reflecting the public's alienation from the Washington establishment, in that the incumbent president was defeated; from this interpretation, it can be inferred that levels of alienation can impact election outcomes. In turn, alienation remained stable in 1988, while the prototypical establishment, Republican George Bush, was elected to the presidency. Shouldn't alienation have increased in 1988, in the face of two candidates who were such typical representatives of their respective parties? Or does alienation *not* contribute to election outcomes? These sorts of questions are most difficult to answer within the limited perspective of two or three, or even ten, presidential elections.

What Does the Future Hold?

Throughout this book we have refrained from personal conjecture about the future behavior of the electorate. Instead, we have sought only to summarize what is known about the electoral behavior of Americans. Political science, depending as it does on survey research and actual election results, is not well suited to predicting events that might occur five, ten, or more years from now. However, by combining some imagination and logic with a little knowledge, we have developed some ideas about the future directions of each of the trends we have discussed in this book.

Some of our predictions will focus on elections in the next decade or so. Others will focus on events that should not fully unfold for thirty years or more. Some predictions are hopeful in nature, while others are dismal. We have greater confidence in some of the predictions than in others. Our greatest confidence can be vested in predictions based on demographic trends that we know will occur (such as the aging of the large baby boom cohort of the electorate) and which involve long-standing relationships (such as the persistent high levels of turnout among middle-aged persons). But all of the predictions that follow are uncertain, and subject to revision and change as the future unfolds.

Partisanship in the Future

Two probable non-electoral trends of the future seem likely to have an impact on partisanship and other political trends. First, the post-World War II baby boom cohort will be the dominant population group in America for the next two to three decades. Assuming normal mortality rates for this group, we can expect it to be the largest chunk of the population for another thirty years at least. Second, it seems certain that government as well as other institutions will be faced with increasingly technical and complex decisions in the future. Two factors seem to insure this outcome: the increased use of computers and other sophisticated analytical devices allow humankind to make policies in areas heretofore inaccessible to decision makers; and technological innovation frequently has by-products that may adversely affect society, the environment, and the individual.

Examples of issues enmeshed with such technical considerations are easy to imagine. What mix of weapon systems should the U.S. military employ in the next 20 years, given the apparent demise of the Cold War? What amount of chlorofluorocarbons can be released into the atmosphere before ozone depletion, and its associated health risks, outweigh the costs associated with developing and using a substitute for these chemicals? What should be the maximum allowable amount of a trace toxic metal in public drinking water supplies? When is a fetus viable outside the womb? The list of technical questions is virtually endless.

We expect that the baby boom cohort and the importance of technical matters will both impinge on political partisanship but perhaps with very different effects. Because we know that attachment to political parties increases as persons become older, as the baby boom cohort ages, its large size in the electorate should result in a more partisan electorate. Only two factors seem likely to counteract this. There could be a new baby boom that would add millions of new voters without strong partisanship into the electorate about the time the baby boom cohort reaches its fifties and sixties. Or the baby boom cohort could defy conventional wisdom and remain aloof from the political parties in their middle and elderly years. The latter seems to be a distinct possibility, given that this cohort entered the electorate with weaker ties to the parties than most other cohorts before or since. It also has reflected lower rates of turnout. Some political scientists have speculated that this stems from the turbulence of the period when the baby boom cohort came of age politically, which included the last days of the civil rights movement, the war in Vietnam, and the drama of Watergate. Exposure to these events may have had a lasting effect on the political behavior of this cohort.

Alternatively, since these events seem to have had little lasting effects on society, the baby boom generation, and those who follow, may reflect on how long it has been since our society has had an experience that truly shaped collective opinion. With the exception of blacks who were influenced by events surrounding the civil rights movement, one must go back to the Great Depression to find an event of lasting political impact. Even World War II had no visible impact save the resulting baby boom and a substantial thrust toward better educational opportunities for (most) Americans. Thus while parental values, attitudes, and partisanship may be passed to succeeding generations, the post-World War II generation may lack the commitment that originally produced the values of those who experienced the Depression.

We expect that technological developments may loosen the bonds of partisanship or at least may weaken parties as influential participants in political decision making. We base this prediction on the belief that technological matters will require governments to rely more and more on technical experts for guidance and direction and less on political parties and other traditional participants in the policy-making process. Political parties are not likely to offer the sophisticated structuring of opinion necessary to guide decisions on such technical issues. The net result may be that the electorate comes to see political parties, and perhaps attachments to party, as anachronisms. Scientists, engineers, and other experts may become the opinion leaders, rather than political figures.

Other factors also point toward the possible further decline of partisanship. One is the increasing attachment of individuals to political organizations that serve as practical alternatives to political parties for some. For individuals that have limited their political interests to one or two issues, there may be a perception that single-issue interest groups are a satisfactory alternative to the political party. The individual opposing abortions, for example, can participate in politics and influence policy making by working through a group such as Right-to-Life. Or an indignant taxpayer seeking tax relief can work through a taxpayers association. Of course, groups like these have always been around as an alternative to parties and have not yet significantly eroded partisanship. But this could change as a more sophisticated use of communications techniques allows interest groups to approach voters directly in greater numbers than ever before. There will always be roles for parties to play, such as candidate recruitment, but parties may lose their hold over many of their followers.

Interest groups will not be the only groups to use the media to undermine partisan control over voters. We expect that political candidates will continue to use the essentially nonpartisan new style politics of media-dominated campaigns to woo voters. If this occurs, and if the political parties do not become willing participants in the new technologies of campaigns (some signs suggest they will become involved), political consultants and other power brokers outside the parties will become dominant forces in electoral behavior. And most of these new political operatives eschew partisanship in their appeals, preferring instead to stress issues or candidate images in their campaign communications. Candidates eager to woo voters away from the other party are increasingly using the strategy of taking partisan appeals out of their campaigns.

In summary, several trends suggest that partisanship may hold little if any appeal for voters twenty to thirty years from today. Partisanship, however, is a habit that the electorate seems to find hard to give up. There have been many predictions of the demise of partisanship before, and many of the forces we see undermining partisanship in the future have been present for some time in the past. We should not be surprised, therefore, if partisanship proves to be a tenacious survivor in the evolution of American electoral behavior.

Political Participation in the Future

Predicting trends in political participation may be the most difficult task we face in looking to the future. This difficulty is illustrated by the puzzling downward trend in voter turnout during the past two decades. In 1960, if we had predicted that the number of years of formal education of the electorate would have dramatically increased by 1988, we would also have predicted a rise in electoral participation. The former has happened but not the latter; despite the increase in the educational attainment of the electorate, turnout has dropped. We have also eliminated many legal restrictions that prevented some from voting. Nevertheless, turnout has fallen with each successive presidential election, except for the stable turnout observed in 1984. In short, we have some difficulty explaining why people vote or do not vote today. And, perhaps as a consequence of that failure, we cannot successfully explain why people are less likely to vote now than they were in the 1960s. It should therefore not be surprising that we are not optimistic about our abilities to predict trends in political participation.

It seems likely that election laws and procedures will be further relaxed in hope of encouraging participation. Such reforms may be accompanied by technological advances, such as two-way cable television, microcomputer networks, and 900 number DIAL-IT telephone surveys, which make voting and other acts of political participation easier. These advances could open the way for more frequent polling of citizen opinion or even more frequent use of binding referendums, in making public policies.

There are already signs of such innovations. In April, 1981, San Diego held a ballot referendum by mail on a proposed $224 million bond issue earmarked for construction of a convention complex in the city's downtown area. Each registered voter in the city was sent a ballot that he or she had to return within two weeks from the date the ballots were mailed. The result was a turnout of 61.7 percent of registered voters, a much higher figure than is typical for bond issues where voters must go to a polling place on a single election day in the traditional manner. Oregon is also experimenting with balloting by mail.

AT&T has experimented with a system for straw polls using ordinary telephones, leading some to coin the term "teledemocracy." The first test of this system came after a nationally televised debate between Jimmy Carter and

Ronald Reagan during the 1980 presidential campaign. ABC television asked viewers of the debate to call a special 900 *DIAL-IT* (the system's proprietary name) number, for which callers were billed fifty cents, to register their opinions about the debate winner. A total of 652,820 voters phoned during the one hour and forty minutes that the telephone lines were open. About two thirds of the callers declared Ronald Reagan the debate winner. Although those calling represented only a fraction of the 40 million people estimated to be watching ABC at the time, and although the opinions of callers were probably not an accurate representation of all viewers, the event was successful in demonstrating the fast developing technology for citizen input and participation.

Obviously, these presently available technologies offer the possibility of making political participation easier than ever before. Some refinements are necessary, of course, before such innovations can be used for actual referenda. For example, we must be sure that only qualified adult voters are using the voting devices and that multiple voting is not taking place. These problems can and will be solved, however; once this is accomplished, teledemocracy and its variants may become the mechanism to increase political participation. Proponents of teledemocracy already are vocal. One such advocate, political scientist Ted Becker, has predicted that "with the help of teledemocratic processes, public opinion will become the law of the land. . . ."[1] Considering that people often do not use "free" ballots for important elections conducted these days, it is somewhat interesting that they will pay to express their opinions in nonbinding straw polls. The current wave of enthusiasm for technological innovations may not last however. It may be that people are initially drawn to these alternatives because of their novelty value. Many Americans love new things, things that seem different and innovative. But after a while, the new wears off and interest wanes. Declines in interest in new forms of voting will probably soon wipe out any initial increases they make in the rate of political participation.

Political Trust in the Future

Political distrust and alienation, which have increased to levels that some observers consider dangerous, will probably *not* change significantly in the next several years. If anything, political alienation could become worse. Despite the fact that trends in distrust and alienation dramatically reversed in 1984, in 1988 they resumed the deterioration observed throughout the 1960s and 1970s.

Several factors seem to rule out a major rebound in political trust. (We refer to a long-term increase, not simply an increase in political trust that typically occurs for a year or so when a new president is elected.) First, we are unquestionably entering an era in which we will confront a variety of problems—social, economic, and technical—that will defy easy solution or any solution at all. We anticipate that the electorate will become increasingly frustrated with the inability of government to resolve such problems, thereby producing continued low levels of political trust.

Second, modern medicine is going to keep more Americans living longer than ever before. This should become most significant when the large baby boom cohort reaches its sixties, seventies, and beyond. If the elderly, as in the past, continue to be the most profoundly alienated and distrusting segment of society, and if the elderly make up an increasingly greater percentage of society, then we can only expect higher levels (or at least stable levels) of political distrust. One issue in particular may stimulate this trend. As more and more politicians speak publicly of the necessity of reforming the Social Security system, the elderly that depend on benefits of the program may become increasingly cynical about efforts to cut their monthly pension checks.

Third, nothing short of an unprecedented era of national economic prosperity seems likely to cause a dramatic upturn in public confidence. The prospects for this scenario seem poor, however, because almost no economists expect the U.S. economy ever to dominate the world again as it did immediately after World War II, creating a generally booming economy during the 1950s and 1960s. America's dominance of the automobile, steel, and other durable-goods industries will probably never occur again, thus leaving many Americans out of work or underemployed. This trend must unquestionably dampen the American spirit.

What is the long-term impact of political alienation? As we noted in Chapter 4, some theorists have suggested that sustained periods of political alienation could spill over into political violence against the system and leadership. Will this happen in the United States? We think not, because no matter how low public confidence has fallen in recent polls, Americans still profess belief that our system of government is best. Sentiment that the system is in need of major overhaul scarcely can be found in public opinion polls. The key to this matter seems to be found in Americans' perceptions of their personal plight. While most citizens are convinced that political institutions have failed the test of confidence, they nevertheless express considerable satisfaction with their personal and family situations, as Everett Carll Ladd has observed.[2] Unless there is some massive upheaval in the private situations of most Americans, they are likely to remain loyal to the nation and its system of government.

The Role of Issues in the Future

While most of the trends in American presidential voting have been either erratic or extremely gradual, the increase among the American public in articulating their preferences for presidential candidates in terms of issues, rather than image characteristics, is dramatic. We have already cautioned against concluding that the American public is therefore now capable of more rational selection of political leaders. For voting to be truly issue based, citizens' preferences on issues must precede preferences for candidates, so that we can infer that the issue preference produced the candidate choice. Ideally, issue positions would likewise precede party identification. These are the most difficult conditions to demonstrate, especially with single-year election studies and without complex and sophisticated statistical models. We have already shown that people are strongly inclined to cast their vote for their own party's candidate. And the available evidence indicates that substantial numbers of citizens cast issue based votes in presidential elections. What is not resolved is whether party identification colors perceptions of issues, producing like-minded voters who prefer the same candidate; or, whether like-minded individuals are drawn to the same political party and the same political candidates.

Let us end on a straightforward note: we cannot predict with any degree of certainty the shape of the American political universe thirty years hence. The Democratic and Republican parties will (probably) still be with us. Turnout will (probably) continue to decline, as will (probably) support for the political system. The electorate will be better educated but perhaps less involved in the political process. In some elections, issues will dominate, in others candidate characteristics, and in still others partisanship.

But through all of these potential changes, the Republic will stand. The political system has endured far more serious crises than declining partisanship, trust, and turnout. And while the connection between public opinion and public policy often seems tenuous, most people do not seem to be especially concerned about it. To borrow from Jimmy Carter, we suspect the government *is* "as good and competent" as are the people who elect it. And in a representative democracy, that appears to us to be quite good enough.

Notes

1. Becker quoted in Michael Malbin, "Teledemocracy and its Discontents," *Public Opinion*, 5 (June/July 1982): 58.
2. Everett Carll Ladd, "205 and Going Strong," *Public Opinion*, 4 (June/July 1981): 7–12.

References

Abramson, Paul R., and John H. Aldrich. "The Decline of Electoral Participation in America." *American Political Science Review* 76 (June 1982): 502–21.

Agranoff, Robert. *The Management of Election Campaigns.* Boston: Holbrook Press, 1976.

Andrews, William G. "American Voting Participation." *The Western Political Quarterly* 19 (1966): 630–39.

Asher, Herbert B. *Presidential Elections and American Politics,* third ed. Homewood, IL: The Dorsey Press, 1984.

Axelrod, Robert. "Presidential Election Coalitions in 1984." *American Political Science Review* 80 (March 1986): 281–84.

Beck, Paul Allan. "A Socialization Theory of Partisan Realignment." In *The Politics of Future Citizens,* edited by Richard G. Niemi and Associates. San Francisco: Jossey-Bass, 1974, pp. 199–219.

Beck, Paul Allan. "Youth and the Politics of Realignment." In *Political Opinion and Behavior,* edited by E. C. Dreyer and W. A. Rosenbaum. Belmont, CA: Wadsworth Publishing Co., 1976.

Berelson, Bernard R., Paul F. Lazarsfeld, and William N. McPhee. *Voting.* Chicago: University of Chicago Press, 1954.

Bishop, George F., Alfred J. Tuchfarber, and Robert W. Oldenick. "Change in the Structure of American Political Attitudes: The Nagging Question of Question Wording." *American Journal of Political Science* 22 (May 1978): 250–69.

Bond, Jon R., Cary Covington, and Richard Fleisher. "Explaining Challenger Quality in Congressional Elections." *Journal of Politics* (May 1985): 510–29.

Bone, Hugh A., and Austin Ranney. *Politics and Voters,* fourth ed. New York: McGraw-Hill, 1976.

Boyd, Richard W. "Decline of U.S. Voter Turnout: Structural Explanations." *American Politics Quarterly* 9 (April 1981): 133–59.

Boyd, Richard W., and Herbert H. Hyman. "Survey Research." In *Handbook of Political Science,* Vol. 7, *Strategies of Inquiry,* edited by Fred I. Greenstein and Nelson W. Polsby. Reading, MA: Addison-Wesley Publishing Co., 1975.

Brody, Richard A., and Benjamin I. Page. "Indifference, Alienation and Rational Decisions: The Effects of Candidate Evaluation on Turnout and the Vote." *Public Choice* 15 (Summer 1973): 1–17.

Brown, Steven R. "Consistency and the Persistence of Ideology: Some Experimental Results." *Public Opinion Quarterly* 34 (Spring 1970): 60–68.

Burnham, Walter Dean. *Critical Elections and the Mainsprings of American Politics.* New York: W. W. Norton, 1970.

Burnham, Walter Dean. "The Changing Shape of the American Political Universe." *American Political Science Review* 59 (March 1965): 7–28.

Bureau of the Census, *Current Population Reports.*

Campbell, Angus, Philip E. Converse, Warren E. Miller, and Donald E. Stokes. *The American Voter.* Chicago: University of Chicago Press, 1960.

Campbell, Angus, Philip E. Converse, Warren E. Miller, and Donald E. Stokes. *Elections and the Political Order.* New York: John Wiley & Sons, 1966.

Campbell, Angus, Gerald Gurin, and Warren Miller. *The Voter Decides.* Evanston: Row, Peterson & Co., 1954.

Campbell, Angus, and Robert Kahn. *The People Elect a President.* Ann Arbor, Michigan: Survey Research Center, Institute for Social Research, University of Michigan, 1952.

Carmines, Edward G., John P. McIver, and James A. Stimson. "Unrealized Partisanship: A Theory of Dealignment." *Journal of Politics* 49 (May 1987): 376–400.

Carmines, Edward G., and James A. Stimson. "On the Structure and Sequence of Issue Evolution." *American Political Science Review* 80 (September 1986): 901–20.

Cassel, Carol. "Cohort Analysis of Party Identification among Southern Whites, 1952–1972." *Public Opinion Quarterly* 41 (1977): 28–33.

Cassel, Carol A., and David B. Hill. "Explanations of Turnout Decline: A Multivariate Test." *American Politics Quarterly* 9 (April 1981): 181–95.

Cassel, Carol A., and Robert C. Luskin. "Simple Explanations of Turnout Decline." *American Political Science Review* 82 (December 1988): 1321–30.

Citrin, Jack. "Comment: The Political Relevance of Trust in Government." *American Political Science Review* 68 (September 1974): 973–88.

Clarke, Harold D., and Marianne C. Stewart. "Partisan Inconsistencies and Partisan Change in Federal States: The Case of Canada." *American Journal of Political Science* 31 (May 1987): 383–407.

Clausen, Aage R. "Response Validity: Vote Report." *Public Opinion Quarterly* 32 (Winter 1968–69): 588–606.

Clubb, Jerome M., William H. Flanigan, and Nancy H. Zingale. "Partisan Realignment Since 1960." Presented at the 1976 meeting of the American Political Science Association, Chicago.

Congressional Quarterly Almanac 44 (Washington, D.C.: Congressional Quarterly, Inc.: 1989).

Converse, Philip E. "The Nature of Belief Systems in Mass Public." In *Ideology and Discontent,* edited by David E. Apter. Glencoe: Free Press, 1964.

Converse, Philip E. "On the Possibility of a Major Realignment in the South." In *Elections and the Political Order,* edited by Campbell et al. New York: John Wiley & Sons, 1966.

Converse, Philip E. "The Concept of a Normal Vote." In *Elections and the Political Order,* edited by Campbell et al. New York: John Wiley & Sons, 1966.

Converse, Philip E. "Change in the American Electorate." In *The Human Meaning of Social Change,* edited by Angus Campbell and Philip E. Converse. New York: Russell Sage Foundation, 1972.

Converse, Philip E. and Gregory B. Markus. "Plus Ca Change: The New CPS Election Study Panel." *American Political Science Review* 73 (March 1979): 32–49.

Converse, Philip E., and Richard Niemi. "Non-voting among Young Adults in the United States." In *Political Parties and Political Behavior,* second ed., edited by William J. Crotty, Donald M. Freeman, and Douglas S. Gatlin. Boston: Allyn & Bacon, 1971.

Philip E. Converse *et al.* "Stability and Change in 1960: A Reinstating Election." In *Elections and the Political Order,* edited by Campbell *et al.* New York: John Wiley & Sons, 1966.

Cook, Rhodes. "The Nominating Process." In *The Election of 1988,* edited by Michael Nelson. Washington, D.C.: CQ Press, 1989.

Cotter, Cornelius P., James L. Gibson, John F. Bibby, and Robert J. Huckshorn. *Party Organization in American Politics.* New York: Praeger, 1984.

Crotty, William J., and Gary C. Jacobson. *American Parties in Decline,* second ed. Boston: Little, Brown, 1984.

Dawson, Richard E. *Public Opinion and Contemporary Disarray.* New York: Harper & Row, 1973.

DeClercq, Eugene, Thomas L. Hurley, and Norman R. Luttbeg. "Voting in American Presidential Elections: 1956-1972." In *American Electoral Behavior: Change and Stability,* edited by Samuel A. Kirkpatrick. Beverly Hills, CA: Sage Publications, 1976.

Dennis, Jack. "Trends in Support for the American Political Party System." Presented at 1974 Meeting of the American Political Science Association, Chicago.

DeVries, Walter, and V. Lance Tarrance. *The Ticket Splitter: A New Force in American Politics.* Grand Rapids, MI: William B. Eerdmans Publishing Co., 1972.

Downs, Anthony. *An Economic Theory of Democracy.* New York: Harper and Row, 1957.

Dreyer, Edward C. "Change and Stability in Party Identification." *Journal of Politics* 35 (November 1972): 712-22.

Easton, David. *A Systems Analysis of Political Life.* New York: John Wiley & Sons, 1965.

Easton, David. "A Re-Assessment of the Concept of Political Support." *British Journal of Political Science* 5 (October 1975): 435-57.

Easton, David, and Jack Dennis. *Children in the Political System.* New York: McGraw-Hill, 1969.

Eisinger, Peter K. "The Pattern of Citizen Contacts with Public Officials." In *People and Politics in Urban Society,* edited by Harlan Hahn. Beverly Hills: Sage Publications, 1971.

Eubank, Robert B. "Incumbent Effects on Individual-Level Voting Behavior in Congressional Elections: A Decade of Exaggeration." *Journal of Politics* (August 1985): 58-67.

Fenno, Richard. *Home Style.* Boston: Little, Brown, 1978.

Finifter, Ada. "Dimensions of Political Alienation." *American Political Science Review* 64 (June 1970): 389-410.

Fiorina, Morris. "The Case of the Vanishing Marginals: The Bureaucracy Did It." *American Political Science Review* (March 1977): 177-81.

Fiorina, Morris P. "An Outline for a Model of Party Choice." *American Journal of Political Science* 21 (August 1977): 601-26.

Fiorina, Morris P. *Retrospective Evaluations in American National Elections.* New Haven: Yale University Press, 1981.

Flanigan, William H., and Nancy H. Zingale. *Political Behavior of the American Electorate.* Boston: Allyn and Bacon, 1975.

Foster, Carrol B. "The Performance of Rational Choice Voter Models in Recent Presidential Elections. *American Political Science Review* 78 (June 1984): 678-90.

Franklin, Charles H. "Issue Preferences, Socialization, and the Evolution of Party Identification." *American Journal of Political Science* 28 (August 1984): 459–78.

Franklin, Charles H., and John E. Jackson. "The Dynamics of Party Identification." *American Political Science Review* 77 (December 1983): 957–73.

Freedman, Stanley R. "Salience of Party and Candidate in Congressional Elections: A Comparison of 1958 and 1970." In *Public Opinion and Public Policy,* third ed., edited by Norman R. Luttbeg. Itasca, IL: Peacock, 1981.

Gallup Opinion Index and Gallup Opinion Report, various issues.

Gant, Michael M. "The Political Content of Party Identification: Traditional *vs.* Revisionist Perspectives." Presented at the 1984 Meeting of the Southern Political Science Association, Savannah, Georgia.

Gant, Michael M. "The Irrelevance of Abstract Conceptualization for Policy-Based Voting." *Polity* 18 (Fall 1985): 149–60.

Gant, Michael M., and Dennis Black. "The Determinants of Split Results at the Congressional District Level." Presented at the 1987 Meeting of the Midwest Political Science Association, Chicago.

Gant, Michael M., and Dwight F. Davis. "Mental Economy and Voter Rationality: The Informed Citizen Problem in Voting Research." *Journal of Politics* 46 (February 1984): 132–53.

Gant, Michael M., and Norman R. Luttbeg. "The Cognitive Utility of Partisanship." *Western Political Quarterly* 40 (September 1987): 499–517.

Gelb, Joyce, and Marian Lief Palley. *Tradition and Change in American Party Politics.* New York: Thomas Y. Crowell Co., 1975.

Gibson, James L., Cornelius P. Cotter, John F. Bibby, and Robert J. Huckshorn. "Assessing Party Organizational Strength." *American Journal of Political Science* 27 (February 1983): 193–222.

Gibson, James L., Cornelius P. Cotter, John F. Bibby, and Robert J. Huckshorn. "Wither the Local Parties: A Cross-Sectional and Longitudinal Analysis of the Strength of Party Organizations." *American Journal of Political Science* 29 (February 1985): 139–60.

Gilmour, Robert S., and Robert B. Lamb. *Political Alienation in Contemporary America.* New York: St. Martin's Press, 1975.

Goldenberg, Edie N., and Michael W. Traugott. *Campaigning for Congress.* Washington: CQ Press, 1984.

Hadley, Charles D. "Dual Partisan Identification in the South." *Journal of Politics* 47 (February 1985): 254–68.

Hamill, Ruth C., Milton Lodge, and Frederick Blake. "The Breadth, Depth and Utility of Class, Partisan and Ideological Schemata." *American Journal of Political Science* 29 (November 1985): 850–70.

Hill, David B., and Norman R. Luttbeg. *Trends in American Electoral Behavior,* second ed. Itasca, IL: F.E. Peacock, 1983.

Hurley, Patricia A., and Kim Quaile Hill. "The Prospects for Issue Voting in Contemporary Congressional Elections: An Assessment of Citizen Awareness and Representation." In *Public Opinion and Public Policy,* third ed., edited by Norman R. Luttbeg. Itasca, IL: Peacock, 1981.

Jackson, John E. "Issues, Party Choices, and Presidential Votes." *American Journal of Political Science* 19 (May 1975): 161–86.

Jacobson, Gary C. *Money in Congressional Elections.* New Haven: Yale University Press, 1980.

Jacobson, Gary C. *The Politics of Congressional Elections.* Boston: Little, Brown, 1987.

Jacobson, Gary C., and Samuel Kernell, "Strategy and Choice in the 1982 Congressional Elections." In *Controversies in Voting Behavior,* second ed., edited by Richard G. Niemi and Herbert F. Weisberg. Washington: CQ Press, 1984.

Jennings, M. Kent, and Richard G. Niemi. "The Transmission of Political Values from Parent to Child." *American Political Science Review* 62 (March 1968): 169–84.

Jennings, M. Kent, and Harmon Zeigler. "The Salience of American State Politics." *American Political Science Review* 64 (June 1970): 523–35.

Jacob, Herbert. "Contact with Government Agencies: A Preliminary Analysis of the Distribution of Government Services." *Midwest Journal of Political Science* 16 (1972): 123–46.

Katz, Daniel, Barbara A. Gutek, Robert L. Kahn, and Eugenia Barton. *Bureaucratic Encounters.* Ann Arbor, MI: Institute for Social Research, 1975.

Kelley, Stanley, Jr., Richard E. Ayres, and William G. Bowen. "Registration and Voting: Putting First Things First." *American Political Science Review* 61 (June 1967): 359–77.

Kernell, Samuel. "Presidential Popularity and Negative Voting: An Alternative Explanation of the Midterm Congressional Decline of the President's Party." *American Political Science Review* (March 1977): 44–65.

Kessel, John. "Comment: The Issues in Issue Voting." *American Political Science Review* 66 (June 1972): 459–65.

Key, V. O., Jr. "A Theory of Critical Elections." *Journal of Politics* 17 (February 1955): 3–18.

Key, V. O., Jr. *Public Opinion and American Democracy.* New York: Alfred A. Knopf, 1961.

Key, V. O., Jr. *The Responsible Electorate.* Cambridge, MA: Belknap Press, 1966.

Knight, Kathleen. "Ideology in the 1980 Election: Ideological Sophistication Does Matter." *Journal of Politics* 47 (August 1985): 828–53.

Konda, Thomas M., and Lee Sigelman. "Public Evaluations of the American Parties, 1952–1984." *Journal of Politics* 49 (November 1987): 814–29.

Kraut, Robert E., and John B. McConahay. "How Being Interviewed Affects Voting: An Experiment." *Public Opinion Quarterly* 37 (Fall 1973): 398–406.

Ladd, Everett Carll, Jr. *Where Have all the Voters Gone?* New York: W. W. Norton & Co., 1978.

Ladd, Everett Carll, Jr. "205 and Going Strong." *Public Opinion* 4 (June/July 1981): 7–12.

Lazarsfeld, Paul F., Bernard R. Berelson, and Hazel Gaudet. *The People's Choice.* New York: Duell, Sloan & Pearce, 1944.

Luttbeg, Norman R. "Voter Interview Stimulation in the Multiple Sample NES 1980 Study." Presented at the 1982 Meeting of the Midwest Political Science Association, Milwaukee.

Luttbeg, Norman R. "Differential Voting Decline in the American States, 1960–1982." *Social Science Quarterly* (March 1984): 60–73.

Luttbeg, Norman R. "Attitudinal Components of Turnout Decline." *Social Science Quarterly* (June 1985): 435–43.

Lyons, William, and Michael M. Gant. "Non-Voting and Public Policy: The 1972–1984 Presidential Elections." Presented at the 1989 Meeting of the Midwest Political Science Association, Chicago.

Madison, James. "*The Federalist* Number 10." In *The Federalist Papers,* edited by Andrew Hacker. New York: Washington Square Press.

Madison, James. "*The Federalist* Number 47." In *The Federalist Papers,* edited by Andrew Hacker. New York: Washington Square Press.

Malbin, Michael. "Teledemocracy and Its Discontents." *Public Opinion* 5 (June/July 1982): 58.

Mann, Thomas E., and Raymond E. Wolfinger. "Candidates and Parties in Congressional Elections." In *Controversies in Voting Behavior*, second ed., edited by Richard G. Niemi and Herbert F. Weisberg. Washington: CQ Press, 1984.

Martinez, Michael D., and Michael M. Gant. "Partisan Issue Preferences and Partisan Change." *Political Behavior* (Forthcoming, 1990).

Mayhew, David. "Congressional Elections: The Case of the Vanishing Marginals." *Polity* (Spring 1974): 295–317.

Mayhew, David. *Congress: The Electoral Connection.* New Haven: Yale University Press, 1974.

Meier, Kenneth J. "Party Identification and Vote Choice: The Causal Connection." *Western Political Quarterly* (September 1975): 496–505.

Milbraith, Lester W., and M. L. Goel. *Political Participation*, second ed. Chicago: Rand McNally, 1977.

Miller, Arthur H. "Political Issues and Trust in Government: 1964–1970." *American Political Science Review* 68 (September 1974): 951–72.

Miller, Arthur H. "Rejoinder to 'Comment' by Jack Citrin: Political Discontent or Ritualism?" *American Political Science Review* 68 (September 1974): 989–1001.

Miller, Arthur H., Warren E. Miller, Alden S. Raine, and Thad A. Brown. "A Majority Party in Disarray: Policy Polarization in the 1972 Election." *American Political Science Review* 70 (September 1976): 753–78.

Miller, Arthur H., and Martin P. Wattenberg. "Throwing the Rascals Out: Policy and Performance Evaluations of Presidential Candidates, 1952–1980." *American Political Science Review* 79 (March 1985): 359–72.

Miller, Warren E., and Teresa E. Levitin. *Leadership and Change: The New Politics and the American Electorate.* Cambridge, MA: Winthrop Publishers, 1976.

Muller, Edward N. "A Test of a Partial Theory of Potential for Political Violence." *American Political Science Review* 66 (September 1972): 928–59.

Natchez, Peter B. "Images of Voting: The Social Psychologists," *Public Policy*, 18 (Summer 1970): 553–88.

Nie, Norman H., with Kristi Anderson. "Mass Belief Systems Revisited: Political Change and Attitude Structure." *Journal of Politics* 36 (August 1974): 540–91.

Nie, Norman H., Sidney Verba, Henry C. Brady, Kay Lehman Schlozman, and Jane Junn. "Participation in America: Continuity and Change." Presented at the 1989 Meeting of the Midwest Political Science Association, Chicago.

Niemi, Richard G., and Herbert F. Weisberg. *Controversies in American Voting Behavior.* San Francisco: W. H. Freeman & Co., 1976.

Niemi, Richard G., Stephen Wright, and Linda W. Powell. "Multiple Party Identifiers and the Measurement of Party Identification." *Journal of Politics* 49 (November 1987): 1093–1103.

Norpoth, Helmut, and Jerrold G. Rusk. "Partisan Dealignment in the American Electorate: Itemizing the Deductions Since 1964." *American Political Science Review* 76 (June 1982): 522–37.

Ornstein, Norman J., Thomas E. Mann, and Michael J. Malbin. *Vital Statistics on Congress, 1989–1990.* Washington: American Enterprise Institute, 1990.

Page, Benjamin I., and Calvin C. Jones. "Reciprocal Effects of Policy Preferences, Party Loyalties and the Vote." *American Political Science Review* 73 (December 1979): 1071–89.

Peffley, Mark A., and Jon Hurwirtz. "A Hierarchical Model of Attitude Constraint." *American Journal of Political Science* 29 (November 1985): 871–90.

Petrocik, John R. "Realignment: New Party Coalitions and the Nationalization of the South." *Journal of Politics* 49 (May 1987): 347–75.

Plano, Jack C., and Milton Greenberg. *The American Political Dictionary.* Hinsdale, IL: Dryden Press, 1976.

Pomper, Gerald M. "From Confusion to Clarity: Issues and American Voters, 1956–1968." *American Political Science Review* 66 (June 1972): 415–28.

Pomper, Gerald. *Elections in America.* New York: Dodd, Mead & Co., 1974.

Pomper, Gerald M. *Voters' Choice.* New York: Dodd, Mead & Co., 1975.

Pomper, Gerald. "A Classification of Presidential Elections." *Journal of Politics* 29 (August 1967): 535–66.

Powell, G. Bingham. "American Voter Turnout in Comparative Perspective." *American Political Science Review* 80 (March 1986): 17–43.

Ramsden, Graham R. "A Partial Explanation for Black Turnout Patterns: 1952–1980." Presented at the 1988 Meeting of the Midwest Political Science Association, Chicago.

Ranney, Austin. "Turnout and Representation in Presidential Primary Elections." *American Political Science Review* 66 (March 1972): 21–37.

RePass, Davis E. "Issue Salience and Party Choice." *American Political Science Review* 65 (June 1971): 389–400.

Rice, S. A. *Quantitative Methods in Politics.* New York: Alfred A. Knopf, 1928.

Riker, William H., and Peter C. Ordeshook. "A Theory of the Calculus of Voting." *American Political Science Review* 62 (March 1968): 25–42.

Roll, Charles W., Jr., and Albert H. Cantril. *Polls: Their Use and Misuse in Politics.* New York: Basic Books, 1972.

Rossi, Peter H. "Four Landmarks in Voting Research." In *American Voting Behavior,* edited by Eugene Burdick and Arthur J. Brodbeck. New York: Free Press, 1959.

Rusk, Jerrold D. "The Effect of the Australian Ballot Reform on Split Ticket Voting: 1876–1908." *American Political Science Review* 64 (December 1970): 1220–38.

Ryles, Tim. "The Processing of Citizen Complaints in Local Government." Presented at the 1974 Meeting of the Southern Political Science Association, Atlanta.

Schneider, William. "1980-A Watershed Year." *Politics Today* 7, no. 1 (January/February 1980): 30.

Scott, Ruth K., and Ronald J. Hrebenar. *Parties in Crisis.* New York: John Wiley and Sons, 1979.

Seeman, Melvin. "On the Meaning of Alienation." *American Sociological Review* 24 (December 1959): 783–91.

Sellars, Charles. "The Equilibrium Cycle in Two Party Politics." *Public Opinion Quarterly* 29 (Spring 1965): 16–38.

Shaffer, Stephen D. "A Multivariate Explanation of Rising Ticketsplitting." Presented at the 1982 meeting of the Southern Political Science Association, Atlanta.

Silbey, Joel H., Allan G. Bogue, and William H. Flanigan, eds. *The History of American Electoral Behavior.* Princeton, NJ: Princeton University Press, 1978.

Sorauf, Frank J. *Party Politics in America,* third ed. Boston: Little, Brown & Co., 1976.

Stanley, Harold W., William T. Bianco, and Richard G. Niemi. "Partisanship and Group Support Over Time: A Multivariate Analysis." *American Political Science Review* 80 (September 1986): 969–76.

Stanley, Harold W., and Richard G. Niemi. *Vital Statistics on American Politics,* second ed. Washington, D.C.: CQ Press, 1990.

Statistical Abstract of the United States, 1989. Washington: Bureau of the Census, 1989.

Stokes, Donald E. "Some Dynamic Elements of Contests for the Presidency." *American Political Science Review* 60 (March 1966): 19–28.

Stokes, Donald E., and Warren E. Miller. "Party Government and the Saliency of Congress." *Public Opinion Quarterly* (Winter 1962): 531–46.

Sullivan, John L., James E. Pierson, and George E. Marcus. "Ideological Constraint in the Mass Public: A Methodological Critique and Some New Findings." *American Journal of Political Science* 22 (May 1978): 233–49.

Sundquist, James. *Dynamics of the Party System.* Washington, D.C.: Brookings Institution, 1973.

Tarrance, V. Lance. "The Vanishing Voter: A Look at Non-Voting as a Purposive Act." In *Voters, Primaries and Parties,* edited by Jonathan Moore and Albert C. Pierce. Cambridge, MA: Harvard University Institute of Politics, 1976.

Traugott, Michael W., and John P. Katosh. "Response Validity in Surveys of Voting Behavior." *Public Opinion Quarterly* 45 (Winter 1981).

Traugott, Michael W., and John R. Katosh. "Response Validity in Surveys of Voting Behavior." *Public Opinion Quarterly* 43 (Fall 1979): 359–77.

Trilling, Richard J. "Party Image and Partisan Change." In *The Future of Political Parties,* edited by Louis Maisel and Paul M. Sacks. Beverly Hills, CA: Sage Publications, 1975.

Tufte, Edward R. "Determinants of the Outcomes of Midterm Congressional Elections." *American Political Science Review* (September, 1975): 812–26.

Tull, Donald S., and Gerald S. Albaum. "Bias in Random Digit Dialed Surveys." *Public Opinion Quarterly* 41 (1971): 389–95.

Turner, Frederick Jackson. *The United States, 1830–1850: The Nation and Its Sections.* Gloucester, MA: Peter Smith, 1958.

U.S. Congress, Senate, Committee on Government Operations, Subcommittee on Intergovernmental Relations. *Confidence and Concern: Citizens View American Government.* Committee Print, 93rd Congress, 1st Session, 1973, Part I.

Verba, Sidney, and Norman H. Nie. *Participation in American Politics.* New York: Harper & Row, 1972.

Walker, Jack L. "A Critique of the Elitist Theory of Democracy." *American Political Science Review* 60 (June 1966): 285–95.

Wattenberg, Martin P. "The Decline of Political Partisanship in the United States: Negativity or Neutrality." *American Political Science Review* 75 (September 1981): 941–50.

Wattenberg, Martin P. *The Decline of American Political Parties, 1952–1980.* Cambridge, MA: Harvard University Press, 1984.

Wilson, James Q. "The Riddle of the Middle Class." *The Public Interest* 39 (Spring 1975): 125–29.

Weisberg, Herbert F., and Bruce D. Bowen. *An Introduction to Survey Research and Data Analysis.* San Francisco: W. H. Freeman, 1977.

Weisberg, Herbert F., and Bernard Grofman. "Candidate Evaluations and Turnout." *American Politics Quarterly* 9 (April 1981): 197–219.

Weissberg, Robert. "Adolescent Experiences with Political Authorities." *Journal of Politics* 34 (1972): 797–824.

Wolfinger, Raymond E., and Steven J. Rosenstone. *Who Votes?* New Haven: Yale, 1980.

Name Index

203

Subject Index

American Electoral Behavior: 1952–1988

Composed by Pam Frye Typesetting, Inc.
Mt. Prospect, Illinois

The text and display lines are
set in Times Roman

Printed and bound by McNaughton & Gunn, Inc.
Saline, Michigan

Cover design and internal design by
Proof Positive/Farrowlyne Associates, Inc.
Evanston, Illinois